I'M GOING

Also by Maurice Rowlandson

Unexpected Adventure
Let's Have a Film
Life with Billy
Life with the Venturers

I'm Going to Ask You . . .

Maurice Rowlandson

Hodder & Stoughton

LONDON SYDNEY AUCKLAND

Copyright © 1997 Maurice Rowlandson

The right of Maurice Rowlandson to be identified as the Author
of the Work has been asserted by him in accordance with the
Copyright, Designs and Patents Act 1988.

First published in Great Britain in 1997
by Hodder and Stoughton
A division of Hodder Headline PLC

1 3 5 7 9 10 8 6 4 2

All rights reserved. No part of this publication may be
reproduced, stored in a retrieval system, or transmitted,
in any form or by any means without the prior written
permission of the publisher, nor be otherwise circulated
in any form of binding or cover other than that in which
it is published and without a similar condition being
imposed on the subsequent purchaser.

British Library Cataloguing in Publication Data
A record for this book is available from the British Library

ISBN 0 340 65648 4

Typeset by Avon Dataset Ltd, Bidford-on-Avon, Warks

Printed and bound in Great Britain by
Cox & Wyman Ltd, Reading, Berkshire

Hodder and Stoughton
A division of Hodder Headline PLC
338 Euston Road
London NW1 3BH

This book is dedicated to Dr William Franklin Graham, whose ministry accounts for all the stories in this book, and without whom my own life would have been immeasurably poorer. He has consistently given glory to God and faithfully preached the Gospel. Always he has related his ministry to the authoritative Word of God and has based everything he has said and done upon the declaration: 'The Bible says . . .' I thank my God for every remembrance of him and have counted it a privilege to have been asked to collect these stories.

Contents

Preface		ix
Introduction		xi
Acknowledgments		xv
1	If Only One Person … – George Verwer	1
2	Introducing Billy – Tom Rees	9
3	Called to Preach – Warren Wiersbe	22
4	Newscaster – Stuart Hamblen	31
5	Wire-tapper – Jim Vaus	41
	The Harringay Crusade	50
6	The Queen's Warrant – Dudley Brient	52
7	Childhood Response – Derek Hills	62
8	Sacrificing Cricket – Peter Pearmain	68
9	A Doctor's Story – David Rowlands	77
10	Fish and Meat Pastes – Ernest Shippam	86
11	No Longer Alone – Joan Winmill Brown	95
12	Monk to Minister – Alan Wright	112
13	No! The Pizzas are Yours – Trevor Adams	119
14	Escape from the Japs – Richard Galway	128
15	Zagreb – Branko Lovrec	137
16	Rock 'n' Roll Singer – Cliff Richard	147
17	Seven Thumbnail Sketches	163
	Ron E. Perez	163
	Dr Raymond Damadian	165
	Isaac Bonful	167
	Rev. Gipp Forster	168
	Norma Symonds	170
	Tom Bradley	172

	Makoto Yamaya	174
18	A Dangerous Life – Vikta Giovanni	177
19	Second Row, Piano Side – Chonda Pierce	189
20	Diminutive Medium – Eva Close	200
21	Dream Machine – Jean Lupton	209
22	Rock Band Evangelist – Alex Bowler	226
23	Not Easy to Respond – Ian Oliver	234
24	A U-turn – Helen Douglas	244
25	The Greatest News Ever Heard – Billy Graham	252
	Appendix	258
	Notes	260

Preface

No one else in the religious world either carries the respect of international leaders or has the stature of the American evangelist, Billy Graham.

He has been the friend of presidents; he has been welcomed by heads of state throughout the world, and in Britain he has had the privilege on several occasions of preaching before Her Majesty the Queen.

The former President of the United States, the Honorable Jimmy Carter, says:

> Real peace is found through a relationship with our Creator. When you hear Billy Graham speak you discover how you can find real peace. I encourage you to seriously consider the message that he gives.[1]

In an additional brief comment, specially provided for this book, Mr Carter says:

> He has never had an official position with any President of the United States, but he has been a friend and has always been available to us. In times of crisis I knew I had his support in prayer.[2]

Introduction

What possible justification can there be for another book about the ministry of the American evangelist, Billy Graham? This book, however, is not about his ministry; rather it looks at what has happened after he has uttered the now-famous words: 'I'm going to ask you to get up out of your seat and come and stand at the front.' Countless thousands have accepted that invitation – and many of them could tell remarkable stories of the changes which resulted in their lives. Indeed, a whole library of books would be needed if all the stories were to be told!

His crusades (later called 'missions' in the UK) began in Los Angeles in 1949. Since then he has carried the message of 'Salvation through Christ' to more than 185 countries around the world – in person, on film, via books and magazines, by radio and, most recently, over satellite television. The 1995 crusade from San Juan in Puerto Rico was carried worldwide in a programme called 'Global Mission with Billy Graham'. In 1996, the Global Television Series carried a single programme on national television stations worldwide – thus making it possible for the evangelist's message to be received in people's living rooms. This was the first major attempt at home evangelism, and it proved highly successful.

Billy Graham's survival as an evangelist has been remarkable when one looks at the fate of his contemporaries, 'falling like ninepins', with excesses in finance, sex, extramarital relations and other unfortunate affairs. Magnus Magnusson, editor of *Chambers Biographical Dictionary*, states:

[Graham] is a charismatic figure who has been the friend

and counsellor of many in high office ... He has consistently emerged from investigative reporting as a person of high integrity, and his Billy Graham Evangelistic Association as a model of financial accountability.[1]

Such high praise has not been achieved without sacrifice and hard work. Constant personal oversight of all his associates and staff, and his concern for his own personal relationships, has cost him his privacy and has been hard on his family. Yet he has willingly submitted to this for the cause of Christ.

A series on 'Televangelism in the USA' appeared in the *Daily Telegraph* on 4 April 1994. In his article, 'The Holy Ghostbuster', Paul Vallely was highly critical of many of the presenters of religious TV. He said:

Whatever makes good television in religion is suspect. If something comes across *great*, then you'd better start worrying. Billy Graham is not that *great* on television. He's kinda boring. That's good. That makes you think the guy is for real. I happen to think that he is one of the few who is.

Many people boast about the good works they do. Billy Graham gives millions of dollars away to the Third World – but he does it anonymously, and most people never find out. Those who have to brag about their giving lead one to ask: 'Is it a cover?'[2]

Billy Graham has said: 'Integrity is the glue that holds our way of life together. When wealth is lost, nothing is lost. When health is lost, something is lost. When character is lost, all is lost.'[3]

Jack Hayford, senior pastor of the Church on the Way in Van Nuys, California, traces six reasons why, in his opinion, Graham has survived. He outlines them in the magazine *Ministries Today*:

money – Graham has never accepted a 'love offering' or an honorarium for work in his crusades.

sexual morality – the Graham team set strict basic rules to protect themselves on the road.

sensationalism – a remarkable absence of the superficial, of hype and of pandering to the crowd marks Graham's preaching.

hyper-emotionalism – Graham merely bows in prayer while seekers come forward – moved by God, not a manipulative appeal.

avoiding digressions – he hasn't allowed himself to be crowded into narrow corners of 'emphasis' that would preclude him from being a blessing to all.

commitment to the whole church – all churches and church leaders are welcome to get involved in his crusades.[4]

In 1984, at a meeting of all the Billy Graham team members (known as the Team and Staff Conference – TASC) held in Phoenix, Arizona, the author of this book noted the names of all the team members present whom he knew personally. He listed 128 names of those who, with their spouses, were present at the conference. Eleven years later, at another TASC in Fort Lauderdale in Florida, the same list revealed that 124 of the 128 were still there! Of the remaining four, one had died; one, who had a wife desperately ill with cancer, had been unable to attend; and one had left to found his own evangelistic ministry, leaving only one unaccounted for. Furthermore, of those 124 names, 87 had been there almost since the beginning of Graham's crusade ministry. Also, God had mercifully protected those 124 from marital breakdown, separation and divorce.

It is important, too, to note that Billy Graham has never been sidetracked by peripheral ministries such as healing, signs and wonders, and good works. He has remained true to his central ministry. God called him to present Christ in the power of the Holy Spirit, and to leave the results to God. Billy Graham has consistently preached the Cross of Christ. He has never shirked from declaring the power that is to be found in the shed blood of Christ. And he has always preached for a decision. That is the message which is at the core of this book.

From the tens of thousands for whom Billy Graham has been the catalyst which has changed their lives, we have selected just thirty examples. They span the forty-five years or so of Billy Graham's crusade and mission ministry. Some of their names are well known. For some, his ministry has resulted in their conversion. For some, he has so influenced their lives that their whole direction has been changed. For some, who were already committed Christians, it was the influence of Billy Graham (or of members of his team) upon their lives for which they are eternally grateful. In this book, many claims about God's goodness to them and the change that He has made in their lives come from their own lips.

The reader may identify with the experience of one or another. If that is so and if, as a result, another life is changed, then that is ample justification for this book. It is commended to you for that purpose.

Julian Huxley wrote:

> By speech first, but far more by writing, man has been able to put something of himself beyond death. In books an integral part of the individual persists, for it can influence the minds and actions of other people in different places and at different times. A row of black marks on a page can move a man to tears though the bones of him that wrote it are long ago crumbled to dust.[5]

If the stories herein can move a man, not only to tears, but to find a Saviour, the labour of writing will have been abundantly worthwhile – long after 'the bones of him that wrote it are long ago crumbled to dust'!

Maurice L. Rowlandson

Acknowledgments

So many have been involved in the compilation of this book that it would be impossible to acknowledge each of them individually. There are some, however, who have been indispensable in helping in the practical elements of compiling a book of this nature.

First I want to acknowledge the love and support of my wife who has lived with an author whose mind is often elsewhere – on the story he is currently writing! Conversation so often centres around those stories. In addition, she has read every chapter as it has been completed, and has made many helpful suggestions.

Then there has been the team of secretaries who have typed much of the manuscript again – and again – and again! Alison Carr (who has also worked many times for the Billy Graham Evangelistic Association) has been involved since the beginning. Latterly, Sue Bridge has not only taken over the typing, but she has also done a word-count, checked the spelling, the grammar and, sometimes, the content, to ensure that it is both correct and readable. She was also responsible for the final typing and has done a sterling job.

To each of the persons whose stories have been told, my special thanks. They have submitted themselves to interview; read the draft of their story; made their corrections, deletions and additions, and have finally agreed to the story being published. For the time and effort it has taken each one of them, my sincere thanks.

Then special thanks must go to Roger Palms and his staff at *Decision* magazine for the help and advice they have given me with chapter 16. Roger has always encouraged me, and I appreciate that.

Many members of the Billy Graham Team – not least Mr Graham himself – have given me advice and help, and I am grateful to each one of them.

Others who should be named for their part in researching these stories are:

Dan Wooding, for his help in obtaining President Carter's endorsement;

Sir David McNee and Colin Sinclair, for their help in locating Dr Oliver;

John Pollock, for many factual details he has given me;

Neil Innes, for research on other Scottish names;

Joan Winmill Brown, for allowing me to use so much of her book;

Branko Lovrec, for submitting himself to long-distance interview;

Chonda Pierce, likewise. Her chapter was a delight to write;

the two pseudonyms, for allowing their stories to be told;

Miss Jean S. Wilson, for help in the Eva Close chapter;

Joyce Nasgowitz, Bob Shuster and Lois Ferm, for their welcome to the archives of the Billy Graham Center in Wheaton and for so readily allowing me to use material gleaned from that source. Story after story has been unearthed there, and a highlight of writing this book was a visit to the Center, where I was given such help.

Some names will inevitably have been missed but, to everyone who helped, my sincere thanks are due.

1

If Only One Person . . .

George Verwer, UK/USA, 1951
The press were agog! Their reporters had been summoned to
a press conference called by the committee of the Greater
London Crusade, to introduce a young, unknown and unheard-
of American evangelist, Billy Graham, to them.

His chief claim to fame, as far as they were concerned, was
that 'questions' about him had been asked in the House of
Commons a few days earlier. There had been a demand that
he should not be allowed to land at Southampton when he
arrived. The trouble stemmed from a sentence which had
appeared in the annual calendar issued by the Billy Graham
Evangelistic Association in Minneapolis, Minnesota, USA. The
calendar had said:

> There will always be an England. But will it always be
> the England we have known? . . . Something tragic
> happened during the war years. Through fear-haunted
> days and never-ending nights, the German bombs turned
> England's homes and churches into fire-blackened heaps
> of rubble. And when the war ended, a sense of frustration
> and disillusionment gripped England, and what Hitler's
> bombs could not do, socialism with its accompanying
> evils shortly accomplished.[1]

Hannen Swaffer of the *Daily Herald* declared: 'Billy Graham
has more gravely libelled us than anyone has dared to do since
the war.' It was the MP Geoffrey de Freitas who raised the
matter in parliament, but the storm quickly subsided when one

of Graham's aides pointed out that 'socialism' was spelt with a small 's' – the American equivalent of 'secularism' – and that no slur was intended upon the British Socialist Party! But the reports did ensure a large attendance at the press conference!

One journalist asked the question: 'How many converts do you expect to make?' To which Billy Graham replied: 'None!' He went on to explain that it was not he who converted those who responded, but the Spirit of God, working in the heart of the enquirer. He then added: '*If only one person* comes to Christ because of the Greater London Crusade at the Harringay Arena, all the effort and expenditure would be worthwhile.'

The significance of that statement can be put into the context of another special 'one-off' meeting, which had been held in New York a year or two earlier. One man who responded to the invitation to accept Christ as Saviour and Lord in that campaign, was a young man named George Verwer.

Verwer was only thirteen years old, a student at the Ramsey High School in New Jersey, when a Christian lady decided to pray for the students at the school. She had done this for twelve years when, in the name of her son, she sent a Gospel of John by mail to young George and challenged him to read it.

The American evangelist Jack Wyrtzen had invited Billy Graham to a one-off 'campaign meeting' at the Madison Square Garden in New York as part of Jack's 'Word of Life' campaign. Mainly out of curiosity, George attended that meeting. 'At the time,' he says, 'I owned three small companies and had dated thirty-two different girls!' On the night in question he actually took his 'date' with him. 'I thought that she needed religion and could use the message,' says George! 'But as I listened to Billy Graham, the Holy Spirit worked in my life and I was convicted of my sins. Billy called on people to repent and to humble themselves and to be born again. To my surprise I found myself walking down to the front of the arena with thousands of others.' As Billy Graham gave the invitation to come forward, George was one of those who responded.

'It was then that I gave my life to Christ,' he says.

Soon afterwards, the enormity of what had happened came home to him. He was not a man who let the grass grow under his feet. George had no idea where that simple decision was going to lead him, but he was so excited with what had happened to him that he started to witness among his friends at Ramsey High School.

'I gave them Gospels, books, tracts and any other literature I could lay my hands on. It was those early days of seeing what the printed word could do that convinced me of the power of that means of evangelism. That conviction has never left me.'

There followed a period at college and, later, at the Moody Bible Institute; but it was during his days at college in a town called Maryville, in Tennessee, that George became very sure that God wanted him to take the Gospel to Mexico. 'I persuaded two other students to come with me (one of them was Dale Rhoton, who still works with us today), and together we went to Mexico to distribute tracts and sell Gospels and other literature from door to door.'

George tells of the way in which a newly formed church in his own home town sent him out to perform this ministry. 'I will never forget the occasion, as it was at a mid-week prayer meeting where I was given the privilege to share my vision – even though I was only nineteen years old. Then they sent me forth, the same as we read in Acts 13. Ever since then I have believed that the local church is the key for local evangelism and follow-up worldwide.'

There followed a very successful ministry. Later, while he was at the Moody Bible Institute, he began to challenge other students about the needs in Mexico. As a result, four of them set out for Mexico for the second time in the summer of 1959. They also began to look at the closed country of Spain. It was during his time at the Moody Bible Institute that he met and married his wife, Drena.

'I thought it was about time we got ourselves properly organised,' says George, 'so we set up a ministry which we

3

called "Send the Light". We incorporated it and ran it from my home in Wyckoff, New Jersey, with my mother acting as secretary and office manager.' His mother would say that she was doing most of the other jobs too!

After graduating and getting married, George and Drena spent six more months in Mexico, and the work there grew very quickly. In September 1960 they responded to the Lord's leading to move to Spain, and by the next summer they had entered the Soviet Union. There, George and his partner, Roger Malstead, were arrested for 'Bible smuggling'. George says: 'Actually we were on a trip to take Scripture into the Soviet Union but, due to my own mistake, we were arrested by the secret police and held by them for a couple of days. However, it is my conviction that failure is the back door to success, and that particular incident led us to a day of prayer.'

They ended up by being deported and spent the day in Austria. 'As we prayed, a clear understanding of what the Lord wanted to do came to me. It was then that the name Operation Mobilization came to me and was adopted.'

That was the beginning of a regular summertime ministry, which later extended to Italy, Germany, Austria, Belgium, France and Great Britain. 'There was an excess of enthusiasm which George exuded, and which inspired us all to get involved,' says one of the young people involved in a team to France.

Each summer George recruited teams, generally between the ages of seventeen and twenty-three, to go out to these countries. 'We had a strong conviction that these young people should be thoroughly trained in order to carry out the evangelistic ministry,' says George. 'It was not easy for them. They had to raise their own keep, and sometimes the accommodation provided for them was terribly Spartan – sleeping bags, groundsheets, with or without tents, were the order of the day. But that was all part of it. They had to learn that serving Christ demanded sacrifice.

'I went around Britain to get British young people moving

4

out by the hundreds. I wanted to get the Germans out as well and I said, "Let's unite and get old vehicles so that people could move out and we could carry literature." God gave us about thirteen vehicles that summer in 1962 and about 200 people.'

More than 90,000 young people have since been trained in this way. In the intervening years many of them have become pastors and Christian leaders in their own countries. Operation Mobilization teams have visited more than a hundred countries in this ministry. George says, 'Most of our long-term workers are sent out by their churches so that things "may be done decently and in order" [1 Corinthians 14:40] and so that proper training may be given to them in the country in which they will work. We long to see effective discipleship training programmes that will produce the workers needed both by the church locally as well as around the world.'

Then in 1964 a team headed overland into the great subcontinent of India – the start of a work there which now encompasses more than 280 workers, most of whom are nationals.

'I couldn't rest,' says George. 'While out there, there were countless thousands who had never heard that Jesus Christ could save them from their sins. I *had* to tell them the good news, and I believed that that could best be done by leaving some literature in their hands. From the very beginning, books, tracts and other printed material have been a major part of our ministry. After all, the printed word lasts longer than the spoken word, and I firmly believe that when material is paid for – however low the price – it is more likely to be read and saved than if received as a free handout.'

Years later, that was to prove very evident when George Verwer was invited to be one of the speakers at the great Bible convention in Keswick, Cumbria, in north-western England. Each time he was on the programme, he always commenced his talk by commending to the audience a number of books. Philip Hacking, who at the time was the chairman of the convention, was a little concerned that it might look a little 'commercial' if books were always being recommended from the platform! So, on the last night when George was due to speak, Philip Hacking said to him: 'George! Only two books tonight!' (George had been in the habit of recommending five or six books each night!)

When the time came for him to speak, George went to the rostrum and said: 'I'm under great constraint tonight. The chairman has said that I can only recommend two books to you – but there are so many I would like to tell you about. How do I select just two out of the myriad of marvellous books that are out there?' Then George held up one book: 'I thought about recommending this one by Ron Dunn on "Prayer", but then I thought, "No, I won't tell them about that one." Instead I considered this one by . . .' And so it went on, until at last George got to the 'two books' that he had decided to recommend that night! By then the platform was in hysterics! George had 'done his own thing' and, while following the chairman's instructions, had nevertheless succeeded in mentioning five or six books in passing!

Another feature of George's method of recommending books was his practice of putting three or four books together in a plastic bag and offering all of them for the usual price of one or two. This habit created chaos in the convention bookstall – but they soon found a way of going along with him, and book sales soared!

Another compulsion which resulted from his commitment to books was a desire to make literature more easily available around the world – especially in those countries which might be closed to missionaries and to the Gospel. Yet he had vivid memories of the gruelling two-month trip across bleak wastelands and over dirt roads that had been faced by those early pioneers to India.

'It was in 1964,' says George, 'that I shared with my colleagues the vision I had of a ship which could sail around the world with Gospel literature. It could go to places that we would never reach by land.' The more he thought about the possibilities of this, the more excited he became.

Six years later, in 1970, God answered that vision by giving to Operation Mobilization the opportunity to buy a 2,319-ton ocean-going vessel. The M/V *Logos* was purchased and has since visited more than 186 countries and over 500 ports of call around the world. Later a second vessel – the *Doulos* – was added to the fleet and continued the evangelistic and literature ministry of the *Logos*. (The original *Logos* has since been replaced by *Logos II*, following the loss of the first ship by shipwreck off the coast of South America, the full story of which is told in the book *The Logos Story* by Elaine Rhoton.)

To make the ships acceptable in ports hostile to Christianity, an 'Educational Book Exhibit' was created, mainly of secular books in English which were quite rare in African and Asian ports. Operation Mobilization staff would go ahead of the vessel and organise church support and secure government approval. Media-wise, the ships attracted great coverage wherever they went. This in turn attracted visitors, and an average of 40,000 visitors go aboard at each port. This means that more than 8 million visitors have been aboard in the eighteen years the ships have been operating. Of these, 370,000 have attended meetings on board, and more than 2 million have come to on-shore conferences. Workers from the ships have trained more than 19,000 Christian leaders and pastors. More than 73 million pieces of literature have been distributed, including over 5 million educational books, 3 million Christian books and more than a million copies of the Scriptures.

With such a positive story, it is sometimes surprising to discover that the ministry is nevertheless human! There have been the disappointments . . . the setbacks and the times of discouragement. George says: 'The great disappointment is when people, whom you think are going to become great disciples, get side-tracked. Sometimes it is a moral problem; sometimes it may be doctrinal extremism – or just the fact that, as the movement gets bigger, you don't have the time to sort out problems.

'We've had other disappointments and tragedies, too. One

of our workers was shot on his doorstep in Turkey. One worker just disappeared in Afghanistan. Just recently we've had two sisters killed in a hand-grenade attack on the *Doulos* in the Philippines. We had a warehouse in Bombay burnt down, and another warehouse in Carlisle also burnt down, a ship on the rocks – but, if we look at thirty-five years of ministry, God has been very good to us.

'What we are doing is just a tiny drop in a vast ocean. The task is so great. The burdens and goals are almost overwhelming; but God does use people at all levels who are fully committed to Him, who experience His grace, and who intersperse all their activities with prayer.'

George's personal ministry has taken him all over the world. He has preached on every continent, and God has used his ministry to reach many thousands of others. George still has an overriding passion for books, and he has written several himself! He remains a great believer in the power of the written word, and he never fails to draw attention to worthwhile publications which, in themselves, may result in changed lives. The story of his ministry goes on! Whole books could be written about any single aspect of the work.

'If only one person . . .' All of this ministry grew out of one man's response to the Gospel. At the Harringay Crusade, 38,447 enquirers were recorded, many of whom made a first-time decision for Christ – and some of their stories are told in this book. At that one-off New York campaign in 1955, around 250 enquirers were recorded, of whom George Verwer was one. Had he been the *only* one, it could be said that the meeting was abundantly worthwhile.

That 'one person' has, in this case, been a catalyst in the lives of many thousands of others. God alone knows the potential in the life of any individual who comes to Christ. George Verwer says: 'Don't miss God's plan for your life. Become self-disciplined. Seek the will of God – not token commitment, but total commitment.'

2
Introducing Billy

Tom Rees, England, 1948

Billy Graham first came to Britain in 1946. He returned in 1947, and on that second visit he brought with him Cliff Barrows and Cliff's wife Billie and their friend, George Wilson. They spent six months travelling and preaching all over the UK. It was one of the coldest winters that Britain had ever experienced, and the cold was exacerbated by a fuel crisis and strikes. Electricity was unavailable for heating, and nor was there any coal or other fuel.

Nevertheless, for Billy Graham and his colleagues, it was unbelievable discomfort. Bill Martin in his book *A Prophet with Honor* recalls their reaction:

> The winter was bitterly cold. The worst in decades, and economic conditions had improved little since the first visit [the year before]. To save money, the group frequently boarded in homes rather than in hotels, and Graham and George Wilson often slept in the same bed fully dressed and wearing shawls over their heads to keep warm. On occasion they spoke in stone churches so cold and dank that fog obscured part of the congregation from their view![1]

They could not have known that those cold six months were a valuable preparation for Billy Graham's later ministry in the United Kingdom. Billy preached in countless churches and chapels around the country. From time to time they held big meetings. Because he was here for so long, many people later claimed that 'Billy Graham spent his first night ever in England in my home in 1947!' They all genuinely thought that they were the first! In reality his first night was spent in the home of Oliver Stott, who lived quite near Southampton, where Billy had disembarked. From there, they travelled daily to locations all over England, Scotland and Wales.

That same winter, the outstanding evangelist, Tom Rees, had a vision. Conscious that, like him, other young British people had led deprived lives during the spartan days of the recently ended war, he decided to buy the vast Kent mansion, Hildenborough Hall, and convert it into Britain's first Christian Bible Holiday Conference Centre.

He determined that everything there should be of the highest quality. The furnishings, the service and the food were exceptional and he provided some of those luxuries never enjoyed by young people in wartime – like cream!

But he couldn't help the coldness of that 1947/8 winter. The staff there at the time still remember the ghastly conditions. Says Mary Amies (Jean Rees's secretary): 'In the winter it was mainly staff, with only occasional weekend conferences run by other organisations, but in that winter of 1947/8 we didn't have many conferences because of the lack of heating. Those of us on the staff wore our thickest clothes – and an overcoat on top. To keep warm, Joyce Silcox (Tom Rees's secretary) and I tried to type letters wearing gloves! It was awful!'[2]

Tom Rees had done his best to help, but really there was nothing much that could be done. One day he sent one of the men on the staff out to scour Kent to try to find fuel of any sort. It was with great glee that the man returned with a car packed full of wood logs that he had spotted in the garden of a house down a tiny Kentish lane. Negotiations with the owner had confirmed that 'everything is for sale – at a price!'

'At least we had a few warmer evenings as we conserved that precious stock of wood,' says Mary.

Eventually news of the ministry of Billy Graham and his colleagues filtered through to the Christian press and one day reached the ears of Tom Rees. He called together the staff at Hildenborough Hall and read to them a paragraph from *The Life of Faith*, which told of the ministry of this young evangelist from America. It said that he had been conducting meetings around the country, and that he would be speaking in London at Westminster Chapel on 31 March 1948.

As an evangelist himself, Tom Rees was deeply interested. He was the first prominent post-war evangelist and had already attracted a large following of young people. He first preached at London's Royal Albert Hall in 1944 as part of a team of evangelists for the series of meetings called the 'Faith for the Times' campaign. Inspired by the obvious hunger of young people for evangelism, and convinced that the day of the old-style evangelism had gone, Rees had the vision for a month-long series of meetings. They would be 'geared to young people' and would be held in central London, with himself as the sole evangelist. In fact he was to be more than that! He was MC, song-leader, sometime soloist . . . and the evangelist! The committee for 'Faith for the Times' did not share his vision, so Tom Rees 'went it alone' and booked London's Westminster Central Hall for the entire month of September 1945.

His enthusiasm proved infectious, and that series became one of the most important of the post-war series of evangelistic meetings. Several further series followed, culminating in an evangelistic rally in the Royal Albert Hall on every Saturday evening throughout the winter of 1947. Every meeting was packed out. Tom Rees used to call the Royal Albert Hall 'our little mission hall in Knightsbridge'! Although he did not know it, he was already laying the foundation for a ministry that was later to be continued by Billy Graham.

The Royal Albert Hall is a strange building. At the time when the hall was built, money was raised by selling boxes and seats inside the hall. These would be owned in perpetuity by the donors. Although more than a hundred years old, that provision still applies. The current owner of a seat still has priority right to use it. Consequently, whenever any organisation or individual hires the hall, the booking includes all seating – *except* those privately owned. As there are around 1,500 such seats, and as the owners often don't use them, when the hall is 'sold out', there are always dozens of empty seats and people wonder why.

It is possible, however, to make an '<u>exclusive</u>' <u>booking</u>. At a price, the hirer can 'buy out' all the private owners. Then the entire seating in the hall is available for use. Tom Rees always took an exclusive booking, so when the hall was packed out – it really was!

As he read that report in *The Life of Faith*, it was not the first time that Tom Rees had encountered the name of Billy Graham. In 1946 Tom had been invited to conduct a citywide campaign in Winnipeg, Canada. For that campaign the local committee had invited, as vocal soloist, a young man named Bev Shea. This was the first time Tom Rees had met Mr Shea, and he returned to Hildenborough with glowing stories of the wonderful voice of this bass-baritone singer. Bev and Tom had 'hit it off' and had got on well together. Occasionally Bev Shea had mentioned the young Youth for Christ evangelist Billy Graham, who was taking America by storm; Bev Shea had sung for him often. Bev Shea added that Tom Rees should try to meet this man.

On 9 April 1947 Tom Rees's diary records: 'I had breakfast with Rev. Billy Graham at the Penrose Hotel. Had long discussions with him about appeals etc. He has had 7,000 conversions since he went to England a few months ago.' Three days later, Tom Rees attended a Youth for Christ meeting in New York. It did not appeal to him: 'It was a sort of Christian entertainment, exalting a movement more than Him! I was to have had thirty minutes to preach the Gospel. After two hours there were only eighteen minutes left. Then their chairman took over. He crooned, coaxed and harassed the crowd for twenty minutes. It was not something that I appreciated.'[3]

Those comments were to become very relevant later on,

when Billy Graham came to Harringay. Tom Rees was dreadfully fearful that a similar pattern might be followed by Billy Graham.

Tom Rees read to his staff that report in *The Life of Faith*. He suggested that a group of them should drive up to London and go to hear this young evangelist. He himself was unable to go as he had already been booked to speak at a youth rally the same evening.

Jean Rees recruited a small group to drive to London with her to hear Billy Graham. There were five of them in the party, including the author and Tom's pianist Lex Smith, both of whom were to have their lives completely changed by that first contact with Billy Graham. The attitude of those who went was a little cynical and sceptical – possibly because they were all loyal to, and believed in the ministry of, Tom Rees. Could any *American* possibly come up to the standard of their beloved Tom?

Mary Amies says, 'We got into the car outside the front door of Hildenborough and, as we were about to depart, Tom came out and banged on the roof of the car. With mock severity he said: "You're all going with the wrong attitude. Now remember, whatever you may think about this man Billy Graham, he *is* God's messenger. So don't go in a critical attitude! Rather, pray for him as you drive up to London that he may preach with great power and that folk will find Christ." Duly chastened, we went on our way up to London.

'As was her custom, when we started to get into London, Jean (who was driving the car) started praying for the meeting. No eyes closed or anything like that. I was a bit worried when she started praying and I took a surreptitious sideways look to make sure she was still looking where she was going!'

A few years earlier, Billy Graham himself had caused similar concern to Dr Donald R. Brown when he was a student with Billy Graham at Wheaton College. Donald Brown was a member of a gospel team quartet which sang at Billy Graham's meetings. 'We would drive in Billy's old Plymouth,' he says, 'and the five of us would pray all the way to the service. When Billy prayed, he often said, "Is it OK if I keep my eyes open while I drive and pray?" '[4]

The journey into London continued with all the party praying for the meeting and for Billy Graham. When they arrived, they were slightly surprised to find Westminster Chapel completely full. Jean had telephoned in advance and had asked for some seats to be kept for the party, and the stewards led them to a pew not far from the front.

The team taking part comprised four members: Stratton Shufelt (the song leader), Chuck Templeton, Torrey Johnson and Billy Graham. Torrey Johnson was a leader in Youth for Christ – the organisation which had arranged the meeting. Chuck Templeton was later to be the catalyst in Billy Graham's own ministry. In his book, *A Prophet with Honor*, William Martin recalls: 'After completing his studies at Princeton and serving for a time as a successful evangelist ... Templeton recognised he was no longer a believer in any kind of orthodox sense.'[5] In sharp contrast, his friend Billy Graham (after talking with Templeton) '... made a conscious resolution that he would never again entertain any doubts whatsoever about the authority of Scripture'. This decision galvanised his faith and 'gave power and authority to my preaching that has never left me'.[6] That event is commemorated at Forest Home, California, on a Stone Witness where Billy Graham had accepted, once and for all, the absolute authority of the Scriptures.

The first part of the meeting was somewhat brash, loud and typically American in style. However, when Billy Graham rose to speak, the atmosphere changed. From his opening words he totally captured the attention of his audience. He was clearly a man to be reckoned with! They listened, captivated, as he preached the Gospel with a strong emphasis upon what the Bible said. 'The Bible says ...' he declared repeatedly. It was powerful stuff and it moved each of the party from Hildenborough. The two men in the Hildenborough party both responded to the evangelist's invitation to commit their lives to the service of Christ by travelling to study and train at the Northwestern Bible School in Minneapolis. At the time Billy Graham was President (Principal) of the college. For those two alone, the trip to London would have been abundantly worthwhile.

When the group returned to Hildenborough, they impressed Tom Rees with their conviction that Billy Graham was 'God's man for the hour'. Tom declared that he was going to invite Billy Graham to come and speak at one of his meetings. Still, before doing that he invited the American to visit Hildenborough Hall – possibly to 'check him out' before issuing the invitation!

Billy came and spent the day at Hildenborough, and he and Tom were closeted together for prayer for much of the day. When the time came for Billy to leave, he and Tom had formed a bond of friendship that endured over the years, as they found a real affinity of spirit in their respective ministries.

It so happened that the BBC was planning to broadcast a Sunday evening hymn-singing programme, which was to originate from Tom's meeting at the Royal Albert Hall. This seemed an appropriate occasion on which to invite Billy Graham to be the speaker.

The occasion was an immediate success. The response to his invitation led many to commit their lives to Christ. Tom Rees was convinced that Billy Graham would have a great future in the British Isles, and he told him so.

He did, however have two reservations. He was still worried about his experience of the 'appeal' in New York. He was fearful that this might be Billy Graham's style. Always an advocate of total honesty and openness at that point in the meeting, he felt that this standard was lowered in the appeal that Billy made. 'All heads bowed, and all eyes closed: no one can see you. This is between you and God,' said the evangelist. People were then encouraged to raise their hands if they wanted to become Christians. Then, when that was all done, they sang a hymn, during which Billy Graham encouraged those who had put up their hands to come and stand at the front. It was not as bad as it had been in New York, and Tom's worst fears were not realised.

Tom's second reservation concerned the Americans' passion for statistics. Tom always felt that statistics could be put to use adversely for his ministry. He advised Billy Graham to stop giving out the numbers of 'converts' resulting from his meeting. Instead, he urged that they should be regarded as 'enquirers'. No one really knew exactly why each person had come forward, save for their desire to find out more. Tom Rees took the view that they were 'enquiring' about the Christian faith and that at that stage they had not necessarily been converted.

Billy Graham's humility was shown by the way in which he both accepted and acted upon these criticisms. He changed the style of his appeal from then onwards and used his much more familiar style of asking people to come to the front right from the very beginning. He saw a clear biblical principle for this, in so far as 'everyone Christ called, He called publicly – and I'm going to ask you to confess Christ publicly tonight, by getting up out of your seat and coming to the front'.

As for statistics, from then onwards both Billy Graham and all the members of his team refer only to 'enquirers'. It is the press who refer to 'converts'.

Because of that meeting at the Royal Albert Hall, the Evangelical Alliance, under the leadership of its secretary, Mr F. Roy Cattell, called together a conference representing nearly 250 of the Christian leadership in Britain. They held this conference at Church House, Westminster, under the chairmanship of Lieutenant-General Sir Arthur Smith. In his brusque yet friendly manner, he governed that meeting and kept it securely on track. He said that Billy Graham had a 'holy audacity that prompted him to try new approaches. In God's name he even sanctified the media to communicate the Gospel of Jesus Christ',[7] and that impressed the leaders who listened to him. Tom Rees recorded in his diary: 'We had a super talk from Billy on "evangelism and the churches".[8]

16

'There followed a discussion whether or not Billy Graham should be invited to London. Most thought "yes"; some of us did not know. I still don't know. Guide, dear Lord!'

The treasurer of the Evangelical Alliance, Mr John Cordle, had visited one of Billy Graham's crusades in the USA, and he spoke warmly of his reaction to the evangelist's message and style. 'It is,' he said, 'a style and method which would be very acceptable here in Britain. It is devoid of the emotionalism so often associated with evangelists from America. His preaching is centred around the Bible.' Mr Cordle was later to be instrumental (through his friends, Lord Westmorland and Lord Burleigh) in securing the first invitation that Billy Graham had to preach before members of the royal family.

It was as a result of the meeting at Church House that the firm invitation was extended to Billy Graham to hold a six-week crusade (later doubled to twelve weeks) in London. This was the birth of the Harringay Crusade: in a sense, Tom had been the midwife.

However, his own ministry was greatly changed after Billy Graham's first visit to Britain. When they were planning the Harringay Crusade, Tom put all his records at the disposal of the Crusade committee. He encouraged his stewards, personal workers and choir members to get involved. The personal workers, although carefully trained by Tom Rees, needed a different type of training for the Crusade evangelism, and they had to get used to a change of name to 'counsellors'. They were therefore enrolled in the 'counsellor training classes', led by Charlie Riggs and Lorne Sanny.

Tom also put his own large supporters' mailing list at Billy Graham's disposal. He was willing for Billy to overshadow his own ministry and humbly stood back – but not without drawing criticism to himself. Tom came to Harringay Arena on the opening night of the crusade and on one or two further nights towards the end of the twelve weeks. He had believed that he should leave London clear for Billy's ministry, while he himself would undertake evangelistic 'campaigns' (as he called them) in other parts of the country. Apart from the last two weeks, throughout the twelve-week period of Harringay Tom was involved in these other missions. His absence from the platform was noticed, however, and it was wrongly assumed that Tom Rees had had his nose 'put out of joint' by Billy's successful ministry at Harringay. In reality he was busily engaged in a similar ministry himself, but elsewhere.

Billy Graham says of Tom Rees's support: 'He was with us from the very beginning. He did everything he could to help towards the success of the Harringay Crusade, and we deeply appreciated his love and support as we came to London.'

Tom Rees had been a forerunner to Billy Graham. In many ways he had prepared the ground for Billy's coming. The ten years of evangelism from 1945 to 1955 led by Tom Rees had been significant in many ways, not least in orientating the thinking of church leaders towards a new style of youth evangelism. Tom's influence over those years had provided an atmosphere of acceptance for a ministry by Billy Graham. It was, in a way, the culmination of everything for which Tom Rees had prayed and worked.

However, for Tom Rees it was never to be the same again. This was partly due to some news given to him by David Rennie on 15 April 1954. David said that the Harringay committee had decided to invite Billy Graham to return to London in June 1955. Tom Rees records: 'The news that David Rennie gave to us was, in a way, sad news because the June visit would conflict with our own series in the Royal Albert Hall [earlier in 1955].'[9]

He met personally with each member of the Crusade committee, and on 5 May he met with Major-General D. J. Wilson Haffenden, the chairman. That evening, and on one or two following evenings, he went again to Harringay. He received a 'diplomatic letter from Billy Graham'[10] and met him personally after one of the meetings. They had prayer together and discussed the dilemma in which Tom found himself. Should he, or should he not, continue with his plans for the meetings in May?

In the end, encouraged by Billy Graham, he decided to go ahead. But, he records, 'my worst fears were realised. We ought not to have had these when Billy Graham was coming so shortly afterwards.'[11] The final meeting was 'the smallest meeting we have ever had in the Royal Albert Hall. It was, I think, the last Royal Albert Hall meeting I shall be conducting, maybe ever.'[12] And so it was.

Although he continued his evangelistic ministry, London was much more of a closed book to him. Still, he and Billy Graham remained very close in the following years. There was never any hint of any breach of fellowship between them – for there was none. For example, when Billy Graham arrived at Southampton some years later on a visit to England, he specifically asked that Tom Rees should be taken to meet him as the boat docked, and that the two of them should drive to London. They spent a precious two hours of fellowship together, sharing their burden for the British Isles and praying that God would continue to use both of them in that ministry.

That prayer was answered for Tom Rees as he conducted his campaigns in other parts of the country. Billy Graham's encouragement of him largely influenced and led him to a significant ministry in the Mission to Britain. Tom Rees and his team conducted evangelistic rallies on a tour which took them to 156 cities, towns and villages throughout the British Isles. They visited every county and the offshore islands of Jersey, Guernsey, the Isle of Wight and the Isle of Man. Nor was Ireland forgotten – both north and south. The team which travelled throughout Britain included Tom and Jean Rees, Ian Cory (as the organiser), Gordon Brattle (pianist), Nigel Cooke and Tony Groom (who travelled the whole circuit on his motorcycle). The baritone soloist from Atlanta, Georgia, Frank Boggs, also joined the party for part of the tour.

They held a service of dedication at St Paul's Cathedral on 4 October 1958, and the thanksgiving service, at the end of the series, was held at the Royal Albert Hall on 16 May 1959. Between those dates, they had travelled continually (with a short break for Christmas). Many places they visited had never had an evangelistic meeting within living memory. Some of them were too small to sustain an evangelistic series. It was a case of 'you name it . . . we've been there!'

This series was extremely successful and the knowledge of it travelled extensively. As a result, an invitation came for a similar series of meetings throughout Canada; a year later, the team went off to Canada to travel across the length and breadth of the province.

The influence of Billy Graham upon the life of Tom Rees was incalculable! He had encouraged Tom in his ministry and had opened new vistas of evangelism which – humanly speaking – would never have opened had Billy Graham never shared with him his heart's concern for the British Isles and, indeed, for the world. There are those in Britain and Canada who look back to those days of mission when they committed their lives to Christ.

Equally, Tom's influence upon Billy Graham was by no means insignificant. The part he had played in introducing Billy to the British Isles – and to London in particular – had been strategic. Heaven alone will reveal the extent of the influence these men had upon each other! The last time they were to appear together on a platform was during the Greater London Crusade in Earls Court in 1966. *The Christian and Christianity Today* recalled the event in its issue of 10 June that year. It reported (complete with a picture): 'British Evangelist Tom Rees, who was invited to read the Scriptures at the Crusade, instead recited them by heart, last Friday.'[13]

This was so typical of Tom Rees, who knew most of the New Testament by heart. In his own evangelistic meetings he always asked those who were invited to read the Scriptures to commit them to memory and to recite them by heart. Unless you were prepared to do that, the invitation did not stand! It was a marvellous discipline for which countless people – who were the 'young people' of those days – have cause to be grateful to him.

In New York, in April 1970, he was staying with his friends, Stephen and Heather Olford, in a room at the Salisbury Hotel. At the time, Stephen was pastor of the Calvary Baptist Church in West 57th Street, and the hotel was part of the church's property.

On 20 April, with his Bible open upon his knees – and in the midst of his normal practice of scripture memorisation (from the Epistle to Timothy on that day) – a massive heart attack overtook him and he quietly passed into the presence of his Saviour. It was the way he would have wanted to go – busy in his work for the Lord!

3
Called to Preach

College Professor Warren Wiersbe, USA, 1948
One of the speakers in 1990 at the famed Bible Convention, 'The Keswick Convention', in England's beautiful Lakeland, was an American. He chose as his subject 'Three approaches to sin', using Proverbs 28:13 on which to hang his theme. He told how salvation and sin were the two most costly things in the world. Salvation because it cost God His only son, and sin because it can rob us of all that is beautiful, blessed and holy. 'He who conceals his sins does not prosper, but whoever confesses and renounces them finds mercy,' declares the text. The speaker pointed out first how we can *conceal* our sin. 'It is our first inclination,' he said. 'Cain did it; David did it; Ananias and Sapphira did it; and all of us do it.'

Secondly, we can *confess* our sin. John, in the Bible, says, 'If we confess our sins, God is faithful and just to forgive us our sins and will cleanse us from all impurity.' David the King confessed his sin, but Saul was good at excuses. Our first instinct is to make excuses. But David said: 'God will not despise us when we come to loathing ourselves because of our sin.'

Thirdly, we can *conquer* our sin. We can do that by walking in the light 'as He is in the light'. For then 'the blood of Jesus His Son – the work of Calvary – purifies us from all sin'. He said that God is waiting for us to turn our sin over to Him and He will hurl it into the depths of the sea, and it will be remembered no more. 'We can do that,' he said, 'by the grace of God!'

Warren Wiersbe was already well known to the British

audience, for he had written more than a hundred books. They were popular commentary books on a variety of biblical subjects, usually prefaced by the word 'BE . . .' (*Be Mature, Be Victorious, Be Real, Be Hopeful,* etc., etc.).

Those who listened to him, however, never knew that he might not have been a speaker at Keswick that year, had it not been for the influence of Billy Graham upon his life. As a youngster he had attended the Swedish Covenant Church that his great-grandfather had founded. Because of the family connection, there was never any question whether or not he should attend Sunday school – he just went! And later he was confirmed.

It therefore came as something of a shock to him – or, perhaps, an 'eye-opener' – to discover that, in spite of all his 'churchy' background, he was still not a Christian. He thought he was, of course. He had done everything that was right. Nor was there anything in his life to make him think that he was any great sinner! But he was to discover that all his earlier experiences were not enough to make him a Christian.

Warren Wiersbe says: 'When I was growing up, teenagers were just being discovered! Any spiritual ministry to them was not the big thing it is today.' Then along came a whole crowd of people with new ideas to 'reach the young'. In 1931 Percy Crawford had started a radio programme specially geared towards teenagers. A few years later, in 1940, Jack Wyrtzen started his 'Word of Life' radio programme, which exploded across the airwaves with an impact that had never been felt before.

So popular were their programmes that both men tried to find other ways of reaching young people. To both of them – gifted evangelists first and foremost – came the idea of starting summer camps which the young people could attend. One feature of these holidays was the opportunity to meet the two broadcasters in person. Because of their popularity, this was something of an attraction.

At about the same time in the mid-1940s (when most of

Europe – and, indeed, much of the rest of the world – was engulfed in a ghastly war) another group of young men got together and prayed. The result of that prayer-time was another explosion which was to rock the youth world both at the time and for decades afterwards. It became known as 'Youth for Christ' and it was spearheaded by young, energetic and visionary leaders such as Bob Cook (who was to become the movement's president), George Wilson (in Minneapolis), Torrey Johnson (in Chicago) and a young preacher called Billy Graham.

'Youth for Christ' meetings were innovative and exciting. In Minneapolis, George Wilson conceived a variety of programmes, which included such events as a hundred grand pianos all playing gospel music at the same time! Specifically the target of 'Youth for Christ' was to reach the many young servicemen walking the streets of Chicago, and on 24 May 1944 'Chicagoland Youth for Christ' was born.

Master of Ceremonies of that meeting was a Chicago pastor, Torrey Johnson. Bob Cook was the song leader and Billy Graham became the speaker. The meeting was an immediate and outstanding success. When Billy Graham gave the invitation to accept Christ, many young people responded and eventually, on American Memorial Day of that year, they moved their rally to Soldier Field in Chicago and more than 75,000 attended. At that, America began to sit up and take notice!

In the following year, the tentacles of 'Youth for Christ' reached overseas, and the first 'Youth for Christ International' rallies were held in London's Westminster Chapel. They were exciting events for the rationed, war-bored, and deprived young people of Britain. 'Youth for Christ International' adopted as its slogan 'Geared to the Times, Anchored to the Rock', and that inspired slogan is still relevant over 50 years later.

In the small town of Indiana Harbor, in Indiana, USA, lived the Wiersbe family. Young Warren, just sixteen years old, was quite a character. Even at that age he knew he was going to be a preacher. After all, he was equipped! He had been going to the Mission Covenant Church as far back as he could remember. But he *wasn't* a Christian!

In the spring of 1945 an unofficial meeting was called to invite a 'Youth for Christ' team to come to Indiana Harbour. They booked the Washington High School auditorium for three successive Saturday evenings and asked the Chicago office of 'Youth for Christ' to send them speakers.

Someone got the idea of printing the publicity on shiny-backed blotters. 'Why? I can't imagine,' says Warren. 'Not many of the kids I knew used fountain pens, but all of us in the Mission Covenant Church youth group who attended the school passed out these blotters all around. And many other church youth groups did the same in their schools.' So when the great night came, there was a very big crowd of people and the meeting was a great success.

Warren was asked to help with the organisation of the meeting. 'After all, I was one of the best Christian boys my friends knew,' says Warren. 'I volunteered as an usher and passed out songbooks. All my friends felt that this was a job I could do well *as a Christian*.' Neither they nor he knew that it was just a façade.

Torrey Johnson had been booked by the Chicago office of 'Youth for Christ' to be the speaker at that meeting. In the event, he sent the young Billy Graham along instead. 'Torrey often did that for his younger colleagues in YFC so that they could get a hearing and become better-known,' Warren says. 'That in itself was a great ministry of Torrey's, for the world is short of people who will direct glory away from themselves and let the opportunity fall to others.'

It is reminiscent of what the beloved Lindsay Glegg used to do in Britain at around the same time. Lindsay often turned up at a meeting (to which he had been invited to speak) with a young man in tow. 'I've asked so-and-so to bring you the message tonight,' he would say, thus exposing to the Christian public a new, up-and-coming young man who might otherwise never be known. Many of the leading evangelists and Bible teachers of the 1980s and 1990s are the young men whom Lindsay Glegg brought forward in those early days. It was a unique and self-effacing ministry, in which he had a special calling from God.

So it was that Billy Graham came to Indiana Harbor to speak. In those days very few people knew who he was, although he had been heard by some on the Sunday evening radio programme, 'Songs in the Night'. That programme itself had been started by Torrey Johnson, but he had handed it over to Billy Graham to run. Eventually he convinced Billy Graham that it would be right for him to resign from the ministry in his own church and become 'Youth for Christ International's' first full-time evangelist.

To the young Warren Wiersbe, Billy Graham was something different! 'I was busy ushering,' he says, 'and I was helping behind the scenes. But when Billy Graham began to preach, I was captivated. I stood against the back wall of the auditorium, unable to move and unable to take my eyes off the preacher. I heard every word he spoke and every Bible verse he quoted, and everything he said went right to my heart. Sure I had heard it all before, but *for the first time* it came together and made sense. I saw that in spite of my character, my confirmation, my church attendance, and my host of religious relatives, I was a lost sinner who needed to trust Jesus Christ.

'I didn't wait for the public invitation to be given. Right where I stood, I asked Jesus Christ to come into my heart and save me, *and He did*! I didn't raise my hand for prayer, I didn't fill out a card, I didn't even go forward when the crowd sang "Just as I Am," but I did trust Christ and become a child of God.'

That was a great evening for Warren. It marked the change of direction – though not a change in his calling. Even though (as he had now discovered) he was not a Christian, he always knew he wanted to be a preacher. Torrey Johnson once asked him: 'Young man, what do you plan to do with your life?' Warren replied, 'I told him I wanted to go to school and get some Bible training and then preach the Gospel. He then gave me a great piece of advice that I've tried to follow: "Young man, find the one thing you do that God blesses, *and stick with it!*" '

Later on, Warren was to learn that Billy Graham had left that meeting feeling very discouraged. It turned out that a few pastors, zealous to maintain their denominational individualism, had criticised him for not 'preaching baptism'. Warren says: 'I wasn't baptised until three years later, but I want you to know that God saved me that night.'

So what did he do next? One of the first things he felt he had to do was to give his testimony at the Mission Covenant Church. 'I was able to tell them that their prayers were answered, for many of them had been praying for me.' Later Warren told them that he had been called into the ministry, and they were especially excited about that. 'My great-great-grandfather had prayed that there would be a preacher of the Gospel in every generation of our family, and there has been.'

Warren soon started receiving invitations to take part in various aspects of the ministry at his church. One day, between the morning Sunday school and the worship service, one of the deacons stopped him and asked if he would read the Scripture that morning. 'It was Luke 3:1–9,' says Warren, 'and it was heavily seasoned with words like "tetrarch", "Ituraea", "Trachonitis", and "Caiaphas". I didn't have a self-pronouncing Bible, so I stumbled through the reading the best I could. It was embarrassing, but I learned two valuable lessons from that experience: 1. Never read the Scripture publicly unless you're prepared; and 2. Never draft anybody in at the last minute to participate in a public service, unless the person feels he or she can do it.'

These are great lessons to be learnt both by the participant and by the speaker!

During those early days, Warren Wiersbe equipped himself through personal study. He also spent one (boring) year at Indiana University, before eventually going to the Northern

Baptist Seminary in Chicago. His five years there gave him the training he needed to serve the Lord as a preacher.

As the years passed by, he became so much more than just a preacher. His gifts expanded to embrace writing, teaching and conference speaking, which ultimately led him to that engagement at the Keswick Convention.

In his autobiography, *Be Myself* (published by Victor Books), he tells much more about the result of the decision which he took under Billy Graham's ministry; it revolutionised his whole life. In the hundred-plus books he has written, he has discussed so many matters of guidance and teaching, on a variety of spiritual topics, that to rehearse them here would be superfluous.

But the Keswick Convention was not alone in the special outlets for his ministry. His experiences were to come 'full circle' when he found himself ministering to Billy Graham and his team in a similar way to that in which Mr Graham had first ministered to him.

From time to time the Billy Graham associates meet for a three-day conference. Bible teaching, reports, fellowship, fun and relaxation form the essential elements of these encouraging and inspiring times together. High on the agenda of each Team and Staff Conference (TASC) is the prominence of the Bible, with expository teaching from a leading Bible teacher on each occasion. In years gone by this position has been filled by such people as Stuart Briscoe and Howard Hendricks. In 1995 it was to be the turn of Warren Wiersbe. The man who had been converted through the ministry of Billy Graham was now to return to minister to Billy Graham and the team.

That year, on the Florida shore of the Atlantic Ocean, in the holiday resort of Fort Lauderdale, the TASC brought together team members, staff, board and international representatives (with their wives or husbands) to share in this time of blessing and fellowship. Morning after morning they sat enthralled as, on each of the three mornings, a Bible exposition was given by Dr Warren W. Wiersbe; formerly a pastor of three different churches, he is currently in great demand as a Bible teacher in similar conferences and assemblies all over the world.

In Florida, Warren Wiersbe took the story of the Apostle Peter for his expositions. He pointed out that the story of Peter covered three facets of our spiritual experience – those of faith, hope and love.

Three times Peter was distracted in his faith: first, as he looked *at himself* when he caught a great host of fish (Luke 5:1–11); the second time, as he looked *at the circumstances* surrounding him when Christ told him to walk on the water and he looked around and failed to have faith in Christ (Matthew 14:22); and, thirdly, when he looked *at others* instead of at Christ when expressing concern about what would happen to the Apostle John (John 21:19).

Warren Wiersbe told how Peter had a constant hope. For example, in Acts 12, Warren pointed out that Peter was able to sleep because he had hope for the future. He knew (from John 21:19) that he was to die from crucifixion – not from having his head cut off! So he was able to sleep peacefully even though there was the imminent possibility of death confronting him.

Peter's demonstration of love was made three times over: when Christ asked him three times if Peter loved Him. Three times Peter had denied Christ, and three times he affirmed his love of his Master (John 21:15–17).

As the team and staff listened to him giving those three biblical expositions, they were rather like the audience at the Keswick Convention of five years earlier. Until he told them so, they were unaware that, but for Billy Graham, he might not have been the featured speaker at those meetings.

Billy Graham himself was among those who listened to the three talks, and he expressed to Warren Wiersbe the thanks of all those assembled for the excellence of the Bible teaching that had been given. It was during the course of the expositions that Dr Wiersbe had paid tribute to Billy Graham and had recounted how, in those far-off days of 1945, it had been Mr Graham's ministry that had brought him to faith.

It seemed fitting that it should have been one of Billy Graham's earliest converts who now returned with messages containing such a blessing to the TASC. 'Cast your bread upon the waters and it shall return to you after many days!' Once again the seed sown by Billy Graham had produced an enormous harvest over many years. Warren Wiersbe says: 'I shall be eternally grateful for that young preacher from Western Springs, who was drafted – in the place of Torrey Johnson – to preach the sermon that led me to Christ!'

4

Newscaster

Stuart Hamblen, USA, 1949

It all began in 1949. At the time, Billy Graham was President (Principal) of Northwestern Bible College in Minneapolis, Minnesota. He had become such not through academic excellence (he would be the first to disclaim that), but because of the insistence of the founder and President of the college, Dr William Bell Riley. Calling Billy Graham to his sickbed, Dr Riley told Billy Graham that it was his express wish that Graham should succeed him as President of the College. He invoked Scripture and said it was his personal conviction that this was God's will. 'Beloved, as Samuel appointed David as King of Israel,' he said, 'so I appoint you as head of these schools. I'll meet you at the judgement seat of Christ with them!'[1]

This left Billy Graham with little choice but to accept. He did so with some reluctance, fearful that such a commitment might interfere with his true ministry of evangelism.

One of the first things he did as President was to bring his close friend, Dr T. W. Wilson (known affectionately to all as 'TW'), to the college as Vice-President.

The author, who attended Northwestern during Graham's presidency, affirms that the introduction of TW to the school was a stroke of genius. The latter's constant presence during Graham's continual absences was a stabilising factor, and it is largely due to TW's support and leadership that Graham's presidency can be said to have been hugely successful.

It was from Northwestern that the backbone leadership of the original Billy Graham team was formed: T. W. Wilson as his closest associate, George Wilson (no relation), then business manager of Northwestern, as the administrative head of all of Graham's work, and Jerry Beavan (Professor of psychology, theology and Hebrew),who had a talent for public relations and publicity, as his associate in that field. Graham quickly involved all of them in his future plans for evangelism.

Dr J. Edwin Orr, a Bible teacher from the UK who at the time was living in the USA, came to Northwestern College during 1949 to conduct a series of devotional 'chapel times' for the students. His ministry was both remarkable and far-reaching. On the fourth day of his meetings, as soon as he had finished speaking, a student stood up and started to pray. No sooner had that one finished than another followed, and he in turn was followed by another. Indeed, so strong was the experience of the presence of God in the gathering that the impromptu prayer meeting went on and on. Shortly before midday, TW came to the platform and announced that classes would be abandoned for the rest of the day, and that the prayer-time would continue. Students left and returned throughout the day, and the prayer meeting did not conclude until early in the evening.

There were prayers of confession and repentance and, as the day went on, they turned to petition and commitment. Petition was heavily centred around the forthcoming Los Angeles Crusade (which had just been announced). There was a deep concern from all the student body that Mr Graham's ministry should be effective.

This was to be the first crusade that would set the style for decades to come and reflected a growing desire by Billy Graham to move on from the gaudier aspects of the 'Youth for Christ' days and to present a style which demonstrated a growing maturity. His conviction that training constituted an important prerequisite for a crusade had come from lesser crusades in Charlotte (in 1947) and in Augusta (1948). It was also heavily influenced by several visits to England (1947 to 1949). As a result, the crusade in Los Angeles was carefully prepared and, for the first time, involved Dawson Trotman and the Navigator team in the training of counsellors.

Stuart Hamblen, a well-known and notorious newscaster on American radio, promised to publicise the crusade on his programmes, and he was true to his word. Nevertheless he was disturbed to discover that the crusade was to be extended by several weeks, for he realised that he was getting close to personal involvement. He had been to the meetings on several occasions but had insulated himself against the message. One night he presented himself at Billy Graham's apartment in a drunken stupor and begged for help in straightening out his life. In the ensuing Bible-reading, prayer and counselling session, Stuart Hamblen declares, 'I heard the heavenly switchboard click.'

Hamblen's upbringing had been by parents who were God-fearing, hell-believing people, and the family lived in the parsonage, so the message of the Gospel was not entirely strange to him.

Stuart loved music and, while still very young, purchased an old guitar. Accompanied on the piano by his sister, Oberia, he quickly learned to play some of the secular songs of the day – songs like 'Yes, sir, that's my baby'. His father came home and, hearing this worldly music coming from the parsonage, said, 'This will never do. What will people think? From now on, you must play only good religious hymns!'[2]

Their repertoire increased and, while they still included tunes like 'Wabash Blues' and 'Tipperary', they could slip into 'Bringing in the Sheaves' and 'Dwelling in Beulah Land' when they saw their dad approaching the parsonage![3]

His father never let an opportunity pass to emphasise the importance of faith. On special occasions (like birthdays) Mr Hamblen Senior would write the boy a letter:

Dear Stuart: This is your birthday and here is a little tie. But this is not just an ordinary tie, for this one can talk. Here is what it says: 'Stuart, I am right from the warm hands of your Father and Mother. When you put me around your neck, remember that their arms would be glad to hug your neck and kiss your brawny face and tell you of the wonderful night, not many years ago, when you came to brighten our lives. It would tell you of how your parents knelt by the bed and dedicated you to the Lord; it would also tell you of the great dreams and fond ambitions they have for you and how they lift you up each day to the Throne of God and ask that you be kept from this wicked world.'[4]

The years went by, and Stuart's skills in music led him to California and Hollywood. On the way, his heart had been broken – several times! – by young ladies with whom he fell in love. But one by one they failed to live up to his expectations. One such occasion occurred over a girl called Mary. Stuart was singing and crying over his lost love, then one day the Mary Stuart he was singing about appeared in the studio. Instead of the willowy, dark-haired vixen Stuart had left in Texas, there stood a matronly woman trying to keep 230 pounds in check. That taught Stuart a lesson and, from then on, he 'just loved 'em and hoped they'd never show up again for recognition'.[5]

Then, one night, Stuart telephoned home and told his family that he had met *and married* the sweetest girl in all the world. Her name was Suzy Daniels and he loved her with all his heart.

'Praise the Lord,' his mother shouted, for now they knew that someone else would have to cope with the idiosyncrasies of young Stuart. And Suzy did, for she stayed with Stuart for the rest of his life.[6]

There were days of anxiety, however. Suzy, aided and abetted by Oberia, tried so hard to bring a change to the rather wayward life of their husband and brother. In the end, after many attempts at trying to change him, both of them agreed that only God could make the true transformation that Stuart needed.[7]

Suzy herself had discovered a deeper spiritual meaning to life. Oberia says, 'Once I saw her in such a silent, prayerful attitude that it alarmed me to the point that I timidly told her one day that I was afraid she was going to die. With a girlish twinkle in her pretty brown eyes she reassured me quickly by replying, "Oh no, I'm not, Obee; I've just begun to live." [8]

Then one day the papers announced that Billy Graham was coming to Los Angeles. 'If we can get Stuart out to hear Billy Graham, he'll be converted!' Suzy exclaimed. Oberia didn't think it would be as simple as that.[9] Nevertheless, all over the nation people were praying for Stuart's conversion, so something was bound to happen.

To Suzy's joy, Stuart eventually agreed to go to the meetings – and he went on several nights. 'Billy Graham aimed his messages directly at me,' Stuart complained, and Suzy knew that the battle for his soul was going on. He was literally like the rich young ruler and he was about as stubborn.[10] ' "You're going to hell," is what he always shouts, and points directly at me,' Stuart would protest.[11]

Finally it was announced that the following Sunday night service would conclude the series of meetings. Suzy was devastated when Stuart went off on a hunt. Here it was, the last night of the meetings, and Stuart was still not saved.

To their astonishment, Billy Graham announced that evening that the meetings would continue for another week. 'Suzy and I had the assurance that God had held the ending over just for Stuart,' says Oberia. 'When Stuart came in from the hunt that night, we casually mentioned that the meetings were going on for one more week.'[12]

Stuart's own words tell the story. 'I knew that I couldn't last another week,' he says. 'I'm not afraid of any man. But for the first time in my life I began to shake when my Lord Jesus said, "Hamblen, that's the last chance you get. That's it."

'Boy, I was scared. I opened the door, and up the stairs I went and switched on the light. My wife Suzy was in bed and I yelled, "Suzy, get out of that bed."

'She sat up in bed and said, "What in the world is the matter with you?"

'I told her, "I don't know, but let's pray." You know, my wife is a little slow – but you should have seen her scramble out of that bed!

'I was praying and I was in earnest, but I wasn't getting any results. I said, "Let's call Billy Graham."

'She said, "Honey, he is a tired man."

'I said, "He's responsible for all of this. He's torn me up mentally, he's torn me up physically, and I'm going to call him."

'It was three-thirty in the morning, but I called him. I said, "Billy, something's terrible; I want to pray."

'He said, "Thank God! Come on down." '[13]

When they got to Billy Graham's there wasn't a parking space, so Stuart made one by parking on a red line. When he knocked on Billy's door, he felt, 'Boy, now my trouble is over. When I went in I said, "Billy, let's pray."

'He said, "No, wait a minute."

'I said, "Do you mean to tell me that you caused me all this hell and then you are not going to pray with me?"

'He said, "No."

'For a moment I thought of busting him one. A man who had torn a man up like he had me and then not pray with me! I said, "Why won't you pray with me?"

'He said, "Stuart, I will not get on my knees with you until you promise to give up everything that is mean and vile and wicked in your heart."

'I said, "Billy, let's pray."

'He said, "No, you've got to make that promise."

'But I said, "No, I can't do it."

'And do you know what went through my mind? It was this: "My race horses," and I'd loved them.[14]

'He said again, "You've got to give up everything that is mean and vile in you." He didn't enumerate my horses, but God told me it was my horses immediately.

'I started counting the cost, and, boy, I was sick. Finally I said, "OK, Billy, OK. I'll give them up."[15]

'Now mind you, this was about four o'clock in the morning.

Billy has got a ringing voice. I wondered what those people in that apartment thought was going on up there. Then Grady Wilson prayed and my wife prayed and when it came my turn to pray, boy I was ready. I thought they'd never get through but I remember my first words to my Lord and Jesus and I'll always remember. I said, "Lord, you're hearing a new voice." And boy, I heard the switchboard click. I knew I had Him on the line that time, man. You can't take that away from me. And when we got through talking – and I did most of it – the Lord just said, "Yes, Hamblen, I love you." '[16]

The next day Stuart went back to the studio as usual, but he had a new direction in his life. In America, the newscaster not only reads the news bulletin, he is also responsible for the advertising slogans of the product of his sponsor. Stuart Hamblen was retained by Camel cigarettes, and he was required to advertise their product. When he came to the advertising 'spot' he first told how he had become a Christian the night before (through Billy Graham). He said that he believed that Christians were not supposed to smoke. Jim Vaus tells how he heard it over the radio as Stuart Hamblen continued: 'Folks, smoking won't do you any good at all! In fact, you might just as well quit. But if you've already got the habit, well, you'd better buy Camel cigarettes; they're the best of a bad bunch! But if you aren't smoking now, there's no use in starting!'

This cost him his job, but the news of his conversion was no longer a secret. Indeed, when the film star John Wayne remarked upon the transformation in Stuart's life, Stuart replied, 'It is no secret what God can do.' John Wayne suggested that he should write a song about it and, using those words, Stuart Hamblen wrote – and sang – the song which has become a standard in country music.

> It is no secret what God can do.
> What He's done for others
> He'll do for you.

With arms wide open,
He'll welcome you
It is no secret what God can do.

'There are a few things that the American public, *en masse*, will speculate about,' says Oberia. 'Things like the outcome of the World Series, a coming presidential election, the prospect of war, and now the probable reasons as to why my brother Stuart was leaving his radio programme after twenty-one years of broadcasting.'

When it came to his final broadcast, there was a long line of sympathetic and interested friends who waited in the rain outside the radio station. They wanted a chance to get into the studio to say 'Goodbye' to their favourite broadcaster. It was very moving and inspiring. While thousands of his fans registered intense disappointment that he should be leaving the air at the peak of his popularity, Stuart felt sure that the Lord had had a hand in flicking the dial that would silence his voice. Says Oberia, 'I became convinced that there was a divine purpose behind it all and an unseen hand was writing in clear, bold letters across Stuart's life the words, "God moves in a mysterious way His wonders to perform." ' Although thousands of fans wrote in, begging him to go back on the radio, Stuart stood firm in his decision.

However, with an offer to go on a national hook-up, he had Suzy and Oberia wondering what his reaction would be. Stuart's reply to the national hook-up offer was most satisfying to the many hearts who had for so many years lifted his name in prayer: 'I can't go on the radio for a barn dance,' he said. 'I can't afford to dilute my testimony. I know now a self-managed life is a self-damaged life. I choose Jesus – He's good enough for me!' That one decision convinced Suzy and Oberia and all the others that Stuart had completely stepped out of himself into Christ.

From that day onwards Stuart turned all of his time and efforts into service for the Lord. Out of his conversion experience came such beautiful songs as 'He bought my soul', 'It is no secret', and many others which are still being sung all over the world. Stuart travelled constantly right across the nation, holding evangelistic services, and he spoke at many of the 'Youth for Christ' meetings. There was a tremendous change in him as he grew spiritually.

Stuart could never be depended upon for details. He would forget something whenever he left home for one of his missions for the Lord. If it wasn't for Suzy's scrutinising eye, he might easily have flown away in his pyjamas! 'On his last trip East,' says Oberia, 'we were all standing in a circle while Stuart was leading in family prayer. He was leaving on a plane and it was about time for it to depart. While I peeked in admiration at my brother's soulful expression as his lips moved, asking for God's protection, my eyes roved down his complete costume and came to rest at his feet. I was horrified to see what shoes he had on! They were a pair of big old hob-nailed boots! I could hardly wait for the final "Amen," when I screeched, "Stuart, your boots!"

' "My boots," he stammered. "Oh, my boots." With trembling hands he thrust some crumpled bills into my hand and motioned towards the door. "Go," was the only word I heard him utter.

'Racing wildly into town, weaving in and out of the cars, I finally reached the shop where he had his boots shined, only to find the door closed and the iron grille locked in place. Desperately, I asked an elderly man standing nearby if he knew where the shoeshine boy was.

' "He's just left, ma'am, and he went that way," the man replied, pointing towards the liquor store.

'Not hesitating a moment, I barged in just as the surprised black boy was sitting down. I yanked him fiercely on the shoulder and threatened him with these words, "If you don't come with me at once and get my brother's boots, he'll miss the plane and hundreds of people will be lost."

'Leaving the bar with the wide-eyed shoeshine boy, I glanced back to see a line of bewildered, befuddled patrons trying to figure out just what had happened!'

There was a broadcast meeting in Los Angeles at which Stuart had to speak to more than 500 preachers. He announced that he was going into evangelistic work. Oberia says: 'On his first trip for the Lord, he spoke to 10,000 people at a Minneapolis "Youth for Christ" Rally and over a hundred converts hit the sawdust trail. He followed that up with a capacity crowd at the Town Hall in Philadelphia, and he spoke at the Hollywood Bowl. There, although there was a bus strike on, over 20,000 eager souls managed to arrive to hear my brother Stuart.'

His readiness to travel thousands of miles in any kind of weather, as an ambassador for the Lord Jesus Christ, convinced those who knew him that he had fully consecrated both himself and his God-given talents to God's own will.

For over forty years Stuart's testimony never faltered from that significant day in 1949. 'He is in Glory now,' says Oberia, 'and I am sure he is among the glorified who have made a triumphant entry into the Holy City. I am sure that the Book of Life will include the name of my brother – Stuart Hamblen – thanks to the prayers of Suzy and so many others and to the faithful ministry of God's servant, Billy Graham.'

5
Wire-tapper

Jim Vaus, USA, 1949

Arch-criminal Jim Vaus was another of those whose lives were changed through the Los Angeles Crusade of 1949. Like Stuart Hamblen, he had been reluctant to go, not least because he was doing very well, thank you very much, from his wire-tapping activities, which became notorious across the United States.

Jim Vaus worked for gangster Mickey Cohen – a name to be conjured with in the criminal fraternity; at the time Cohen was the West Coast 'boss' of crime. *Time* magazine in 1949 described him as 'the undisputed boss of Los Angeles gangdom'.[1] He soon heard of Vaus's skill in the electronics field and came up with a suggestion which was to net vast profits for him and his gang. The technique developed by Vaus was to tap into the telephone wire which brought the bookies the results of all major horse-racing events.[2] By so doing, Vaus and his cronies could delay transmission long enough to enable a colleague to place a last-minute bet on (what they now knew to be) the winning horse. This device made them large sums of money, and they were all living very well.

At this time Jim Vaus had his own business, called 'Electronic Engineering – Consultants'. His offices were in the same building in which Mickey Cohen maintained a haberdashery shop – an excellent and unspectacular 'front' for his real business.

Through his business, Jim Vaus soon became involved in shady affairs, and his skill in tapping telephone wires was used to spy on people in high places. Several court cases ensued, and before long the name of Vaus began to appear in the newspapers. It was sleaze and scandal of a high order, and Vaus was at the centre of its exposure and ultimately he served a term in prison.

All of this brought him to the notice of Mickey Cohen, who felt that Vaus's skills were being wasted in small-time activities. Cohen saw that there were larger fish to fry if Jim's talents could be enlisted. In particular Cohen felt sure that his apartment was being 'bugged' – possibly by the police – and he asked Jim to investigate.

That evening, Jim came home and told his wife: 'I went out to Cohen's place and found the bug.' Most of Jim's electronic activities were a mystery to her, and she asked him how he had managed to do that. 'I've a high-frequency transmitter and receiver which sends signals into the ground and returns signals if any metal object is picked up. Then there's a highly sensitive meter that computes the depth at which the metal object is buried. Within ten or fifteen minutes after I arrived at Cohen's place, I had found that the bug was concealed in a section of a built-in wooden box.'[3]

Jim told his wife that he had disposed of the bug and that Cohen had paid him well for finding it and getting rid of it – 'And I don't mean too few bucks!' he said.

Alice was not overly impressed. She told him: 'You'd better stay away from that man.'

Jim found that it was the police who had put the bug in Cohen's flat. He claimed that his activities were more legal than those of the police, since it was in any case illegal to plant a microphone.

From then on, Jim Vaus found himself doing more and more jobs for Mickey Cohen, and gradually the opulence of his home grew. He hardly ever mentioned Cohen's name at home because to Alice it was 'like a red rag to a bull'. His jobs for Cohen included the installation of a special alarm system which surrounded Cohen's house and protected him by giving adequate warning if someone was approaching his premises.

Meanwhile, at home Alice was worried. She felt that the things her husband was doing were very near to the bone. She did not like Cohen or his activities, and she felt that her husband would be better without the business that came from him. At the same time she enjoyed the new furniture and the better equipment in the kitchen – and the wonderful barbecue in the back garden where they entertained their friends.[4]

One day, when Alice was just about giving up hope of ever reforming her wayward husband, Jim came home and out of the blue announced that he wanted to go to church. Alice said, 'I was sure it was bravado on Jim's part, to prove to his friends that he had done nothing to be ashamed of, and that he could attend church *if he was in the mood*!'

Jim Vaus was no stranger to the Christian message. In earlier days he had attended the famous Bible school of Wheaton College, and he had also attempted to study for the ministry at the Bible Institute of Los Angeles. However, he was expelled from the latter for wire-tapping the girls' dormitory. He had developed a skill in electronics which he now diverted to criminal ends.

When they got to the church, it was interesting to note that, while Jim's special friends were as pleasant as ever, all too many members of the church looked askance at him. They had read of his shady activities in the newspapers. To Jim everything was 'above board', so he held his head up high.

Alice, on the other hand, was discouraged. 'The unfriendly attitude of so many of the church members worried me anew. If the Christians did not welcome him to church, how would he ever be convinced to change his ways and drop his associates?' She wondered what if anything could get below the surface to a Jim Vaus who needed God. That was where matters stood in the late summer of 1949.

Then one day Alice picked up the newspaper. Emblazoned across the front page was the big headline: REVIVAL HITS LOS ANGELES. The article was all about a campaign in central Los Angeles that was attracting enormous crowds. Not only was the Los Angeles newspaper covering the story, but prestige magazines like *Life* and *Time* were also carrying articles about it. The speaker was a man called Billy Graham.

The *Los Angeles Herald-Express* reported: 'At thirty, Evangelist Billy Graham is hailed by churchmen as a modern Billy Sunday. His six-week-old tent revival here is called the greatest in the history of Southern California. Converts number in the thousands.'

That night Alice turned to her husband and said, 'Let's go hear Billy Graham. Your mother has heard him and says he is most interesting.'[5] Jim responded that, if he could find the time, he was prepared to go. Alice did not read that as a good sign. Jim had often agreed to do things with her which he really didn't want to do, and then never got around to doing them.[6]

But this time a strange sequence of events was to change the course of Jim's life. First of all, they had the news that Jim's uncle had died unexpectedly. 'It was a hot and sticky day, that 6th November,' says Alice, 'but we felt we should drive to the mortuary to see the coffin and pay our respects. The coffin was open, of course, in the usual American style, and Jim looked down at his uncle's body. I could see he was touched and that his uncle's sudden death had given Jim the feeling of how suddenly one can be cut off.'

As Alice and Jim walked back to the car, Jim was very subdued. Alice thought that it might be passing through Jim's mind that he could be next! The day was getting hotter and stickier, and they decided to take in a movie; they knew that the cinema would be air-conditioned. The film they saw was called *Pinky* and was about a girl who pretended to be something she was not. It seemed that this film hit Jim in a weak spot because he knew that, for much of his life, he was bluffing – appearing to be an upright person and as good as the next fellow, when in his heart he knew it was not true.

'When we came out of the cinema,' says Alice, 'we drove towards the beach. But even there it was a cloudy, sticky day.' They stopped and ate on the way home, passing Mickey

Cohen's place. It seemed that some invisible force was driving them on and on.

Suddenly, as they reached Washington Boulevard, Jim suddenly turned to Alice and said: 'Honey, how would you like to go to the big tent and see what this fellow Graham is like?'

Alice replied, 'Anything you say, dear,' trying not to sound too anxious. She felt that if she appeared to be pressurising him, he would back off and change his mind. But Jim drove on to find a car parking space, and they walked across to the tent. When they got there, they found it was jammed with more than 6,280 people – its nominal capacity. They managed to find a couple of seats on the side and near the back.

Later Jim confessed that he was critical of everyone and everything that happened. But Alice enjoyed it all. She was moved by the music and by the tall young Cliff Barrows, who led the singing. Then Billy Graham began to preach. He was six-feet-two with a shock of blond wavy hair and burning eyes that captured the attention of everyone in the audience.[7] 'It was a wonderful evening,' says Alice, 'and when the preacher got to the invitation I felt "This is for me!" And I prayed "for Jim too, Lord, please".'

Alongside Alice, Jim sat, apparently unmoved. Alice feared that the evangelist's message had not touched him. She felt that if this message had not touched her husband, nothing would. And then the choir started to sing: 'Almost persuaded now to believe.' Alice's fervent prayer was that Jim would be persuaded.

In those far-off days there were still little earnest men who would go around a congregation, tapping people on the shoulder to ask if they were 'saved'. One of these men – later identified as 'Uncle' Billy Scholfield – did rather more. He grabbed Jim by the arm. Jim turned and glared at him. Scholfield bowed his head and started to pray for Jim and, when he looked up again, Jim muttered: 'I'll go!'

And with those two simple words, the spiritual transaction

was completed. Alice followed Jim down the aisle to the front. Her prayer was that Jim would really mean everything he said and did that night, that it would not be just an empty experience. At the front was the newly assembled team of trained counsellors, one of whom met and prayed with Jim. Afterwards Jim said: 'I didn't remember or hear much of what was being said. All I knew was that something had got beneath that ever-smiling surface which so often had said, "I'll get by." ' For once, however, Jim wept. And for a man who so rarely showed his feelings, those tears held a rainbow of promise for Alice.[8]

Jim prayed: 'Lord, I mean business with You, but You've got to mean business with Jim Vaus, for the road ahead is going to be a rough one. It's going to be almost impossible to straighten out this bewildered, tangled life of mine. But if you'll straighten it out, I'll turn it over to You – all of it.'

Next morning, the Los Angeles newspaper had the headline: WIRE-TAPPER VAUS HITS SAWDUST TRAIL. There could be no turning back now! Jim knew that he would have to stop associating with Mickey Cohen. He knew, too, that he would have to pay back money that had come through illegal means. There was no knowing how far-reaching Jim's decision that night would be.

He had stolen equipment from the telephone company, Warner Brothers' Broadcasting Station, the Bleitz Camera Company and lots of others. He began making a list of the money he must pay back – going as far back as 1939. When he totalled it all up, it came to $15,000 – a vast sum in those days. Alice exclaimed: 'But, Jim, where will you ever get that much money?'

He replied, 'Honey, I don't know. Believe me, I don't know. But I do know I'm going all the way with the Lord, and these are things I have to make right. I'll do everything I can, and the Lord will provide the rest!'

It was the beginning of a total change in lifestyle for the Vaus family. Each day they seemed to have less and less money.

They only bought the food they *had* to have. In the end, Jim only had enough petrol to get the car to a parking lot downtown. From there he telephoned the finance company and told them to come and get the car. He phoned Alice and told her, and she immediately asked, 'But how will you get home?'

'I'll hitch-hike,' he replied.' To Alice it was more than she could bear to picture her proud Jim using his thumb to hitch a ride. It was an enormous surprise to her when, just a little later than his usual time, a car drove up and out stepped Jim. As he came into the house he gave Alice a box. It contained clothes for the two children, Denny and Madeline, clothes that they needed but which she could not afford. It was a new experience to learn what other Christians could do to help. It was the first time a stranger had ever given her anything for nothing. 'It was so wonderful,' she says, 'to learn how Christians will give when they want to help someone.'

Then Jim showed her two $5 bills. He explained, 'Billy Scholfield got me the ride and pushed this into my breast pocket, and Alfred Dixon, who drove me home, put this in my Bible, which was lying on the seat between us. I'm not going to take this money. They're hard-working men, and I've squandered my share.'

It hurt Jim's pride to take from others, but Alice reminded him, 'You said you'd trust the Lord to provide. You have to let Him choose the way. Besides, Jim, maybe this is God's way of making you humble.' In the end, they prayed and sincerely thanked the Lord for the money – and kept it!

In the past Jim had often had dinner with the Cohens, but after he had become a Christian he decided he had to go and see them once more. When he arrived, he was shown into Cohen's den. It was a long room with rich cabinet-work furniture. There were huge brass lamps, flowerpots and trailing ivy. LaVonne, Cohen's wife, stood at one end of the room, and several prominent men, whom Jim recognised as gangsters, at the other. One of them called to him: 'Jim, is it true that you've got religion?'

Jim replied, 'You might call it that, though I prefer to say I've found Christ. Anyway, something has happened to me and I have peace in my heart since I've settled things with God.'

LaVonne glanced at Jim, looking a little puzzled. Then she turned away and, staring out of the window, said, 'I could use a little of that religion myself.' At that moment Mickey Cohen walked into the room. He and Jim left the room, and Jim told Mickey of his decision. 'There's a lot of people that won't like what you're doing,' Mickey said. 'They'll figure you're running out on them.' But as for Cohen himself, he told Jim that, even if the whole world turned against him, 'there's one little guy who thinks a lot of you for the decision you've made. Promise me you'll never go back to your old way of life. Quit it for good!'[10]

Jim made that promise, and he never went back on it. From that time on, his whole life was changed. As the years passed he was invited to speak at innumerable meetings all over the United States – and, indeed, the world. Everywhere he went, he told of the Grace of the Lord Jesus Christ in his life and of the change that had come so suddenly, as he committed himself to Christ at the great Los Angeles Crusade.

Since then, two books and a film have been written and made about his life. His own story, in *Why I Quit Syndicated Crime,* is a testimony in his own words to the journey from crime to Christ. *They Called My Husband a Gangster* is Alice Vaus's observations both before and after her husband's conversion. It also traces the moving story of their courtship and marriage, and the birth of their children. She tells things that Jim was unable to tell in his story, and she holds the reader enthralled by the wonderful workings of the Lord in their lives.

Wiretapper is the story of Jim Vaus told on film. This dramatic movie was made by World Wide Pictures and has been used over the years – particularly in prisons, where its message is especially relevant. No holds are barred and no punches pulled as Jim's association with the gangster world is superseded by his association with Billy Graham's ministry.

Jim Vaus's story goes on, for in the years between he has been deeply involved in evangelistic projects himself. In the city of New York he has organised and promoted evangelism in New York's gangland. Only as a former gangster himself could he reach and understand these youngsters whose lives had been overshadowed by crime.

In the spring of 1958 he founded an organisation called Youth Development Inc. He set up a small store-front club for boys in order to try to reach youngsters in the forty or so known armed gangs in a square mile of the city housing nearly 250,000 people.

From the first group of ten gang leaders, nine committed their lives to Christ, and one even became an employee of the federal government, while another became an elected official in the City of New York. Jim's original intention was to stay only a few months in the city, but he remained there for fifteen years, before returning to the West Coast. There, in spite of Parkinson's disease and diabetes, he continued his work and opened (and ran) sixteen homes for children in the San Diego area.

More than 30,000 calls a month are received on a telephone hot-line for children. Through his electronic skills Jim was able to design a computer-driven system that allowed each of the calls to be forwarded to the appropriate volunteer among the hundreds in the churches and across the nation who had promised to help in this task.

Through the message he has preached – the same message that Billy Graham had preached to him – countless dozens of young people have come to a knowledge of the saving power to be found in Jesus Christ. As they have put their faith and trust in Him, so their lives have been changed – as was Jim's. He was only one person, but through him the message goes on – and on!

The Harringay Crusade

London, England, 1954
No single religious event can have had greater effect than the visit of Dr Billy Graham to London from March to May 1954. Many books have been written and many stories told about an event which has shaped the cause of the Christian Church in the UK.

In response to the question, 'What has been the long-lasting effect of the crusade?', it is probably more significant to ask, instead, 'Where would the Christian Church in the UK be today had Billy Graham never come?'

The indisputable fact is that, in the latter part of the twentieth century, the Evangelicals in the Church are in the ascendancy. Evangelical churches of all denominations are largely full churches: in the Anglican Church there are more evangelical bishops than ever before. The Evangelical Alliance, promoters of the Harringay Crusade, now has more than a million members. Evangelicals are a force to be reckoned with.

Of the twenty-three crusades and missions (including Spre-e 73) which Billy Graham has held in the UK (see Appendix, p. 258), the one with the most long-lasting effect has undoubtedly been that at the Harringay Arena. It is appropriate, therefore, that of the thirty stories which comprise this book, seven should originate from the Harringay Crusade. Six of the seven subjects are still alive and active in the Christian ministry. The seventh burned himself out by travelling throughout the country in order to be a peripatetic evangelist himself, while still maintaining his duties at the head of a major food-manufacturing company.

The incalculable results of Billy Graham's own preaching, plus the positive response from the many clergy and ministers, and the testimonies from lay persons, leave little doubt that the influence of Harringay has been felt over four decades and several generations.

Such was the impact of Harringay that the *Oxford English Dictionary* at one stage included the word as a definition of 'an evangelistic spiritual experience'. The *Encyclopaedia Britannica* has also included it in a descriptive paragraph.

Through the message of these chapters, may the blessing continue!

6

The Queen's Warrant

Dudley Brient, England, 1954

Fast! That is the Dudley stationery company's slogan and keyword. In everything they do, they seek to be 'Fast and Efficient'. But without Dudley Brient's enthusiasm it might not have been like that.

In September 1945 Dudley was a young man, just demobilised from the army. With his gratuity he bought up a stock of surplus envelopes, which he re-banded, renamed, and sold as the first product of his infant company, which he called 'Dudley Stationery'. 'I also negotiated with the army for their old and surplus Ordnance Survey maps, which I had cut up and manufactured into envelopes,' says Dudley. 'They were a vital commodity in a severely controlled, post-war situation.' It was an example of his entrepreneurial flair and originality, and it was something which marked out his company for success in future years.

His only ambition in life was to build up his own company for the benefit of his two sons, and to make enough money to enjoy himself. He had a lively life, a lovely wife, and those two young sons – Trevor and Alan. His philosophy in those early days, he says, 'was to be successful. I just hoped that everything I attempted would not backfire on me. The ideas I had could have spelt disaster. But somehow or other the plans I made just seemed to catch on. Someone must have been looking after me "up there", but I didn't know much about that.'

Gradually he built up his business by buying more and more bespoke stationery at an economic price. He repackaged the same items under his own company's name and sold them at a profit. At first the business operated from the front room of his home. Later, as the work expanded, he moved to the ground floor of premises in Carlisle Street in the heart of London's Soho district, close to his potential customers. Later he also took over the basement. By 1954 his annual turnover was in the region of £50,000.

From the very beginning Dudley had been a great marketer. He believed in putting the availability of his products before his customers, and allowing them to make their decision and selection on the quality, the price and the speed of delivery. Hence 'Fast' was his watchword. In those early days, if you ordered in the morning, you got delivery by the afternoon. Fifty years later, delivery is still effected for most items by the next day – and the company's *monthly* turnover is more than £4 million. Over eighty-five years of age, Dudley does not let up! He still scours the telephone directory for likely customers, and he is continually bombarding his sales force with 'leads to follow up'! He has been described as 'the tiger that growls occasionally in the background'!

He was a 'different' man. The eccentric and the extrovert about him led him into business enterprises he had never expected. Although he was an extrovert – especially in his dress – he was still a very shy man, and he often found himself in a situation that he had provoked but which he could not handle. Even at his son's wedding he found the occasion full of stress and was almost ill. Nevertheless, he used his talents to their full advantage – although on occasion he felt that he had bitten off more than he could chew!

He had no religious convictions. He was into life for a good time – and that required money. So he set out to make his business as successful as possible from the very beginning.

That was, until 1954, when Billy Graham came to the Harringay Arena. Dudley's two boys persuaded him to go to one of the crusade meetings. In their wildest dreams they could scarcely have imagined the catalytic result that would follow.

Dudley's wife, Myra, had always tried to bring a religious

influence into the lives of their two sons. Both Trevor and Alan had attended camps organised by the Varsity and Public Schools movement (a part of the Children's Special Service Mission and Scripture Union). There, they had been confronted by the Gospel and had reached a point of choice. Were they to put all that behind them – or did God have a place for them and a part to play in their lives?

What they learned at VPS camps was backed up by the teaching they received week by week in their Crusaders' Union class. Aimed at reaching boys outside the churches, this weekly Bible class had grown to many hundreds of groups all over the country. Their friend, the young Horace Webber, was deeply involved and had a concern that Trevor and Alan should be regular attenders. He picked them up from home each week. 'The man is here,' Dudley would call out to Myra, who got the boys ready to go each week. Dudley, of course, had to pay the bill for the camp fees year by year. He was very glad to do that because he thought it 'was good for the boys'.

As time went by, the two boys grew in spiritual stature and became concerned for their father. So when Billy Graham came to Harringay, it seemed to be a God-given opportunity to invite their father to attend. They knew that he appreciated well-organised and successful events, and by all standards Harringay quickly proved to be that. So Dudley accepted their invitation and went.

It was Trevor who had said, 'Dad, go and hear Billy Graham,' which he did. But it was not long before the boys grew slightly worried. They found that Dudley was going every night! At first they thought that 'the old man' was 'going round the bend'.

It was at Harringay that Dudley's life changed. He never 'went forward' in response to Billy Graham's invitation, but it was there that he discovered a new dimension to his life – a dimension which meant that in the future his life would be governed by Bible principles and his business would be dedicated to the service of God.

Of that time Dudley says: 'Until I went to Harringay I was doing a job that I enjoyed and my sights were set on a successful business. I was respected for what I did, and that counted for a lot to me. But, after Harringay, I discovered that there was so much more to life. Billy Graham made the Bible come alive. He related it to the nitty gritty of life and he showed me that there was a better way.'

From then on, the direction of the firm was changed. Dudley determined that it would be a company with a Christian ethic. He would endeavour constantly to witness to his customers in whatever way he could and by whatever means he could.

In 1964 he established the company's colour of vermilion orange because he happened to see a van like that one day. It stood out among the many other vans and he said to himself, 'That's the colour I want for my company.' Nevertheless it was none too easy. The manufacturers of the vans pointed out that this was not a standard colour which their company used and they said that his van would have to be painted specially. Dudley says: 'I told them to buy a lot of that paint, because I had the vision for more than one van.' Today they have over 50 of them (including an 'artic' lorry), and the vermilion colour is still a hallmark of the company. It is hard to drive through London during the daytime in the 1990s and not pass at least one Dudley van. In the late 1940s Dudley would never have dreamt that his company would grow so big – but he lived in hope!

In the early 1960s tragedy hit him: Myra died and he was left to struggle with bringing up his two sons alone. At first it seemed like a disaster and he found himself questioning his new-found faith in God. Then, even in that extremity, he found that God had met him, and he was able to survive and rise above his loss.

'God is no man's debtor,' says Dudley, 'and He had a plan for my life that I could not possibly know about. Into my life came Norry Chandler, a wonderful lady with two teenage daughters, Dawn and Heather, both a bit younger than my sons. A short while later, my family became complete again as we got married. For Trevor and Alan it meant two ready-made delightful sisters, something they had never had hitherto.'

When they married, Norry was not a committed Christian. She knew of Dudley's faith and was happy to accept it in him. Dawn and Heather, however, had taken part in a ski-ing holiday in Switzerland which had been organised by Tom Rees and the people at the Christian Conference Centre, Hildenborough Hall. During that holiday, both of them discovered what it meant to become a Christian, and they committed their lives to Christ. That decision made them anxious about their mother. They were keen that she too should find the same satisfaction to life that they had found. They prayed for her constantly.

Then Billy Graham came to Earls Court (in 1966 and 1967). In preparation for that crusade training classes were held all over the country – and one of these was in north-east Essex. It was conducted by Charlie Riggs, a member of the Billy Graham team. During that time he got to know Dudley and Norry and encouraged them to attend the crusade at Earls Court.

They got tickets and, when they arrived, Dudley says, 'We were sent up into the gods. They were seats right up at the top in Earls Court. Billy Graham looked like a matchstick on the platform! However, when he preached, his sermon was as powerful as ever. It evoked many memories as I thought back to the time I had spent at Harringay.

'Billy Graham had scarcely finished speaking when I was conscious of a movement next to me,' Dudley says. 'Norry was up and off! She was on her way to the front and I had to call after her and say, "Hey! Wait for me. I'm coming with you!" '

When they got to the front, they found Charlie Riggs there, and he introduced Norry to a counsellor who shared with Norry the simplicity of the Gospel. 'It is as simple as A, B, C,' the counsellor said. 'That is the way in which the Bible lays it down for us. A – admit that you are a sinner; B – believe that Jesus Christ died on the Cross to forgive your sins; and

C – come to Him. Commit your life to Him and ask Him for forgiveness.'

That clear explanation of the Gospel helped Norry to understand what it was all about. She committed her life to Christ in a simple prayer and was quite sure of what she had done. 'To cap it all,' Dudley adds, 'her decision for Christ certainly made our marriage. It made us more considerate of each other's wishes, and we have never looked back. What a difference that visit by Charlie Riggs made!'

Dudley counts it as almost a miracle that it was through his two sons that he became a Christian, and now Norry had found the same faith through her two daughters. 'How important to us are the prayers of our children,' says Dudley! 'For both of us the catalyst that brought about the change in our lives was the preaching of Billy Graham.'

From that time, Norry brought an added spiritual depth to the family as the years went by. The four children got on well together and in later years it was hard to realise that they were not blood relatives. Dawn Chandler worked for the Billy Graham Evangelistic Association for some years in both London and Amsterdam, until the time of her marriage to an army doctor. Heather Chandler met and married an officer in the army, and together she and her husband, Colin Brown, have often been involved in the ministry of Billy Graham. The whole family is very close.

Both Dudley's sons developed as committed Christians and they have shared with him the many activities that have grown out of the firm. Trevor was first involved in overt evangelism in 1957, when he accepted an invitation to visit Germany with a team taking Billy Graham films to show to units of BAOR (the British Army of the Rhine) stationed in Germany. Both members of the team were appointed as 'honorary colonels' for the duration of the tour, and they enjoyed accommodation in the Officers' Messes in each of the army and Royal Air Force camps they visited. Once they went in to breakfast in one of the messes and cheerfully greeted the assembled officers with good wishes for the morning. They were met with a stony silence! It was only later that they discovered that the mess had a strict 'silence' rule at breakfast time! All the officers took refuge behind their morning papers!

Trevor was not a conventional person and did unusual things. The army gave the team a 'rest day' every four or five days. On one of those days the team was accommodated at the Park Hotel in Dusseldorf. Their rooms were on the fifth (top) floor, about five or six doors away from each other.

In the morning, Trevor phoned his colleague to say that he was ready for breakfast and that he would come along to the other's room. His colleague waited for the knock on the door, but it never came. Instead, there was a knock on the window! Trevor had climbed out of his window and walked along a five-inch-wide parapet (five storeys up) from his room. His colleague chided him as he visualised what might have happened had he fallen.

A second heart-by-pass operation early in 1995 proved too much for him and he passed into the presence of his Saviour.

The magazine of the Crusaders' Union paid this tribute to him:

> Those who knew him best will always remember him as much for what he was as for what he did. Ebullient, fun-loving, popular and generous, he was a wonderful witness to the joy of Christian faith in action. We all loved him for his good humour, wise advice, friendship and teaching.

For Dudley, he will always remember that it was Trevor, with Alan's encouragement, who persuaded him to go to Harringay.

Alan, Trevor's brother, was also involved in Christian matters, but in a different way. He became deeply involved in the Crusaders' Union, whose local class had helped him so much in his early days. Both Dudley and Alan had their homes at Frinton-on-Sea, and there was already a class in the town. This was a class that had its roots in the late 1930s and after the war was run by Charlie Voyle, a young man fresh home from the forces. Eventually Charlie moved on to another town, and Alan became the crusader leader in succession to him. It was essentially a Bible teaching class and Alan found it very stimulating. He remained leader for the next thirty-three years.

Trevor and Alan were deeply involved – commercially – in Billy Graham's Greater London Crusade at Earls Court in 1966 and 1967. With Dudley's support and encouragement Trevor suggested that the major part of the printing for the crusade could be done by Dudley Stationery. His promise of a 'fast' service was accepted, and he maintained high standards throughout the two years.

Early one morning, Alan had a call from the Greater London Crusade office to say that Billy Graham had decided to write a letter to all the crusade supporters, which he wanted to go out the next day! Alan was told that it would be a double-sided letter (in two colours, because Billy Graham always liked his signature to be printed in blue so as to look more personal). Some 75,000 copies would be needed that same night. Printers normally demanded a week to complete most jobs, and Dudley's were no exception. But they pulled out all the stops. Dudley says: 'As I recall it, we got the job done as Alan and Trevor got behind the printers and pushed them to the limit. The 75,000 letters were delivered that same evening!'

As the years went by, Dudley's offices in Soho became too small and the company moved to a larger factory and warehouse in Kingsland Road, in East London – only to find that twelve years later they had outgrown those premises too, necessitating a further move to gigantic premises in Bow. There, with little trumpeting or razzmatazz, this family-owned office-supplies concern has edged its way into the front rank of to-day's superdealers. They have become the second largest stationery distributor in the United Kingdom – yet, through it all, they never lost their Christian influence.

Dudley has long since retired from the company, but the strategy he devised is still applied within the company today. God has honoured the fact that He has been put first in all the planning for growth and expansion.

Dudley says that after his conversion at Harringay he became a very 'churchy' Christian. In 1959 he was appointed churchwarden at his church – a post he held until 1968. He was always the distinguished man in the black pin-stripe suit with a white carnation in his buttonhole who welcomed the churchgoers at the door. Indeed, he was the epitome of all that was 'proper'; life, for him, was both boring and pedantic outside his business commitments.

It was only after that time that he found a new release to his life as he discovered the power of the Holy Spirit to set his life ablaze. 'They never talked about that at church. Why not?' he asks in puzzlement. 'It is surely the next step for the Christian to realise that, once Jesus Christ has become his Saviour, it is the Holy Spirit which communicates with him on a daily basis, through the Bible, which is God's word.' He goes on, 'When I discovered that, I found a new satisfaction in my Christian life, and suddenly life became exciting and meaningful. No longer was it boring!'

From time to time the Brients held 'open days' at their factory and warehouse, when they would invite their many customers to visit their premises. They gave them lunch and showed them around. After lunch there was a limited amount of speech-making, and it was a rare occasion when one or other of the Brient family did not refer to their Christian faith. Their customers could be left in no doubt that God was at the centre of their business. On occasion a tongue-in-cheek suggestion is made that their success stems from Divine guidance. Alan Brient clearly finds the thought faintly amusing. He explains that he and his family *are* Christians who prefer to work with those of a similar conviction. 'Accordingly we have attracted a lot of Christians into the firm. I believe that I am doing the job God intended me to do.' Alan goes on to say, 'God needs

Christian businessmen as much as He needs missionaries and clerics.'

Most of their activity as a business is run by computer nowadays. However, personal contact with the customer is still needed, and a series of 'teams' spend the whole day answering phones. In spite of this, calls can build up and they cannot deal with them as quickly as they come in, so Alan Brient has devised a system of 'traffic lights on the wall, and if they ever turn red the panic signals flash,' he says, adding, 'All of this adds an element of fun to the operation and takes the boredom out of work.' He firmly believes that the success of the company is due to hard work, enterprise, enthusiasm, honesty and integrity – and he places particular emphasis upon the last two.

It was in 1995 when Dudley heard that the ultimate accolade had come, when his company was awarded the Queen's Warrant as a supplier of goods and services to Buckingham Palace. Not content with that, they also received a Royal Warrant from the Prince of Wales's office for similar services, thus becoming one out of only two of fifty-four firms to obtain more than one royal warrant in that year. The accolade came at the time of the firm's fiftieth jubilee.

Dudley would be the first to give glory to God for the success of his (private) company. He says: 'I have never looked back since that time when, night after night, I attended the Harringay Crusade and heard the remarkable Billy Graham. He was so young, yet he was a powerful and authoritative preacher. I had never heard anything like it. I dare not think what my life might have been like without that influence upon it. I had the privilege of meeting Billy Graham in later years – and his lovely and dear wife – and I am overwhelmed that God has kept him faithful to his cause over all the years.

'If it had not been for our children, and Billy Graham, God might have had some other plan to touch our lives; but, as it is, I am eternally grateful to Billy for showing us a better way.'

7

Childhood Response

Derek Hills, England, 1954

Derek Hills was never far from Christian influence as a small boy. Brought up in a committed Christian home, it might have been construed that nothing further was required of him.

Southborough Lane Baptist Church, Bromley, was the church his family attended and, at the time, it was pastored by a lay pastor, Bert Hughes. His heart was in evangelism and he was deeply supportive of Billy Graham when he heard of the crusade which had been organised at Harringay Arena. It was a natural extension of his interest that he should get his own church involved, and on 27 February 1954 – two days before the crusade commenced – he invited one of the Billy Graham team members to come and speak at his church.

He did not know that Grady Wilson, who accepted that invitation, was the team member closest to Billy Graham himself. The two of them had been inseparable since college days, and Grady and his brother, T. W. Wilson (always known as 'TW' or more colloquially by his closest associates simply as 'T'), would be of tremendous importance to Billy Graham throughout his ministry. For many years, 'T' was an aide to Billy Graham and always accompanied him on his overseas ministry. It was his important task to watch over his welfare and to manage his programme.

Grady, however, almost always fulfilled a preaching ministry, and his quick-fire sermons were effective in bringing many to find the Lord Jesus Christ as their own personal Saviour. Grady also fulfilled another role. He was a man full of fun, with a highly developed sense of humour. If his life had taken a different route, he could well have been one of the world's greatest comedians! But God sanctified his humour and allowed it to be used for His glory. To the Billy Graham team he was a catalyst, using his humour to weld together the vast Billy Graham organisation as he recounted story after story of events that had happened in his ministry. He was, essentially, a 'human' man whose personality compelled those who heard him to listen attentively.

Derek Hills was an eight-year-old boy when he went to his church that Saturday evening in February. Only eight he may have been, but the fiery presentation of Grady Wilson captivated him, and he listened carefully to the message of the evangelist.

Derek realised that the simple fact that he came from a Christian family did not automatically make him a Christian. As Grady Wilson spoke, a chord vibrated in young Derek's heart. Grady Wilson moved on to the end of his message and to his appeal for people to come to the front to indicate their desire to find Christ.

Almost immediately Derek's sister, Vivien, was on her feet and pushing her way to the front. But Derek had a problem. He also wanted to go to the front but he was sitting in the middle of the row – about as far away from the aisle as he could possibly be – with most of his family between him and the exit.

'I was determined to go to the front,' says Derek, 'and I started to push my way along the row. Then my mother stopped me. "You don't have to go because Vivien went," and she laid a restraining hand on me. I said, "Get out of my way, I've got to go," and I pushed by them all and went forward with many others.'

In a sense, that was the first stage of his conversion. The second stage came a few days later when, with a party from his church, he went to spend the day at the Harringay Stadium and the Arena.

The Saturday morning was a very special day for youngsters.

The famous cowboy, Roy Rogers, with his wife, Dale Evans Rogers, and his horse, Trigger, was present, to the delight of all the children.

Roy and his wife were dedicated Christians – even in the show-business world (somewhat unheard of in those days) – and often gave of their time to help with children's evangelism during a Billy Graham crusade.

It was an exciting and eventful morning, capped at the end of the day by Derek's first visit to the Harringay Arena. He was captivated by the forceful and compelling singing of the crusade soloist, Bev Shea, and the beautiful and fluid singing of the black soloist, Myrtle Hall. But above all he was deeply moved by Billy Graham's dynamic preaching.

Derek's response to Grady Wilson a few days previously all came together suddenly, and now he fully understood the decision he had taken at the earlier meeting. He did not go forward again at Harringay, but when he got back to his own church his pastor, Bert Hughes, took him under his wing and did the follow-up with him.

In those days Derek was a serious kind of boy. Perhaps he was a little shy, and this serious demeanour, coupled with his readiness to talk about his Christian experience, soon led to his nickname of 'Joe' at school. As the years went by, that embryonic Christian faith developed and never faltered. He grew from strength to strength – and that eventually led to his conviction, many years later, as to the importance of evangelism to children.

'I believe that there is an appropriate response to Christ at every age,' says Derek. 'For me it was a response as a child, and there were further appropriate responses as I grew up. There was a response to be made when I considered my career; another when I came to get married; yet another when I had children – and I'm sure there will be another when the grandchildren come along! A long way off yet, though!'

As a teenager at school, preparing for his school leaving exams (in those days called the 'O-' and 'A'-level exams), he had chosen the subjects of Economics, History and French. One day his French tutor called him in and said to him, 'Hills, you are wasting your time! You'll never make the grade in this subject, because your heart is elsewhere.' He suggested, and arranged, for Derek to be transferred to John Edgeler, another teacher, who also happened to be the secretary of Bromley Baptist Church. The latter transferred Derek's speciality to Religious Studies and, in one year, pushed him hard in order to reach the A-level standard he required. He gave enormous support to young Derek.

Derek wrote many essays under his direction, and his abiding memory of those times is of the red circles on the corrected essays. John Edgeler had circled every 'h' in the words 'he' and 'his' whenever they referred to God, the Lord Jesus Christ or the Holy Spirit. 'You are referring to the Lord God Almighty,' said John Edgeler. 'You must accord Him the privilege of a capital letter!' And that memory has never left Derek. 'There is a tendency today to downgrade the creator of the universe, and to try to make Him as one of us. And He is not! He is the Almighty God – although He is still our heavenly Father.'

But it was Jeremiah 1:6 which ultimately showed Derek the way in which God was calling him to go: 'I do not know how to speak; I am only a child . . . "Do not be afraid . . . I am with you," declared the Lord.' Derek never forgot the impetus which came from the decision that he took at Harringay. He was determined to use his life to serve Christ wherever and however he could.

He became a teller at the National Provincial Bank until that text from Jeremiah made it paramount to him to become a messenger of the Gospel. And for the past twenty-five years he has been pastor at one of three Baptist churches, and is currently the senior pastor of a team ministry at Tonbridge Baptist Church in Kent.

Now (in 1996) fifty years of age – with more than half his life gone – he is as committed as ever to the ministry. And he has never forgotten his own conversion at eight years of age. Because of this, he has a strong conviction that the children within his congregation are of supreme importance. 'I believe,' he says, 'that that part of the morning service during which the children are present should reflect their understanding and style of worship. Once they have departed for their own classes after the first fifteen minutes of the service, we revert to a style of worship more suitable to the adults. But for that first fifteen minutes, the children have priority.'

His wife supports him in his ministry. It was almost a different scenario, however. When he was twenty-five he was very keen to learn to play the piano, and he was the pastor of a small Baptist church. He had been pastor there for four years, and was a bachelor throughout that period. The church organist was a lady of over seventy years of age, and she gave lessons in playing the piano. Arrangements were made to harness Derek's talents and for this lady to give him lessons. That was in the days when boys were taught by men and girls were taught by ladies. However, as she was over seventy, it was felt 'safe' for him to learn from her.

The lessons proceeded apace and he progressed well. Then one day he was both astounded and embarrassed when she turned to him and proposed marriage to him!

Derek recalls, 'I remember thinking "I'm only twenty-five! This is disgraceful. Anyway, she's got varicose veins!" She was one of three sisters – all of them eccentric. I don't know how, but somehow or other I managed to talk my way out of it!'

Years later he met a young girl called Alison, who was a member of the youth group in his church. 'She was the first person I ever baptised,' Derek says, 'and having had no practice or previous experience, I didn't make a very good job of it. To this day I still tell her that our disagreements are due to the fact that she was not properly initiated!'

They were friends for some years before, eventually, they got married in 1975. 'Since then,' Derek says, 'she has been a tower of strength to me.' They now have two children – a boy of seventeen and a girl of sixteen. Both of them have committed their lives to Christ, so the effect of Billy Graham's ministry goes on to another generation in yet another family. If he was unpractised in baptism, he was also a novice in weddings!

Can a man like that go through life without any periods of doubt? Derek Hills says, 'I've never had any doubt about my faith, but there have been times of doubt about specific things. I believe that God allows doubt as a means by which he prevents my faith from becoming superficial. In that sense, doubt is a healthy thing to have.' He added, 'I suppose my biggest doubt has been how professing Christians, who have been on the road for many years, can act in a way which is, so often, un-Christian. Sometimes that can even be to the point of discouragement. But God is faithful and doesn't allow that doubt to persist.'

Derek Hills says: 'I've never regretted the decision to follow Christ – although it came at so early an age. Nor have I ever regretted the fact that it was through Billy Graham that I came to faith. Life has been fulfilling and satisfying, and I have faith to believe that God will continue to give me similar experiences in the years ahead.'

8
Sacrificing Cricket

Peter Pearmain, England, 1954

Ivy has a lot to answer for! She was a hard-bitten ward-ress from Holloway Prison, but she had a heart softened by love. She also had a burden for the young people of her church – not least for sixteen-year-old Peter Pearmain. At the time he was not aware of the fact that he was the focus of her prayers. He did not discover that until several years later.

Peter lived with his family in Highbury. He had been born in a house right across the road from the Arsenal Football Club stadium, so it was no surprise to discover that he was an avid supporter of the Gunners. It was hard to say which sport he favoured more: cricket or football. Until, that is, he got invol-ved in playing cricket for a top club and seemed destined for a career in professional cricket. He even had coaching from a Middlesex professional. He continued playing in cricket matches until he was forty.

He was very happy with his life and was quite content with the way that everything was going. He had no great burden of sin sitting on his shoulders and he never gave a second thought to anything even remotely religious.

He had, however, been going to a youth club at Camden Road Baptist Church in London, partly because a number of the boys from his school went there – and they seemed to have a good time – and partly because the leader of the group was a Yorkshireman who made a big impression on him. Yorkshire was, after all, the *real* cricketing county!

Then one day Ivy's prayers were about to be answered. Billy

Graham came to the Harringay Arena to hold the Greater London Crusade.

The young people from Camden Road Baptist Church were invited to go in a bus party to one of the nights of the crusade. In fact they were only a twopenny bus ride (in those days) from the Harringay Arena. There was something special, however, about going in a chartered bus. So Peter Pearmain was one of the fifteen or so who agreed to go.

His home was a normal home. Religion was not talked about much and, as a general rule, the family did not go to church, so there was no pressure from his parents to go to Harringay with the party. Peter himself had been a little reluctant about going and, on the way there, he was a little fearful. He did not know what he had let himself in for, but he thought the trip might be good for a laugh.[1]

As he came through the entrance into the Arena, he just could not believe his eyes. He had been here before for wrestling, ice hockey and the circus, but he had never seen such a vast crowd. It seemed to him that every seat was filled.

On the platform was a young man in a light-blue suit, wearing an unspeakable tie and holding a trombone. And there was singing! Such singing as he had never heard before. The words were strange and the music unfamiliar, but it was catchy, and Peter's attention was grabbed from the very beginning.

Everything that happened appealed to his theatrical instinct. He had done quite a bit of acting in amateur dramatics and he was overwhelmed by the excellence of the whole production. As a result, his interest was captured and he watched and listened to all that went on.

Not much of the preliminaries sticks in his memory, 'But when Billy Graham got up to speak,' he says, 'I was captivated by him. All that he said made so much sense – and he spoke with such authority – that I was compelled to listen. I had been to church from time to time, but this was the first time I had heard the Gospel.'

Billy Graham was at the podium, and preaching. 'We need

to be converted for entrance into Heaven. Jesus said, "Except ye be converted and become as little children, ye shall not enter into the Kingdom of Heaven." I did not say it; Jesus said it. Do you think Jesus was lying? You haven't been converted? Then you will not get to heaven. That is what Jesus said.

'You say, "Oh, we will make it somehow, for God is a wonderful God. He is a God of love and He is a God of mercy. Certainly He is going to get us there." Yes, He is a God of mercy, He is a God of love, not willing that any should perish but that all should come to repentance.'[2]

This was strong stuff, and it made young Peter sit up and take notice.

Billy Graham continued. 'But if you go on rejecting Christ and go on without conversion to Him, there is nothing God can do about it, because you sin away the mercy and the grace of God and there remains nothing but judgment to come.

'God compares you to Jesus. He compares you with His Son. And there is not a person here who can stand up and say, "I'm as good as Jesus." If you come short of Jesus, you are a sinner. You must recognise that. You must acknowledge it, and then there is a change of feeling. But any change that God makes in your life is a permanent change! Old things pass away; your life is different. A change takes place when you come to Christ, and God brings about this tremendous transformation that we call the new birth.

'Can you say, "Jesus is my Saviour. I am trusting in Him and Him alone for salvation. I am not trusting in anything or anybody but Christ. By faith I surrender to Him. I am willing to obey Him and follow Him from this moment on." You must be willing to say, "I *will* receive Christ." Christ appeals to the will of men. Jesus said, "Ye will not come to Me that ye might have life." Jesus didn't say, you couldn't come. He said, "Ye *will* not come." You will not come.

'There are hundreds of you here that ought to come and give your life to Christ. But Jesus says, "Ye will not come." You are not willing for your will to be surrendered to the will of Christ. If you haven't come, if you haven't met Christ, I am asking you to do it now.'

When Billy Graham came to the end of his talk, he invited those who wanted to to come to the front and accept Christ. 'I wanted to go forward,' says Peter, 'but it was a struggle. I got up out of my seat to join the many others going forward.'

He was a little surprised that he was the only one of the group who responded in this way, and when he got back to the bus he found that they were all waiting just for him. 'It was a little embarrassing,' he says. 'But by then my mind was in a whirl!'

At the front, Peter had been carefully counselled by one of the trained counsellors. Instead of doing any other follow-up work himself, the counsellor put Peter in touch with someone from Oakwood Baptist Church, which is near Cockfosters where Peter and his family lived at the time.

Although they had moved to Cockfosters, Peter continued to travel back and forth to the youth club at Camden Road week after week because he had so many friends there. Looking back on that situation, Peter is today so thankful that he did that, because otherwise he might have missed out on the visit to Harringay.

There was another important reason why he stayed there. Among the Christian Endeavour group at the church was a rather special young lady named Elsie. One day a member of the church asked her, 'Have you met Peter?' She had to confess that she didn't know who he was talking about. It was not long, however, before she found out who Peter was, and in due course they met. He had only just begun to get interested in her – and she in him – when he announced that he was going off to college. Elsie was devastated, especially because she had only just succeeded in weaning him away from his interest in another girl in the group. She knew that she was much more right for him than the other girl! So they laughed and said that CE stood for Courting Encouraged (instead of Christian Endeavour), and their relationship blossomed from that day.

It was not easy, because Elsie herself was a teacher and she lived in St Albans, but each weekend she would come back to her parents' home because her father's health was deteriorating. And she went along to the Camden Road church. By then they were both too old to continue as members of the youth club, but they managed to see each other as often as possible. In due course they fell in love and were married.

At the time of attending the Harringay meeting, Peter was working in the City of London in an insurance company's head office. 'It was only a very junior job,' he says, 'but I was immensely proud that I was "working in the City".'

His immediate reaction to his decision at Harringay was to invite a friend to come with him the next night. His friend worked at the Midland Bank, and he agreed to go with Peter.

The meeting was in every way as impressive and compelling as it had been the night before. Billy Graham preached a different sermon – and it was remarkable to young Peter that it could be so good. He was hooked on preaching as he listened to Billy Graham. During those moments – although he was unaware of it at the time – the first seeds of his future career were being sown.

He couldn't believe that, when the invitation was given, his friend did not go forward as he had done. 'Oh yes,' his friend had said, 'I'm tremendously impressed by it – but it's not for me.' It was the first lesson Peter learned that, however faithful the preaching is, it may not always bring the results we hope and pray for.

The next day he went back to work. A number of other people worked in the same office as Peter, and it did not take him long to discover that four of them were also believing Christians. He had always thought of them as 'rather religious', but now he recognised something in them that chimed with him. It was remarkable that God had put him into that prepared situation.

At home, it was not quite so easy. For Peter, his whole life had gone through a transformation. It was hard for his parents to understand what had happened to him. 'I began to grasp more clearly what had happened,' he says. 'No longer was *self* the controlling factor, I discovered, for Christ had really invaded my personality and captured my heart.'[3]

His commitment to his church at Camden Road was total. He went to the Sunday morning service; stayed on for lunch and, because Sunday school was held in the afternoon and he was a teacher, he stayed on for that too. He was then often invited to stay for tea, and that led on to the evening service. 'You're never home!' his parents complained, and he had to recognise that this was true. Despite that, however, he cannot imagine what life would have been like had he never taken the stand for Christ at Harringay.

On the other hand, to teach in the Sunday school at his church had cost him a considerable sacrifice. Cricket was still a big part of his life. He knew that to advance in the cricket world required playing every Saturday and Sunday. When he decided to become a Sunday school teacher, he had to give up playing on Sunday – and that spelt the death-knell to any aspirations he may have had to be a professional cricketer.

An early test of his faith was soon to come, when Peter was called up to do his National Service in the RAF. He spent two years in the service of his country. Once again, he found that God had prepared the way for him and, in years to come, he was very thrilled to learn that, during the two years he had served, four of those he had met in the RAF had gone on to become ministers like himself.

Back at the insurance company, which by then had moved to Dorking, he told them that he was leaving and going 'into the ministry'. The news quickly got around the typing pool – only they misinterpreted it and, before long, the news was all over the whole office that 'Peter Pearmain is going into a monastery!' He quickly put them right by explaining that he was going to become a minister, not a monk! Peter did not mind the long commuting journey to Dorking each day. The three

73

hours on the train gave him an opportunity to read and study for his 'O' and 'A'-level exams.

He applied to, and was accepted by, Spurgeon's College in Upper Norwood. This essentially 'preaching college' was very selective in its students: generally those accepted had at least two years' experience of lay preaching. Nor did Peter have any academic qualifications which would have commended him to the college. But he did have his cricket!

His only previous preaching experience had been in various youth activities and in the RAF. It was true that he had preached three sermons – several times each – but in college terms he was inexperienced. Nevertheless they accepted him!

Today he is president of the same Spurgeon's College Conference and has been a member of the college council for eighteen years. 'Today,' he says, 'I've turned down applicants with better qualifications than I had! It was remarkable that they accepted me. I saw it as the hand of God.' Currently he is the senior minister of a team ministry at Ashley Baptist Church near New Milton in Hampshire.

He didn't shine in college, but he kept on at his cricket and also joined a musical 'skiffle group' – the Venturers – which had been founded and was led by another college student, Bryan Gilbert. The college rather frowned upon their activities, but despite this they had persevered, with openings and opportunities in all sorts of places, from prison to the open air.

It was traumatic for Elsie to lose the man to whom she had so recently become attached. Soon after they had courted in the Camden Road Baptist Church, Peter was off to college, and they had the opportunity to meet only on occasional weekends and in the vacations. Nevertheless their relationship flourished and on 25 August 1962 they were married at Camden Road.

From the time of Harringay onwards, Peter always looked upon Billy Graham as his 'spiritual father', although he had never met him. In 1973 he did a three-month exchange of pulpits with a minister in Virginia, USA. As he was leaving to go over to America, he wrote to the Minneapolis office of the Billy Graham Evangelistic Association. His enquiry was to ask if there would be a crusade he could attend during his stay in the States. To his surprise they replied with an invitation to him to travel, at their expense, to Atlanta, Georgia, where Billy Graham's next crusade was to be held.

His responsibilities in his 'exchange church' were such that he was able to accept that invitation only for four days. Those days included the 'School of Evangelism' – an event held during most crusades that Billy Graham conducted. Billy Graham himself was one of the speakers at the school, and Peter found the experience uplifting, instructive and inspiring. However, Billy Graham's heavy commitment to the crusade activities meant that he was able to call in only briefly to speak at the school and he left immediately afterwards. So still Peter was unable to meet him.

After fourteen years of ministry at the Kirby Muxloe Baptist Church in Leicester, Peter was moved to St George's Place Baptist Church in Canterbury. As one of the prominent ministers of the town, his ministry at the church carried with it a chaplaincy at Kent University. As a result, he and his wife were invited to the installation and enthronement of Dr Robert Runcie as Archbishop of Canterbury.

Among those present at the ceremony was James Runcie, the Archbishop's son. Elsie was aware that Billy Graham's ministry during the mission at the University of Cambridge had been instrumental in some sort of reconciliation between James and his father, so she was not altogether surprised to find that Billy Graham was one of those invited to attend. As she and Peter came through the great west door into the cathedral precinct, they realised that Billy Graham was standing just behind them.

Summoning up his courage, Peter turned around and introduced himself. Thus, for the first time in his life, he found himself face to face with the evangelist through whom his conversion had taken place. Peter met and talked with Billy

Graham and was able to tell him of the impact upon his own life that Mr Graham's ministry had had. As a result, the enthronement ceremony for the Archbishop carried a special significance for Peter Pearmain.

In response to the question, 'Have you ever regretted the decision you took as a sixteen-year-old youngster?', Peter Pearmain replies, 'I can't imagine how life would have been, had I never been to Harringay. Everything that has happened to me since then has slotted into place and I have seen God's hand at work in my life ever since. It has been like a thin "gold line" through my life, for everything that has happened to me – my work, my time in the RAF, my marriage, my calling and my present ministry – stems from that initial decision I made at Harringay on that memorable day in 1954. I can only say, to God be the glory!'

9
A Doctor's Story

David Rowlands, New Zealand, 1954

It is impossible to speculate upon what would have been the moral and spiritual condition of the British Isles today had there never been a visit from Billy Graham. Post-war, the secularisation of life threatened to engulf the whole of the nation. It was into that secular society that Billy Graham came with his Harringay Crusade of 1954. The influence of the 38,447 'enquirers' at that crusade permeated every corner of the country, and its tendrils extended to many other places throughout the world.

Take Billy Graham out of that syndrome, and we might have had a far worse society today than we already have. Despite the promiscuous society of the 1960s, the humanistic society of the 1970s, the selfish society of the 1980s and the multinational and pagan society of the 1990s, there has always been that core of true believers who have been 'the leaven in the lump' and have saved society from its worst excesses.

In this and the following chapters we trace the stories of four more people from those Harringay days. They are stories of ordinary men and women whose influence far extends beyond the day of their original response to 'get up out of their seats and go to the front'.

In Frank Colquhoun's book *The Harringay Story*, he includes the following story:

> There was the doctor from Kent, married, with four children, who admitted, 'Although I regularly attended church and led an average life by the world's standard,

it was not until I heard Billy Graham that I realised how far I was separated from God and the kingdom of heaven. My life was restless and empty, and I sought satisfaction in hobby after hobby, expensive travel and entertainment.

'Out of curiosity I went to Harringay and for five nights took careful notes. On the fifth night the struggle which had been going on from the beginning came to a climax, and I realised that the answer I sought was to be found in Christ; and so, in humility, I surrendered my entire life to Him.

'In Him I have found peace of mind and soul, a happiness before unknown to me, and the assurance of eternal life. I have become a different person and my standards, motives and interests have changed completely. The books and magazines I now read are quite different. Christ is now the centre of my life and home . . .'[1]

That was in 1954. David Rowlands was that doctor, and what does he have to say about that experience today? Did it last? Was it real? Was it purely the emotion of the moment, or has it stood the test of time?

David told me: 'When I went forward at Harringay, a vacuum in my life was filled. I had not accepted that anything was wrong. But it must have been, because otherwise I would not have gone back to Harringay night after night. That fifth time I attended Harringay was a catalyst in my life – and I have never looked back.'

It is with a degree of amusement that David confesses: 'I went to Harringay on those nights, armed with binoculars, a camera and a notebook! I suppose the binoculars were because I expected the man on the platform to be about as high as a matchstick – and I wanted to see his face. I was intrigued by what it was that attracted so many people to hear him night after night. While my binoculars helped with that, there was no way in which my *camera* could record the changed life that came away from Harringay!'

It was a week after his decision that David told his wife about it. They were walking along Brighton promenade at the time, and he turned to Margaret and said: 'I've got something to tell you. You know that I've been going to hear Billy Graham every other night at Harringay... well, on Wednesday the 10th of March, I joined others going forward and accepted Jesus Christ as my Saviour.' He was very surprised when Margaret, normally a very shy and reticent person, turned to him and said, 'I have been praying for that to happen for the past seven years!' She turned in her tracks and kissed and hugged him, and a new relationship between them started at that moment.

That seven-year wait had been a time of great patience for her. So often we pray for friends and relatives, and nothing seems to happen. We believe that it is inevitable that they will *eventually* find Christ after we have prayed so long for them. We feel like saying to them: 'One day you *will* accept Christ – so why not do so now and make the most of all the time you've got left, to use it for Him?' It is always a thrill when someone for whom we have been praying reaches the point of decision and becomes a Christian. So it was for Margaret.

David Rowlands was 'followed up' by Dawson Trotman, founder of the Christian organisation, the Navigators. Several times he invited David back to his hotel room and allowed him to pose difficult questions to him. 'I told Dawson that I wanted to apply for the mission field, but wisely he steered me on to the right course. He urged me to stay in my medical practice and to witness from there. Looking back from the standpoint of many years later, how right he was!

'Dawson had told Billy Graham about me, and one evening I was invited to the platform by Billy Graham, to tell the people what had happened to me. I told them how I had discovered that Jesus Christ is very much alive in the twentieth century in the lives of those who will accept him.'

In his talk to enquirers after they have responded to the invitation to 'Get up out of your seats...', Billy Graham always says that an important part of becoming a Christian is to tell others. David vowed to try to find ways of doing this. To start with, Margaret and David organised six double-decker buses to take local people to Harringay. To their surprise the tickets sold out very quickly. A call came from the Ministry of Transport to tell him that it was apparently illegal to sell tickets and use the buses in that way. So David telephoned back to the Ministry of Transport. He says, 'It was impossible to get any satisfaction from them, so eventually I went to the Minister of Transport himself to explain the situation. I gave him my testimony about Harringay, and he relented and allowed the plan to use the buses to proceed with his consent! There's nothing like breaking the law with the consent of the law-makers!'

There were a lot of opportunities to witness. It might have been a soapbox on London's 'Skid Row' in company with a London City Missionary. 'I remember that occasion well,' says David, 'because one chap shouted out to me to "hurry up" because he wanted his soup from the LCM van. It was given to them only after hearing the speaker!'

Another way in which David and Margaret were able to witness was by holding 'cottage meetings' in their home. There were often thirty to fifty people present, and many of them became Christians as a result.

David goes on: 'After the crusade was over I went out and bought a film projector and all the paraphernalia necessary to show films. Then I hired the local town hall to show a series of Billy Graham films every Sunday night. To my lasting surprise the hall was always packed. I had managed to persuade Mr Atterbury, a non-Christian friend of mine, to help me. Later he became a Christian and is now the vicar of a North Country church.'

David's enthusiasm for this film programme knew no bounds! He went out at night and pasted large notices on billboards to advertise the show. 'That led to my being arrested by two policemen when I was half-way up a ladder pasting up the notices! It was hard to get released because I had no ID on me. But eventually they let me go!'

David tells a story of one of his patients from those days. She was a lady who had tried to commit suicide by swallowing phenobarbitone tablets. The reason was, she was terrified of getting cancer, and her two brothers had recently died of it.

Her life hung in the balance for a whole week, and when she came out of hospital David received a telephone call. ' "Please can I have a tonic?" she asked. I knew that *that* could have only a temporary benefit. Instead, I called at her home and took her in my car to hear Billy Graham. It was the best tonic I could think of!'

David tells how she was so impressed that she went to crusade meetings on her own several times and, at a subsequent meeting, she went forward to receive Christ as her Saviour. 'She became a radiant Christian,' says David, 'and her fear of dying from cancer completely vanished. So had her need for phenobarbitone. As a result of her newfound confidence she has been able to lead two of her colleagues to Christ.'

The well-known Christian, Fleet Street reporter Hugh Redwood, was a patient of David's at that time. Hugh had left Fleet Street to become involved in Christian work and in writing. One day he telephoned David to say that he was ill; David, with the help of X-rays, diagnosed an obstructive cancer of the bowel. 'The surgeon we had consulted wanted to carry out an urgent operation. However, after Hugh strolled around the hospital grounds, he returned to announce that there would be no need for an operation. Hugh had been praying and he felt that God wanted him to trust in His power to heal. Hugh asked our home group to pray for him on a regular basis, and two or three weeks later the symptoms disappeared and Hugh lived a useful life for the next eight years. He eventually died of a completely unrelated illness.' Hugh Redwood has documented that story himself in his final book *Residue of Days*.

There were sad stories, too! David tells the story of an army major. 'He was forty-four and had no time for God. On the day he came to see me he had a new project which, he believed, would bring him in a considerable sum of money over the next five years. But it would take more energy than he had, so he wanted me to give him some "pep" pills. It was clear that his mounting worries became his daytime enemy, with resulting insomnia at night. He neglected his home life in his pursuit of success.'

David recalls how that urge for success had become the major's god. He now lived from one worry to the next.Then, one day, David had an urgent call to go to his home. The major told David that he had just been declared bankrupt and that he was broken-hearted. While David was there, the major developed a heart attack and died within half an hour. 'I remember recalling our Lord's words: "What good is it for a man to gain the whole world, yet forfeit his soul?" (Mark 8:36 NIV). He had nothing to leave his wife except an empty bank account. He had nothing to hand to God but a bankrupt life!'

His experience was a reflection of many famous people before him. There were those who had found nothing lasting in life. Voltaire, who was an infidel of the worst type, wrote: 'I wish I had never been born.' Lord Byron, who lived a life of pleasure, wrote: 'The worm, the canker and the grief are mine alone.' Jay Gould, the American millionaire who had all the money in the world, when he was dying said,'I suppose I am the most miserable man on earth.' And Lord Beaconsfield, who enjoyed both money and pleasure, wrote: 'Youth is a mistake, manhood a struggle, old age a regret.'

'Where then is happiness to be found?' David asks. 'I have learnt from so many of my patients whose lives have been changed that I can honestly say it is the Spirit of God living within a person that gives inner joy and happiness that nothing can take away. Jesus said: "Your heart shall rejoice and your joy no man takes from you" (John 16:22 KJV). I know of no earthly guarantee to equal that!'

The late Dr W. E. Sangster, minister at London's Westminster Central Hall, encouraged David and his family to accept an invitation to move to New Zealand to take over a medical practice there. Before they arrived, the *Reader's Digest* had carried a story about them, so they were not altogether unknown when they arrived. That story told of the effectiveness of Billy Graham's ministry and included some stories about the lives of others as well as the story of David's life. So, on arrival in New Zealand he quickly found himself catapulted into an active Christian life. He soon became Sunday school superintendent of his local Baptist church.

Then, in 1959, Billy Graham held a crusade in New Zealand. He stayed in the home of a well-known New Zealand Christian businessman, Mr Robert A. Laidlaw (author of the famous booklet, *The Reason Why*, of which millions of copies have been sold). One day David was in his surgery and was looking out of his window. 'I was astounded when I spotted Billy Graham walking up the path of our home with Robert Laidlaw by his side. I looked into the waiting room and saw eight patients sitting there, and I told them that I had an unexpected and important visitor and that all consultations would have to be postponed! There were a few smiles and a few frowns, but they all generously accepted the situation.'

David spent the whole of that happy day in the company of his two visitors, showing them around Auckland and visiting the grave of Dr Harry H. Ironside, the former pastor of the huge Moody Memorial Church in Chicago. The crusade itself was a great opportunity to witness, and David and Margaret were deeply involved in it.

'What a dull and materialistic life I would have had if Billy Graham had never come to London in 1954,' says David. 'I have not regretted my decision, and I know that He, Jesus Christ, saved me from my sin. I know too that by His Holy Spirit He lives in me every day. As the Bible says in 2 Timothy 1:12 (NIV): "I know whom I have believed and am convinced that He is able to guard what I have entrusted to Him ready for that day." I knew that referred to the day when the Lord Jesus Christ would return again, as He had promised.

'As a doctor, I marvel at the magnitude of God's creation. The human brain is a most remarkable computer. The whole concept of genetics involving such things as the miracle of DNA is quite overwhelming. God created us to be healthy and enjoy Him and His world. So often we break His laws, and we suffer physically, mentally and spiritually. When we get right with God, we restore the fine balance of body, mind and spirit, and then God is able to deal with our stress and duodenal ulcers!'

If David has any regrets, it is that he did not respond to his wife's prayers much sooner. Those seven years of her faithfulness were unknown to him at the time. But he is thankful that God answered those prayers and made him sufficiently intrigued and curious about Harringay to want to go and hear Billy Graham. The years in between have been full of constant opportunity, and he has never lived to rue the day when he 'got up out of his seat' and went to the front. He says: 'I did not like to admit it, but for the first time in my life I had the realisation that all was not right in my life. I was, in short, "a sinner", and this fact had separated me from God. Without the personal challenge from Billy Graham I would never have found the peace and satisfaction that comes through Jesus Christ – I would still be searching!

'Now the Bible, which had been a dusty and uninteresting book, became alive and I wanted to read more and more of what God said to me through it. Someone pointed out to me that the Bible itself explained why it was such a deadly book to me. It says in 2 Corinthians 4:4: "The god of this age has blinded the minds of unbelievers so that they cannot see the light of the Gospel of the glory of Christ." But in 1 Corinthians 2:10 it says: "God has revealed [the truth] to us by His Spirit . . . that we may understand what God has freely given us." As the hymn-writer expresses it:

> 'Open my eyes that I may see
> Glimpses of truth Thou has for me;
> Place in my hands the wonderful key

That shall unclasp and set me free.
Silently now I wait for Thee,
Ready, my God, Thy will to see.
Open my eyes, illumine me,
Spirit divine!

'The first thing I did after my conversion was to throw a pile of *sensational* calendars over the rail of London Bridge into the Thames! A suspicious policeman rushed up to enquire what the bundle contained. Little wonder he was a bit sceptical when I replied, "My sins!"

'Now I can say, with Paul, "I am not ashamed of the Gospel because it is the power of God for the salvation of everyone who believes"' (Romans 1:16 NIV).

10

Fish and Meat Pastes

Ernest Shippam, England, 1954

Many a family, gathered around the supper table, has heard someone ask during the meal, 'Please pass the Shippam's.' The unusual-shaped glass jar which contains the much-loved fish or meat paste is so well known! Almost certainly it *will* be 'Shippam's', for that colloquialism has been an advertising gimmick by which the spread has become well known and universally enjoyed. Indeed, the company's letter-heading disclosed, in those days, that they were 'By appointment to HM The Queen as manufacturers of meat and fish pastes'!

What it consists of is a family secret. It is manufactured in the family's factory in Chichester, the home of the Shippam family. Ernest says: 'We've lived in Chichester for years and years and years. I can't think how many hundreds of years. We were, and are, still deeply involved in Shippams of Chichester, who are the manufacturers and suppliers of this delicacy.

'My father was managing director of Shippam's, and I followed him on. Surprisingly, we were a Christian family. On my mother's side – the Priors – as well as with my older relatives it was always "Jesus comes first." '

Because of this, Ernest had a strict Church of England background. Two of his aunts ran Sunday schools, and they reckoned that there were Christians in practically every country of the world. 'I could well believe that,' says Ernest, 'for they were so enthusiastic and tireless in all that they did. They were just superb. I thought I was a Christian too. I went to church, and I read my Bible. I said my prayers – what more do you want?'

When he was sober, Ernest Shippam was in charge of the operations of the company. But there were times when his predilection to drink rendered him incapable of making proper business decisions. He was, in short, an alcoholic.

Partly because of this, things were not happy at home. There were frequent outbursts of temper and abuse. Ernest was normally a placid and temperate man, but when he had been drinking to excess he became so terrible that his children feared to have him around, and at one time his wife had even thought of leaving him.

As a boy, Ernest Shippam was sent to school at Sherborne. From there he gained entry to Caius, Cambridge. He says, 'I think it was at dear old Caius that I first started enjoying my drink. I'm not blaming them, for it was the "done thing" for students there to drink, and I enjoyed it along with the rest.'

It was the start of a slippery path downwards. For years and years afterwards, Ernest almost drank himself to death. He found that he couldn't even start the day without a couple of gin-and-tonics. 'I just found, quite simply, that I could not start a day's work without having some drink in me, and then the time would come during the day when I could not carry on any longer without finding some excuse to get out of the office. I pretended to go to Newlyn (where we had a factory) to do some non-existent work that, I said, had to be done down there. But in reality I ended up in the pub, drinking, drinking and drinking.

'Drink was a frightful problem to me. I hated and loathed myself for it, but eventually I would go home. The amazing thing is that, through thick and thin, my wife stood by me and was absolutely marvellous. When I got home, they sobered me up enough so that I could go out and get drunk again.

'One day I was taken to a place where they proposed to try and cure me. A chap from Harrow came and sat by my bed and told me what the programme was. I said to him, "If you're bloody fool enough to think you can stop me drinking, you can try, but you won't!" He replied, "Oh, yes, we will, don't worry!"

'I thought he was a bit of a chump, and when I left the nursing home he came and tapped on the window of my car and said, "Don't forget that you have the power within you to be the person God intended you to be." And off I drove.'

It made Ernest stop and think, however. He said to himself that, if he determined not to drink, he would be able to resist. Surprisingly it worked, and he was able to stop. 'Life was hell,' he says. 'I had to say "No" to my pals, and they all laughed at me. "Surely you can have one, can't you?" they said. But in the nursing home they had drilled it into me: "One drink is too many." So I didn't.'

It came as a surprise to everyone when, one day shortly afterwards, he readily agreed to go on a company outing to London – an outing which was to include a visit to the much publicised Greater London Crusade with Billy Graham at Harringay Arena.

Ernest liked to be thought of as benevolent to his workforce when it came to his relations with his staff. They knew all about his excesses, and there were occasions when they deemed it wise to avoid him. But when it came to outings, he wanted to be seen as one of the 'family'. So, although it was something of a mystery to him, he was not averse to attending this 'religious circus' with all the others.

'I had heard that Billy Graham was coming,' he says, 'and I thought, "Well, there're lots of chaps and lasses at the factory who want a bit of Christianity. Of course, I'm all right – but it might be of some good to them. I might put them in the charabanc and send them up to town or something." Well, in the end I went up with them, and I was amazed at the enormous crowds there. I don't know what Billy preached about but, right at the end of his message, I appeared to be the only person he was looking at, the only person to whom he was talking. He just said, "If Jesus Christ could carry His Cross to Calvary for you, can't you trust Him with everything you've got."[1]

'I really went through an emotional time then. The Holy Spirit took me through my life and showed me what it was really like. My dirty, spotty, smelly life! And He, the Holy Spirit, prompted me to hand over all my problems to the Lord Jesus. That included the drinking, which was still worrying me, even though my determination to give it up still was working. He even challenged me about my big black Jaguar car, which heaven help anyone who touched it. It was, after all, Ernest Shippam's perfect car.

'I went forward at Harringay with faith that something good was going to happen. Exactly what, I didn't know. What I did know was that Jesus Christ had died on the Cross for *me*. I couldn't really understand it and what it meant, except that it was just one of those wonderful, marvellous things for which we could never say "Thank you" enough. We can only say "Thank you" by the way we live.

'On the way home from Harringay I thought to myself, "Well! I'll wake up in the morning feeling what a Charlie I was!" But when I did wake up in the morning, something *had* happened. There was a different relationship between my wife and myself. Something wonderful had happened. The Ernest Shippam who went to Harringay was a completely different Ernest Shippam from the one who came away from Harringay.' The effect of all that happened remained with him for the rest of his life.

The first to experience the difference were his wife and his family. They couldn't believe that they now had a husband and a father who was mild, good-tempered, moderate, considerate and happy – and who never drank alcohol. At first they thought it was too good to last.

'Not long afterwards I went home for tea one day. Before that I had never been home to tea because I could take just so much of the children – but no more! My wife greeted me at the door and said, "Darling, thank heavens you've come home.

89

The children have been such a nuisance." Now I knew that I couldn't do anything with them; never had been able to! My wife said, "Don't you realise that since Harringay they are asking me all the time, 'What has happened to Daddy?' and, 'Why is Daddy so different?' "

'I discovered that tender, loving care was better than shouting at them, "Shut up, you silly little fool!" I found out that the children really wanted me at home, and really wanted to have tea with me.' But, as time went by, they too discovered that what had happened to him was real and lasting.

It didn't take long for the news to get around. Outside the family, the Billy Graham team was the first to learn about it. Dawson Trotman, the person responsible for the counselling and follow-up programme for the crusade, had met with him and learnt all about what had happened. He quickly told Billy Graham, and shortly afterwards a meeting was arranged between the two.

Once that had taken place, the news started to filter through to church groups and large meetings in Central London and elsewhere, and it was not long before Ernest found himself bombarded with more invitations than he could possibly accept. Nevertheless, he was so excited by the change he had experienced in his own life that he never hesitated to tell others about it, and to commend a faith in the Lord Jesus Christ to them.

Ernest Shippam found himself becoming obsessed by telling other people about what God had done in his life – 'Some people said "non-stop"!' he said. 'But I still had to do it, and I wanted to give up my work and be ordained. But everybody begged me not to, but to go on and preach the Gospel in my own way, both in my work and whenever I had an opportunity to point someone to Jesus.'

He found that his conversion brought about many other changes in his life. He began to show a concern for the health of his employees. He tried to make sure that, when necessary, they could see the right doctor. He was prepared to help them financially when they needed treatment. He also found that an important part of integrity was paying a bill straight away. 'The Bible says you should not owe anybody overnight,' he says. 'Of course that would obviously not apply today. What we have to do is to pay bills promptly. And I even let other people drive my Jaguar!'

He also had a highly developed sense of propriety and honesty. He felt that Billy Graham had done so much for him that the least he could do was to help to keep the Billy Graham Evangelistic Association on the 'straight and narrow path'! He wrote, on 31 July 1972: 'When I was in Minneapolis I was shown with great pride the electric typewriters and the electric signing-machines they had, and I was told that a letter might be received addressed to any member of the Association team. The individual concerned might never see that letter, yet a stereotype letter would go out over his signature and it would be quite undetectable that it was a stereotyped letter and that the signature hadn't actually been signed by that person's own fair hand – dishonest?'

A few days later Ernest had lunch with the director of the Association's work in Britain, who explained to him that this situation simply helped the staff cope with an impossible situation. As for Billy Graham himself, if he saw and answered every single letter – and signed them personally – he would never have time to do the work of evangelism to which God had called him. Many thousands of letters arrived each week, taking a staff of up to ten to read and reply to them. The 'stereotyped letters'[2] were all compiled from paragraphs that had originally been dictated by Billy Graham. Most of the letters received covered similar subjects. There was a data bank available of hundreds of paragraphs, which covered almost every conceivable enquiry and subject. From these a suitable reply could be compiled and sent to the correspondent. The remarkable machine which produced the signatures of Billy Graham and others had originally been programmed by them, so the signature was the right person's – if by proxy. It was simply a device to help cope with the vast correspondence in the most economical way.

Of course, every individual letter *could* have been dictated and signed by hand, but to do so would have involved a large and expensive workforce – not so much of a problem to a commercial organisation (such as Shippams), but a disaster for a charity which tried to limit its overhead costs to around the 7 per cent level of its income! That was explained to Ernest who – perhaps rather grudgingly – accepted it.

It is not quite true to say that the mechanical signature 'would be quite undetectable' in a stereotyped letter. Betty Ruth Barrows was staying in England one Christmas, and numerous letters of greeting arrived from America. With each one she would lick her finger and rub it over the signature. If it smudged, she knew it was real! If it remained perfect, she knew it had come 'via the machine'!

Ernest also took his concern to the Association office in London. On one occasion he wrote: 'In your last letter to me it is signed by you. Then, in tiny little print underneath, that anybody could miss, "Dictated, but signed in his absence." Nearly dishonest? Surely it would be better to start the letter off: "So sorry I shall not be able to sign this myself as I shall be away."

'I am guilty of the same sort of thing when someone says to me, "You will pray for this or that, won't you?" And I glibly say, "Yes," and then forget all about it – dishonest? I believe we, as Christians, have to watch this sort of thing terribly carefully – but then I have a bee in my bonnet!' He was a stickler for making sure that everything coming from the Billy Graham Evangelistic Association was strictly kosher and honest!

He soon lost count of the number of times he gave his testimony but, in spite of the repetitive nature of what he had to say, it never lost its freshness and inspiration. His sole prayer and desire was that others should be brought to the same experience that he himself had had.

With it all he was self-effacing. He did not want publicity drawn to himself. On 11 September 1961 he replied to a letter from Dr Sherwood Eliot Wirt (then editor of Billy Graham's monthly magazine, *Decision*): 'I have been asked to supply [you in America with] a photograph and a biographical sketch of myself to accompany it. To this I am afraid I have to reply "No". In my opinion, by so doing the whole thing becomes far too much of a self-advertisement. On this side of the Atlantic, we do essentially see things in a different light from what you do, and vice versa. This kind of self-advertisement we very much abhor over here, whilst we appreciate that, on your side of the water, nothing is thought of it.'[3]

Sometimes it made things difficult for those who had invited him to speak. They were faced with the problem of making their speaker known, yet without drawing too much attention either to him or to his achievements. Happily, the name 'Shippam' was often enough!

Within Shippams of Chichester he founded a Christian Union, to which he invited any interested employees to come. Often he himself led it, and before long there was a new spirit in the company. His employees now enjoyed having him around and were no longer fearful of him.

It was all the dramatic result of that single meeting with the man from Harrow who witnessed to the power of God to such effect. But that alone would have been insufficient to enable Ernest to maintain his resolution. In the end it was Billy Graham who faithfully preached the Gospel in the power of the Holy Spirit and left the results to God. If Ernest Shippam had been the only person converted at Harringay, the crusade would have been worthwhile for him alone.

'For me it was the turning point in a spiritual pilgrimage; the end of superficial religion. At the time,' he says, 'there were shameful things in my life which I seemed powerless to eradicate. My home was unhappy; our business was my god; my church-going was sporadic and merely a pattern of my social life. Events led me to hear Billy Graham at Harringay.

All I can actually remember him saying was this: "If Christ could carry His Cross to Calvary for you, can't you trust Him with everything you have got?" The Holy Spirit made me realise my need. In a flash I saw what my life was like – and it was pretty rotten; and at that moment seeing the tremendous love of Christ for me, He also filled my heart with such love and trust for Him that I committed all to Him. It was an act of absolute and complete yielding to Christ.'

Ernest Shippam is now with his Lord and Saviour. That firm resolution he made after leaving the nursing home never forsook him. It was strengthened by the faith he later gained from the sermon preached by Billy Graham at the Harringay Crusade. From the day he took that determined resolution, he never took another drink until the day he died. But without the power of the Holy Spirit in his life that testimony might not have been given. The amazing change started with that determination on his part, and it was confirmed in his life as he found the Lord Jesus Christ as his Saviour. As a result, he had a story to tell and he never tired of telling it. The outreach from his ministry as a convert has touched many hundreds of others. As he has told his story again and again, it has reached into other people's lives. So the influence goes on and on from one simple sermon preached by Billy Graham. Without a doubt Ernest's welcome into heaven was a triumphant: 'Well done! Good and *faithful* servant. Enter into the joy of the Lord!' (Matthew 25:23.)

11

No Longer Alone

Joan Winmill Brown, USA, 1954

The audience was ecstatic when the final curtain calls were
taken and the applause was deafening as they stood to give a
standing ovation to the cast. It was a memorable 'first night',
matched the next morning by the endorsement of the critics.

It was always with some trepidation that Joan Winmill
picked up the morning newspapers to read the critics' assess-
ments of their play, so she was delighted when she discovered
that not only had they liked the play but her performance in
particular.

She needed that boost. It gave her temporary release from
the loneliness and from the nagging fear that had encompassed
most of her life. It was a fear that she would let others down
– particularly her fellow cast members.

There was an occasion, a year or two before, when she had
been on the verge of a breakdown, when she had fluffed her
lines and had needed the whispered prompt from the wings.
It took courage to go on and so, somewhere within the depths
of her, she managed to summon up enough strength to survive.[1]

After the first-night performance – very late at night – she
returned to her unglamorous London apartment. She had
rented it furnished. As she looked around at the characterless
furniture, she realised that this was not 'home'; it was merely
a place to sleep and to eat in. But when she was here she had
no need to act; she could abandon herself to her personal pro-
clivities and to self-pity and depression. She had an emptiness
that nothing seemed to satisfy.[2]

The play was *The Chiltern Hundreds*; its author was the

famous William Douglas Home, brother of Britain's one-time prime minister, the late Sir Alec Douglas Home (later Lord Home).[3] The theatre was the Vaudeville, one of London's smaller West End theatres, and Joan's role was based on the story of Kathleen Kennedy, sister of the Kennedy brothers in America.

Later on in the run Joan became more and more distraught, eventually collapsing from sheer exhaustion. The author of the play sent her to Scotland to recuperate at his family home.[4]

In desperation Joan cried out: 'Dear God, please help me!'[5] As she did this, she realised that, after a long time of living in a wilderness, she had at last offered a prayer to God.

On the other side of London, one day early in 1954, a young man named John Mercer was sitting in the offices of the Billy Graham Evangelistic Association. He was an insurance broker: an entrepreneur with a desire to get on in life.

He had been introduced to the BGEA by a Member of Parliament, John Cordle, who was honorary treasurer of the Billy Graham Harringay Crusade in 1954. John Mercer was summoned to their offices to discuss an insurance policy to cover the liabilities of the organising committee. They needed to ensure that, in the event of illness, accident or death occurring to Billy Graham, which might prevent his appearance at Harringay, they would be able to meet their commitments.

It was the first of numerous similar policies that John arranged over the ensuing years. In Manchester, in 1961, there was a claim on the policy when Billy Graham was taken ill just before the crusade at Maine Road Stadium and his brother-in-law, Leighton Ford, took his place for the first two or three days.

This business contact had made John aware of the events at Harringay, and one of the staff members at the BGEA offices had given to him a supply of tickets to use for himself and his wife and for their many friends. Some time before, John's cousin Joy had thrown a party to which she had invited the young actress, Joan Winmill. Joan and John Mercer had met and, over drinks, had talked about the theatre.

Shortly afterwards, at some time in March 1954, John was watching a BBC television programme when Joan suddenly appeared on the screen. He remembered when he and his wife had met her at the party. He said to his wife: 'Why don't we invite Joan to use one of those tickets we've been given for Harringay? We could get up a party. Might be fun!'[6]

The next morning, putting his thoughts into action, he telephoned Joan. 'We saw you on TV last night,' he said. 'My wife and I were wondering if you would have dinner with us next week. We've got some reserved tickets to see Billy Graham and thought we could get up a party to go and see him. Could be a laugh!'

Like most Londoners at that time, Joan was aware of the visit of Billy Graham. She says: 'It seemed that every double-decker bus in London carried the news of his crusade on their sides. After seeing those advertisements I wanted to go, but I wasn't about to let anyone know that!'[7]

Then Joan remembered her capsule prayer a few days previously. 'It seemed as if someone, or something, had stopped me short. That telephone call. Was it God's way of answering my prayer?'[8]

Until that time, Joan's life had been full of traumatic incidents. When she was four years old her mother had died giving birth to a brother for Joan. 'For some time I was not told of her death, nor of the death of the baby,' says Joan, 'only that she had "gone away".[9] But I missed my beautiful, fun-loving mother, who had been my security. It was not until a year later, when I overheard a conversation my grandmother had with a stranger on a train, that I learned what had really happened.'[10]

After her mother's death, Joan and her father moved in with her grandparents: 'fader' (she could not pronounce the 'th' properly) and 'nanny' (as she called her grandmother).[11] Fader was not a religious man and had no belief about the future life. 'So, when he died, it seemed, to me, so very final,' Joan says.

She was only five when her 'nanny' had a breakdown and Joan's father took her to live with her Uncle Hector and Aunt Hilda in Sutton.[12] That move meant changing schools too, but she was then able to stay on there until she was ten years old.

One day Joan's father told her that Aunt Hilda was going to have another baby and that she could no longer look after Joan.[13] 'Daddy told me that he had found a lady who was willing to look after me,' Joan says. 'She was a kind lady and tried very hard to make me happy.[14] But I never felt that I belonged.

'Aunt Hilda had a little baby boy called Stewart. I was very fond of him and he was a child with a sunny temperament.[15] Then, when he was about four years old, he began to feel tired all the time, and his little face was always white.[16] I learned one day that he had leukaemia. He died shortly afterwards and I was taken to see him at the funeral home. He looked like a little angel. I could not believe that he would not open his eyes and say, "Come on, Joan, let's play another game!" '[17]

These were only some of the many traumas that Joan experienced in her early life. It seemed they never stopped, and Joan developed an emptiness and insecurity that were to remain with her for many years.

Shortly after the war ended (during which she had served in the Observer Corps by falsifying her age) she took a variety of jobs but, increasingly, her interest and appetite were leading her towards the theatre.[18]

Joan recounts: 'It was the famous actor, A. E. Matthews, who encouraged me in my ambition. With Joy Elson, a friend of mine from schooldays, I had gone to see him in the play *But for the Grace of God*.[19] The next day we were sitting on the beach when we looked up and there was Mr Matthews walking past us.

'I told Joy that I wanted to get his autograph. "Why don't you go and ask him?" she said, and she dared me to do so.'

Joan protested vehemently but, having found a piece of paper and a pen in her handbag, she nevertheless walked hesitantly up to the actor, then she told him how much they had enjoyed the play and asked him for his autograph. 'He was very gracious and asked us to sit down with him and talk. I managed to say that I had always wanted to be an actress, and he encouraged me to follow that ambition.'

As a result of that meeting, Joan became friendly with the stage director of the play. When it later moved to London, she often went to the theatre and met him. One day he told her that the play was going on tour and that they needed an understudy for the juvenile lead. He encouraged her to try out for the part.[20]

'My application was accepted and I was to read the understudy's part after leaving work one evening. I left my office at 5 p.m. and walked across Trafalgar Square to St Martin's-in-the-Fields. It was a quiet and beautiful church, where I had often gone in my lunch hour.[21]

'I prayed and asked God to help me get the part.' Joan marvelled at the way she readily turned to God in a time of need but did not really have much to do with Him at other times.

'With trembling knees I walked out of the church and took a bus to the nearby St James's Theatre. I had gone to great pains with my appearance. I had bought an emerald-green coat especially for the occasion. I thought it would offset my blonde hair. That afternoon, as I went about my normal work, my make-up had taken quite a share of the company's time!

'Holding my head high, and acting as if I were not in the least bit nervous, I walked through the door – only to find, too late, that there was a step down. As I fell, a raucous "*Whoops!*" escaped my lips, reverberating through the auditorium. That was my grand entrance into the theatre!'

Joan got the job which, through the intervention of A. E. Matthews, led eventually to her playing the juvenile lead in *The Chiltern Hundreds*.[22]

One of the highlights of that run was when the Queen with Prince Philip, together with Princess Margaret, came to see the play. 'I found it hard to believe that Her Majesty, whom I had watched grow up and had grown to love and respect, was sitting there watching me!'[23]

Eventually the pressures of daily appearances began to get to Joan, and the time came when the playwright sent her to Scotland to rest and recover. It was a remarkable experience for an unsophisticated London girl to find herself living in a castle with a real-life earl![24] There she discovered a renewed stability and a strength to return to her role in the play. The only problem, according to her co-star, Diane Hart, was that when she returned she was insufferably snooty, 'talking about tea with the Buccleuchs and breakfast with the earl!'[25]

In some ways that situation was exacerbated by a friendship which developed between Joan Winmill and Bobby Kennedy. She had met him through William Douglas-Home during the run of *The Chiltern Hundreds*. Subsequently they spent much time together whenever he was in London and, although his father disapproved of the friendship,[26] Bobby continued to escort Joan to many engagements. When he returned to America, he wrote regularly to her and, because he remembered that there was a shortage of good clothes in England, he sent her packages of beautiful clothes scrounged from his sisters![27]

Joan came to consider herself to be 'in love' with Bobby.[28] It was a shock to her, therefore, when she received a letter from him which read: 'I am getting married to Ethel Skakel.' This was a girl Joan had been introduced to by Bobby when they had met in her dressing room at the theatre a year or so earlier. It was just one more setback to add to Joan's sense of loneliness. Shortly afterwards, she finally succumbed to a full-scale breakdown.

It was at that 'dead-end' phase of her life that the telephone call came from John Mercer. He had no idea that God was using him to start Joan on life's most important and fulfilling venture.

Joan took phenobarbitone to help her gain the courage she felt she needed to meet John and his wife. 'I had carefully selected what I would wear to the Billy Graham crusade meeting,' Joan says. 'This was to be "Miss Successful" enjoying the company of some friends, and I acted as if nothing at all was wrong with my world.[29] But inside, I knew I was a fake.' There were several in John Mercer's party who dined together that night. Afterwards they made for Harringay.[30]

There was a certain levity among members of the party. 'I can't wait to see all the crying converts,' one exclaimed. They all laughed and agreed that it would be interesting.

Joan says, 'Even as I laughed I sensed a terrible need in my life – but these people would never know of it. Of that I assured myself.'[31]

When they arrived, the vast choir was singing 'Blessed assurance, Jesus is mine'.[32] To most of the party – including Joan – it was an unfamiliar hymn and the words seemed almost foreign to them. One big surprise for them all was the appearance on the platform of Dale Evans Rogers – the wife of the cowboy star, Roy Rogers. She told the audience how Jesus Christ had changed her life and how much she loved Him.[33] It seemed amazing to all of them that this well-known actress from Hollywood should speak like this in front of all these people.

Soon, Billy Graham got up to speak. 'So *this* was the American who had come to tell the British about religion,' Joan thought. She settled down to listen to him, promising herself that she would collect some witticisms to share with the others on the journey home.[34]

'But God had other plans,' she says. 'As I listened to Dr Graham, I was struck by his sincerity. I didn't agree with him at first, but I could see he was sincere.[35] And then he went on to talk about a personal Saviour. What *was* that all about?'

Billy Graham said: 'If you had been the only one on this earth, Jesus would have been willing to die for you – only He was pure enough to be sacrificed for your sins. God loved you so much that He sent His only Son to die for you. All you have to do is to realise your need, acknowledge your sin, and ask Him to come into your life.'[36]

Was this oversimplifying the Bible?[37] Joan wondered whether she had missed the significance of God's love in her quest for happiness and self-satisfaction.

'For what shall it profit a man if he shall gain the whole world and lose his own soul?' Billy Graham continued. 'How many people here tonight have had no time for God because of their ambition for material things?'[38] To Joan, this was a blow between the eyes. *Now* Billy Graham was getting personal! 'But seek ye first the kingdom of God, and His righteousness; and all these things shall be added unto you,' the evangelist continued, quoting Matthew 6:33.[39]

Suddenly Joan came to life. To herself she said: 'Oh, God, I have not put You first in my life. It has all been self-seeking.'[40] Here she was, confronted by Christ, a living Redeemer.

Then Billy Graham said something which made Joan think that John Mercer may have said something to him about her! 'There are many here who believe suicide to be the only answer to their problems.' That was exactly what Joan had once contemplated. But as she glanced at John there was no clue at all from his expression that he knew anything about it.[41]

'You cannot run away from your problems. But by coming to the foot of the Cross and realising your need for forgiveness, you can find a peace that passes all understanding through accepting Christ,'[42] Billy Graham concluded.

More than anything else Joan wanted peace, so she prayed: 'Lord, you know what a terrible mess I have made of the life You have given me, and You know that I have even thought of ending it. Lord, forgive me! But I don't have the courage to face it alone any more. I want to give my life to You, but I'm terribly afraid of what these friends will think. Dear God, give me the courage to turn this life over to You.'[43]

Around Joan, on both sides, were the friends with whom she had come to Harringay. What would they think if she went forward? She knew she might be laughed at – but suddenly she felt herself stand up. 'It was as though God had given me the courage to make this decision, and I stepped out

102

into the aisle!'[44] It was such a simple step, yet it brought a drastic change to her life. There was now a light at the end of the tunnel.

She had no knowledge of what would happen next. All she knew was that, as she went to the front, a tall and good-looking lady came and stood beside her.[45] Joan was about to try to slip away from the crowd because she did not want to discuss with *anyone* what she had done. But the lady moved with her. 'Trapped!' thought Joan and she felt herself enveloped by fear. 'But I sensed that in the lady next to me was someone who really did care. It seemed that an aura of serenity surrounded her and, as I looked at her, I saw that she was a truly beautiful woman.'

Joan followed her, with the rest of the crowd that had come forward, into an adjacent hall. There they sat down next to each other and the lady read to her from the Bible, counselled her and then prayed with her. What then followed was a big surprise!

The lady turned to Joan and asked: 'Would you like to meet my husband?'[46] She led Joan to an unmarked door, knocked and entered – and who should be there but Billy Graham himself! 'My counsellor, unbeknown to me, was Ruth Graham, Billy Graham's wife! I was so overwhelmed that all I could say in reply to his questions was a stumbling "Yes – no – yes – no!" '

Before she left, Ruth Graham told Joan, 'Don't forget, when you walk out of here you'll no longer be alone – Christ goes with you!'[47] On the journey home, Joan sat with her friends, and she cannot recall a word being spoken. If it had been, she was oblivious to it! Something had really happened in her life. As Ruth Graham had said, no longer need she be lonely – Christ would be with her.

Nevertheless, it was not an easy path ahead. Life continued to be a major struggle. She had to disentangle a relationship she had formed.[48] This necessitated finding a new apartment. Temptations she had faced before did not go away. But the memory verses, to which Ruth Graham had introduced her,[49] helped her through the lower days.

With those things taken care of, her spirits soared and 'As David had danced before the Lord, I danced from room to room in my new home, praising God and thanking Him for the release that had flooded through me.'[50]

Shortly afterwards, and before the Harringay Crusade was ended, World Wide Pictures planned a feature film to tell some of the stories of the crusade. Initially entitled *Dateline London*, the film was to tell the stories of three people: a factory worker, a test pilot of aircraft, and a London actress. Joan's conversion had been 'high profile' and Ruth Graham mentioned to the film's producers that Joan Winmill would be an excellent choice for the starring role.[51]

Joan was invited to appear, and she was delighted to accept this opportunity, which she saw as the hand of God upon her life. The film, eventually called *Souls in Conflict*, became one of the most outstanding films ever produced by World Wide Pictures. It was a powerful evangelistic force with an extended message from Billy Graham.

Apart from public showings in churches, town halls and other large auditoria, the film was used extensively in a ministry to the armed services and also in prisons. Between 1956 and 1961 the film was shown by an evangelistic team in every penal institution throughout the British Isles.

One of the strengths of the film was the clear choice offered to the viewer. In one scene Frank, an aircraft designer, was reading a report in the newspaper about the crusade at Harringay and declaring that it was all 'sheer unadulterated nonsense'. Geoff, the test pilot, had been to the crusade the night before, when he had responded to Billy Graham's invitation to accept Christ. Turning to Frank, he answered the other's outburst by saying, 'I was one of those who went forward last night to accept Christ – and I found it the most natural thing I had ever done!' Frank looked at him with incredulity, shaking his head in disbelief.

Yet in the remarks by those two was enshrined the decision that faced the entire audience. Either they would say, with Frank, 'sheer unadulterated nonsense' and reject Christ, or they would say, with Geoff, 'To accept Christ was the most natural thing I ever did.' There is no other choice, and Geoff's conversion was matched by the story of the factory worker's wife and that of the actress. It was powerful and compelling stuff!

A prisoner in Dartmoor prison, who saw the film and accepted Christ, wrote afterwards:

> It is now some months since you visited Dartmoor with your film *Souls in Conflict*. It has taken all this time before I could feel justified in writing to you. You see I wanted to make really sure that I had found God before I started making any commitments . . . Even in here, in my present situation, I think I am happier than I have ever been before. My cell no longer seems dull and empty, but in my quiet moments I feel that God is with me . . . I am working hard to pass on God's message to other inmates of this institution. It is often said in here that prison is the breeding ground of crime. But from my own experience I know that it can also be the birthplace of Christians![52]

On his release from prison, that prisoner sought permission to remarry his wife (who had also become a Christian). She had divorced him earlier for cruelty when he went into prison. However, due to prison regulations, he had to wait six months before the new marriage could take place. He wrote and asked: 'Is it all right if I live with my wife while I am awaiting the wedding?' He was reminded that 'What God hath joined let no man put asunder!' In God's eyes he was still married to his wife. But it is the type of question that would never have been asked in the 1990s!

Twenty-five years later, a 'silver jubilee celebration' was held in London's Grosvenor House Hotel. To it came hundreds of those who had been associated with the Harringay Crusade. As part of the programme, it seemed appropriate to show once more the film *Souls in Conflict*. Everyone was surprised at how relevant the film still was. The fashions had changed a bit, but the story was in every way as applicable to the 1970s as it had been to the 1950s. It was an inspired piece of film-making!

Forty-one years after it was made, the film was shown once more, 'as a bit of nostalgia', to a conference held in Hothorpe Hall near Market Harborough. Even after such a long distance in time the film was by no means dated. Even the fashions had 'come back'! Several of those who attended the conference went away determined to use it in their churches. Reports from those who did so affirm that people were *still* coming to Christ as a result of that remarkable film made in Harringay.

As another result of making that film, Joan was invited to America for a 'personal appearance'[53] tour, which was to be set up and run by a member of the film team of the Billy Graham Evangelistic Association. His name was Bill Brown, and Joan was associated with him throughout that tour.[54] Before long the news came that she and Bill Brown were to be married. Together they made their home in California, where Bill was later to become president of World Wide Pictures. This company was to go on and produce and release such famous Christian films as *The Prodigal*, *Time to Run*, *No Longer Alone* (Joan's own story), *The Hiding Place*, *Joni* and *Cry from the Mountain*.

There was now no looking back for Joan. She and Bill had two strapping sons, and their lives were dedicated to God's service wherever He led them. Joan says: 'I thought of the many times when Bill and I had wondered if any of our spiritual training had rubbed off on our children.[55] As the years went by, it seemed that some had, and I was reminded of something that Ruth Graham has said: "You should never judge a painting until the artist is finished with it." We are content to leave the lives of our two sons in the hand of God.'

Bill and Joan returned to London in 1965 to direct the 1966

and 1967 Billy Graham crusades at Earls Court. 'I never would have dreamt, on that evening at Harringay in 1954, that in twelve years' time I would be back in London as part of another Billy Graham crusade,' says Joan. 'How wonderful God is! He saw us through the dark days of 1967/8 when Bill was suddenly afflicted by cancer. Then I remembered the text in Romans 8:26: "Likewise the Spirit also helpeth our infirmities: for we know not what we should pray for as we ought: but the Spirit Himself maketh intercession for us with groanings which cannot be uttered." I decided to claim that promise for myself, and I trusted God to see us through.[56]

'Bill had an operation for cancer, and when I went to see him he looked so big and helpless, lying in his hospital bed.[57] But we talked and prayed together. Later, when he had recovered, he went back to the hospital for a check-up. The doctor came in and he said: "I've never seen a healing like this one. There isn't even a trace!"[58] Many years have passed since then, and each time Bill has gone back for a check-up he has been given a clean bill of health.'

For Joan it seemed that there were new opportunities for her to use her skills as an actress. One day she received a telephone call from Frank Jacobson, then vice-president of World Wide Pictures. He asked her if she would like to play a role in the new film they were making, *Time to Run*. 'Naturally I was excited,' says Joan, 'and said that I would love to be able to appear in a film again.[59] But Bill was not so sure! He was worried lest people might say it was nepotism. I was not convinced until my son David came home and, when he heard the news, said, "Congratulations, Mom – let's celebrate." This support from David persuaded me that I should accept the invitation, and Bill also then gave me all his support.'

In due course the film opened in London. Bill and Joan were able to be there and, for the opening night, Bill invited many people who had been an influence in Joan's life. Her headmistress from her schooldays was there. Joy Elson Rayner – who had dared Joan to ask for A. E. Matthews's autograph –

was there too, and so was Joy's cousin, John Mercer, who had first taken Joan to hear Billy Graham.[60] 'Lots of members of my family also came, and I remembered the years when they had to watch me go on so blindly. There had been many agonies and very few ecstasies. Now, as I spoke to them all, I hoped I could convey my happiness in Christ.'

A few years later, this problem of nepotism reared its head once more! Joan had written a book entitled *No Longer Alone*. In the book she described the many experiences through which she had seen God's hand at work in her life. It told of her involvement in playing the leading role in *Souls in Conflict* – a story which so easily might have been her own.

As Nick Webster read Joan's book, he felt that the element of loneliness would make a good story for a film. He approached World Wide Pictures, and Bill Brown was once more faced with the agonising decision, whether or not to allow the story to be filmed. It was, after all, the story of his wife's life, and he was the president of the company! At first he hid the script so that Joan would not see it. But Nick was persistent. 'Have you sent the script to Billy Graham?' he asked.[61]

'Bill struggled with his conscience for some time,' says Joan, 'but finally he sent the script to Mr Graham, and Billy said, "OK, let's do it." Larry Holbin, who did the film script, came to me and he said: "Oh, Joan, I'm so excited about doing this, because I've always wanted to do a 'period' piece!" And I thought "A *period* piece! This is *my* life." But when I saw the clothes arriving, and the old cars, I thought to myself, "This *is* a period piece!"

'The film was made mainly in London, so it gave us the opportunity of going there once again. It was always nostalgic to return home – even though California is really my home today. It seemed appropriate to have the world première of the film in London, and arrangements were made for it to be held at the beautiful Wembley Conference Centre. Maurice Rowlandson made all the arrangements and compiled a guest-list which included all the stars of the film – most of whom were able to come. It also included members of my family, lots of our friends, supporters of the Billy Graham Evangelistic Association in Britain, and some other special guests.'

There was a celebratory dinner afterwards to which many of those attending had been invited. James Fox, who was one of the cast, was there, and he recalled that he had become a Christian some years previously. He said that this film was his first for ten years. As a result he had felt somewhat 'rusty'. 'It was not that I had anything against films,' he said. 'I wanted to grow as a Christian and God led me in that way . . . It was a privilege being involved in this story and I thank the Lord who made it possible.'[62] Joan responded to the greetings given to her and she said: 'It was Nick Webster who felt that my story would make a good film. Shooting it provided us with many memories which will live with us for a long time.

'I remember the day we shot the scene in Trafalgar Square and I was feeding the pigeons. That looks easy, but when you're filming pigeons you don't know how many packets of seed you'll have to go through! The pigeons would go one way and I would go the other. We were waiting for the sun to come out and I was standing there waiting, watching out of the corner of my eye for the signal to start acting again. Then a man came up to me and he said in my ear, "Are you lonely?" I said, "No, I'm not, actually!" He said, "Well, I am, and I wonder if you could have dinner with me tonight?" I said to him, "Well, actually this is a film that I'm doing, and a camera is right on you at this moment!" I've never seen a man walk away so quickly!

'It's traumatic, but a wonderful experience, to make a film like this,' says Joan. 'Everyone connected with making it meant so very much to me that, when the shooting of the film ended, it was like a big family saying "Goodbye". We who know Christ have a tremendous bond. We may not see one another for years and years, yet as soon as you see each other again there is this wonderful bond – as though there hadn't been any years in between. And if there's anybody reading this who hasn't known God's love, I just pray that you may know it, because we live in a very very troubled world and I know that I couldn't have gone on, I couldn't have raised two children without Christ.[63]

'Life is like a huge jigsaw puzzle to me. My eldest son is now a police chief in California. But I have one piece of that jigsaw puzzle – his life – in my hand. I'll never give that up until I go to be with the Lord, because I pray for him. It's so wonderful to know that, wherever he is, whether or not in danger, the Lord is with him; and with my son David too.

'Our Creator gave us all different fingerprints and He loves us all so much. I know that I am loved and I look at my fingerprints and I say, "Thank you, Lord, for caring enough about even the finest detail in my life." Nothing is too small in our lives that He doesn't care about.'

Summing up her story, Joan says: 'Our past, our childhood, dominates our future years. We should learn from our past, but not let it tear us down. All we confess to the Lord is forgiven and forgotten. In the Psalms, David said: "As far as the east is from the west, so far hath he removed our transgressions from us. Like as a father pitieth his children, so the Lord pitieth them that fear Him. For He knoweth our frame . . ." (Psalms 103:12–14)[64]

'I have cried out to God in *my* unbelief, and there has always come a peace that is not complacent, but one that is God's. It is not of my own making, for I am a weak woman – but I have a strong God.[65]

'If I ever needed proof that God answers prayer, I have it in my own life. I was alone without hope in that apartment in London, crying out to Him. He heard that prayer and sent along the right people to provide the answer.[66]

'There are those who would say that all these things were coincidences. But I know that the sequence of events – which included Joy, John, Billy Graham and Ruth, my marriage to Bill and my involvement in the work of the Billy Graham

Evangelistic Association, and my children – are all part of the perfect plan of God for my life.

  ' "I will praise the Lord no matter what happens. I will constantly speak of His glories and grace. I will boast of all His kindness to me. Let all who are discouraged take heart. Let us praise the Lord together, and exalt His name. For I cried to Him and He answered me! He freed me from all my fears." ' (Psalm 34: 1–4, Living Bible)[67]

12

Monk to Minister

Alan Wright, UK, 1954

If his beard had been white, he had the perfect build to be a
Santa Claus! Alan Wright was another of those innumerable
young men – and some ladies, too – who have devoted their
lives to the Christian ministry as a result of Billy Graham's
ministry at the Harringay Arena in 1954.

Alan exudes joy and commitment – and that is all the more
surprising because he is just out of a job. His whole life has
been a pilgrimage since Harringay. Until now that pilgrimage
has been within various theological groupings within the
Church of England.

Alan was born in Northampton and it was there that he
went to school. One day a friend of his, a co-member of the
local church scout troop, told him about a trainload of people
from Northampton who were going to London to attend the
Greater London Crusade with Billy Graham, and he invited
Alan to join the party.

Not altogether sure what it was all about, Alan nevertheless
agreed to go. He thought that, at the very least, it would be
an interesting day out. He had no idea at all that, by the time
he returned to Northampton on the train, the whole direction
of his life would have been changed.

Today he does not remember a great deal about the meeting.
All he is sure of is that there was something about the preacher
which compelled both his attention and his response. 'It was
as if I had heard it for the first time,' he says. 'I had *heard* the
message before, but this was the first time I really understood
it. I saw that traditional church-going was not enough. Most

of my life, I had gone to church three times on a Sunday. I'd been a member of the choir and attended Sunday school. Then, too, I had been confirmed. I really had expected that to make a big difference. After all, the bishop had laid hands on me. But still there was something missing.

'Now, at Harringay, Billy Graham proclaimed the Gospel with such clarity that I saw what was missing, and what I needed. When Billy gave his usual invitation to "get up out of your seat . . ." I was one of those who responded.'

Without any doubt the occasion had an immediate impact on his life. A church-goer since the age of three, and a choir-member since six, he had been brought up to say his prayers and to believe that everything he had been taught was right. But when he went back to school, he found some Christian friends who showed him that they had something different from what he had.

'In a way, I had been prepared for the event, because for several summers I had attended boys' camps run by youth-worker David Tryon. "Pioneer Camps" they were called. And there I had heard the Gospel. But I hadn't done very much about it. But the Holy Spirit used all that preparation to make me ready to respond when I heard Billy Graham's message. I was a different person when I went home.'

Alan tells how the follow-up from that crusade meeting almost destroyed the embryo faith he had. 'My actual counsellor was very helpful, but the crusade people had sent my name and address to the local parish church. It was a middle-of-the-road Anglo-Catholic church whose parish priest said to me, "I'll do what I can to help, but nothing like this has ever happened to me!" My counsellor also wrote to me, but he used such spiritual language that I found it difficult to understand what he was saying!'

Two other things happened propitiously to him at that time. He was fortunate in having a born-again Religious Instruction teacher at school, who helped him enormously in his spiritual life. Then his friend from the scout troop pressurised him into

113

joining a cell group to study the Bible. 'And that was a life-saver for me,' he says. 'It was a crucial contribution to my spiritual development.

'In due course I was able to attend a home group, formed by some real believers in my own church. So I continued to go to that church, and it is remarkable that a not-very-good sermon from the curate was used by God to give me a call to the ministry.'

Alan tells of a young lady at that home group who arrived every time with an insatiable stack of questions. She was always to the forefront and her questions were always difficult. Two years later, Alan met her again and she told him, 'I've found Christ and become a Christian now, and I've found the answers to all those questions I used to ask!'

Soon after leaving school, Alan did an apprenticeship for two years, working at a roller-bearing factory, and from there he went on to study for three years at Oxford. Although he read maths and physics, he spent much of his time debating theological subjects. This led him to spending nine months in a monastery, before going to Chichester to study for the ministry. The High Anglo-Catholic ambience of Chichester resulted in his coming out of college heavily influenced by the teaching of the Tractarian Movement.

Alan says: 'I preached the Gospel – in fact it was virtually the same Gospel that the evangelicals (and Billy Graham) were preaching – but I meant something different by it. To me, at that time, the important things were christening (baptism), confirmation and the sacrament of Holy Communion. There was nothing about a personal commitment to the Lord Jesus Christ in it.'

It is strange that, if you take the various approaches to the message, they might be described in the form of a circle. At the very top of the circle is the Anglo-Catholic ministry. Going around the circle, you pass through all the theological varieties of the message until you reach the very bottom of the circle. There you reach the broad church's position: preaching without any – or little – biblical message at all; mostly it is a political or social message. The name of God, the life of Christ, His death, resurrection, ascension and return are subjects rarely mentioned, and there is no message or power in the ministry. Continuing up the remainder of the circle, you move through increasingly warmer and more spiritual messages until you come back to the top of the circle, next to the Anglo-Catholic starting point, where the traditional Gospel, evangelical and fundamental message is paramount. But the circle does not join! Although they have a similar message to the evangelicals, the Anglo-Catholics are a whole circle away! That was a factor which Alan came to recognise.

It was the British evangelist Tom Rees who used to say that there are three elements in the Church of England: the HIGH and hazy . . . the BROAD and crazy . . . and the LOW and lazy!

Alan recalls that there came a time in his life when he accepted a curacy to a church in Edgehill, Liverpool. 'It was of the High Church tradition,' he says. While he was there, he met a lady who had been to a school run by a group of Anglican nuns. Under their ministry she had become a Christian. She had such a lively faith that Alan soon realised that he wanted to spend the rest of his life with her, so eventually he asked her to marry him.

Shortly afterwards they went together to Swaziland, where he became the curate at a large, English-speaking church. On his return to Britain, he once again took a church in Liverpool. This time it was in the Seaforth area, to the north of the Liverpool docks. It was a very depressed area and he found that all his previous experiences didn't work there. The rural dean even had doubts whether the church should be allowed to continue, it was so depressed and in such decline. But it was while he was there that Alan too came to a renewal of his faith and returned to the true preaching of the Gospel.

Life was not easy in Seaforth. Even at the neighbourhood level there were problems. The local authority decided to run a road straight through their garden! When the road was finished, the authority put double yellow lines down each side – right opposite a shopping centre, a church, a school and a park. In spite of the protests of the local residents, nothing was done about the danger of this road and, eventually, the inevitable happened. A boy was knocked down as he crossed the road. So the local residents banded together, and one morning they did a 'lollipop lady act'. Led by the vicar, they stopped all the traffic by standing across the road in the middle of the rush hour! This gave Alan and his wife many opportunities to talk to the neighbours about Christ. One housewife who became a Christian told him that their family life had been transformed. 'Before,' she said, 'it was cornflakes for breakfast, jam butties for lunch and chips for supper.' After her conversion she wanted to do better, and the quality of their life was transformed. Her husband now stayed at home instead of going out and getting drunk – and now he brought her a cup of tea in bed!

Then one day another change was to come into Alan's life. He was invited to a meeting of the Diocesan Evangelical Fellowship, where the programme consisted of a film made of the parish of the Holy Redeemer Church in Houston, Texas, USA.

That day the ministry of the Holy Spirit in his life became real to Alan, and his life and ministry were again transformed. Although he was not aware of any immediate conversions from his preaching, the seed was nevertheless being sown. Eventually, after three or four years, the first conversion happened. Since then, there has been a steady trickle as God has used his ministry in an effective way. Lives have been transformed and the Scriptures have been brought alive. Moving on to a church in Taunton, Alan now seeks to teach only those things which are within the Word of God.

Alan's faithfulness is about to be tested yet again as another transformation to his life takes place. Deeply disturbed by the ambivalent attitude of the Church of England towards morality – and especially to young people living together when they are not married – he feels that he can no longer associate himself with the Anglicans. He believes that the process of rejecting Scriptural teaching, in which he believes deeply, began with the ordination of women to the priesthood and came to a head recently. There was a TV programme on which his bishop, the Bishop of Bath and Wells, was speaking. Alan felt that the bishop had departed from the clear teaching of Scripture when he declared on TV that 'the church has to recognise the pressures of modern life and that living together should no longer be described as "living in sin" '.

Alan felt that, if the Church of England could not give a biblical and scriptural lead from the top, then his own position as a leader of his own people would be seen to be ineffective. He felt, therefore, that, for this and other reasons, he had no alternative but to make a stand – costly as it would be to him – and to resign his living and to trust in God for the future.

His own family life has been impeccable, as he and his wife have sought to live a life which is pleasing to God. They have been blessed with four (now grown-up) children, all of whom have themselves become Christians and are engaged in Christian work. They are scattered around the world, the eldest daughter living in the USA and the second daughter at Bible School in Australia. Their son, having already preached in four continents, has recently returned from a short period of missionary work with his wife in Albania. She is now establishing a Christian kindergarten school in Wellington, and the youngest daughter hopes to do missionary work in Eastern Europe. Thus the influence of Billy Graham's ministry has now moved on to the next generation.

Through it all, Alan has remained a very human person, and the warmth and wonder of his home is a testimony to the way in which he and his wife live. 'Please do not leave the cats in this room and shut the door as the budgie is vulnerable,' says one of the many handwritten notes scattered around Alan Wright's home. It typifies the homely feeling which is immediately noticeable upon entering his home. It is a family home, and the warmth of his welcome is apparent from the minute the front door is opened.

Without Billy Graham it might all have been so different. Everything that has happened since is a long way from the fifteen-year-old boy who was taken by a scouting friend to the Harringay Arena in 1954. Alan is under no illusion that, had that simple conversion not taken place at Harringay, the pressures of life and the studies at college might well have led him on to different paths. But God, having claimed his life, laid His hand upon him and brought him through many experiences, to the point where the Word of God is paramount in his life. He remains eternally grateful to the crusade at Harringay, and to Billy Graham's ministry in his life. He believes implicitly in the faithfulness of the God who has led him all the way in ministry from Billy Graham's 'call' at Harringay until the present time.

13
No! The Pizzas are Yours

Trevor Adams, Australia, 1959

It was 1992 – and 4 a.m. in the morning. Trevor Adams was still out there, driving taxis around the streets of Brisbane and finding there was a whole world of people out there without Christ at that hour of the day.

'God!' he screamed to himself in the cab of his taxi as frustration swept through him. 'What is my future?' He had tried to face life with honesty. The pressures on all sides made him wonder whether God had forsaken him. But no! He could never believe that the God in whom he had put his faith and his trust at a Billy Graham crusade many years before would leave him destitute.

Then, one afternoon, sleeping off the hours of early-morning taxi duty, he was awakened by a phone call at 1 p.m. It was from his friend and mentor, Robert Adsett – a man in the architectural business with whom Trevor had previously worked. Adsett had been involved in the World Explo in Brisbane and was now contemplating a similar ministry in Spain; he was planning to construct and operate another 'Pavilion of Promise'. 'Would you,' he asked Trevor, 'consider going to Spain in 2½ weeks to be the operations manager of the pavilion?'

In a state of total shock, Trevor took a decision, as a result of which he found himself setting off for Spain in three short weeks. He was to be there for the next eight to nine months.

It was a massive task which faced him: it would be his responsibility to assemble a volunteer staff of some 600–700 people to deal with visitors from more than 300 nations.

In the event, he rose to the occasion and, during the tenure of the pavilion, more than 50,000 people became Christians and he received more than 100,000 requests for pieces of literature.

He was only nine years old when, in 1959, he was taken to a Billy Graham crusade in Brisbane, Australia. His home was very committed: his parents worshipped among the Brethren, and it was well-prepared ground into which the seed of the Gospel message was sown.

Nevertheless, he was not ready to take the step of commitment on that first night. When Billy Graham gave his invitation to respond on the second night, Trevor was one of those who went forward.

'It is not possible for a child of nine to know what he is doing,' one sceptic said to another person. 'Oh yes it is,' the other replied. 'I accepted Christ as my Saviour and Lord when I was only seven. I'm seventy now, and the conviction of what I did sixty-three years ago has never left me!'

Trevor could say exactly the same thing. 'I knew what I was doing all right. Even at that age, my conviction of sin and the sense of relief was very real.'

When he was sixteen, he went to hear a local evangelist. It was then that he rededicated his life to Christ and began fully to understand the reality of his decision.

At nine years of age, however, it had not been easy at school. When he returned there the next morning, they soon found out what he had done, and he was teased by the other pupils. But he stuck to his guns and, with the help that he received at home, he developed as the years went by.

Then in 1969 Billy Graham came back to Brisbane, and this time Trevor Adams found himself deeply involved in the crusade. He attended the 'Christian life and witness' classes; he was a member of the choir, and he found his life, and that of his best mate, impacted through their work in the co-labourers' room, where he went to help following each evening's crusade meeting.

The co-labourers corps in a Billy Graham crusade is a team of workers who 'come on duty' as soon as the evening meeting ends. Their work is to process the cards completed by the counsellors as they had talked to enquirers.

It was the job of the co-labourers corps to prepare and send an initial letter, with literature, to each enquirer. They also ensured that news of the response was sent to the appropriate local church minister. The co-labourers corps often worked through until the early hours of the morning. They were a deeply dedicated group whose input added substantially to the number of enquirers who went on with the Lord in the years ahead.

In his daily work he was involved in accountancy, and he had also been trained in the marketing of real estate property – in an unusual context! He was engaged in selling mobile homes (caravans) to potential buyers.

Not finding this occupation entirely satisfying, he also started working with a support team, taking ministry to country towns. And this set him on the path to consider entering the full-time Christian ministry.

At the same time he became interested in Christian radio and was also invited to become a foundation member of the board of a large Christian camp. Thus, little by little, his interests moved away from his daily work, and the conviction grew that the full-time Christian ministry was a special calling from God.

Then he got married! Suddenly it seemed that there might be obstacles in his way to fulfilling that calling, until he found that his wife, Carol, was quite prepared to support him in the training he would require. In 1980 they moved to Auckland, New Zealand, where he went to a Brethren Bible College.

It was while he and his wife were there that his faith was severely tested. One day, out in the country, one of his sons (he and Carol now have six boys!) was attacked and badly mauled by a dog. As a result the child needed more than 140 stitches. On three occasions during the next weeks his life was in danger. Nevertheless, in response to much prayer that went up for him, he survived and recovered.

In 1981 the family returned from Auckland to Australia and settled back in Brisbane, where Trevor returned to his management position. He did not know what other opportunities would open for him in the city. At one time he was faced with some six or seven possibilities in church ministry and in para-church organisations. Yet, as he considered these, he never felt that God was calling him to any one of them. Instead, he continued in business. In 1975 he had helped in the founding of a new church, of which he became an elder. This involved him in a ministry situation, and by 1984 he felt a new and pressing call to full-time ministry. But still he took no decision.

His daily work was all-absorbing, but part of his mind was thinking around this problem of his call. 'You can only steer a ship when it's moving,' he said, so he kept moving ahead and was confident that God would direct him into the situation of His choice. He was torn between full-time ministry and his awareness that there was a real ministry to exercise in the marketplace.

Then in 1984 he could battle against it no longer. He went in to see his boss one day and told him that he had come to give him six months' notice, to start on 1 July. Then he told the eldership of his church that he would be ready for full-time pastorate from 1 January 1985. And so it worked out.

The church was a Community Brethren church in Logan City – a community of 150,000 on the outskirts of Brisbane. And there he stayed until 1988, when a telephone call from Robert Adsett came, asking him to consider working for six months at the Pavilion of Promise which he and David Mainse from Canada were intending to present at the world Expo that year.

Trevor had a real sense that the Lord was leading him to this ministry and, while he still pastored his church, he took on the role of duty manager, responsible for 480 volunteer staff from twenty-seven different countries.

The pavilion featured a high-tech presentation of the Bible.

It lasted for forty-eight minutes and was a multi-media presentation which some 850,000 people saw. Of these, some 4,000 were converted to Christ and counselled. As this ended he returned to the pastorate.

He felt it right to take a sabbatical from his church, and in 1991 he started driving taxis. After the twelve-month sabbatical he did not return to his church but continued in a variety of ministries as invitations came in.

In particular, with Carol, his wife, he founded a Kids' Club in his local area and concentrated on a ministry to children. In two months, sixty-five children came with twenty-five parents (for coffee) to the local community centre.

Throughout 1991 and into 1992 this ministry continued, mainly on a Friday night, when between 160 and 170 kids came, accompanied by some thirty-five parents. So the ministry was not to the children alone but also to their parents. Meanwhile he continued his taxi-driving and also took on a variety of odd jobs.

Then, in 1992, came that 1 p.m. telephone call from Robert Adsett that was to change his whole life – and, eventually, to bring him back into the orbit of Billy Graham and his work. He was asked to become operations manager for the Pavilion of Promise at the 1992 World's Fair in Seville, Spain, where more than 50,000 people made a decision for Christ.

It seemed as though Trevor's troubles were far from over, however. One day, while a few feet up a ladder doing some repairs to his house, he fell down and was on crutches for eight months.

To top it all off, his car caught fire and was destroyed and, while he was recovering from the shock of that, his house was broken into. Then, just one week later, his house was broken into a second time and he and Carol lost almost everything – including the van in which all their electrical equipment was stored.

'Did you ever doubt God during those stressful periods?' he was asked.

He came back with an emphatic: 'Never! Not a doubt – but I did ask the question "Why?"!'

As a result of all this, finances were terribly tight in the family. On 2 September 1994 – 'A day our family will never forget,' says Trevor – one of his sons came to ask him if they could have a pizza for supper (pizza was a family favourite). Trevor had to tell him that, unhappily, pizza was not in their budget for the present. They would have to live on the meagre fare to which they had grown accustomed.

Then suddenly there was a ring at the front door. When Trevor went to answer it, outside was a man from the pizza company. 'I've got four large pizzas and Cokes for you,' he announced.

Trevor replied, 'There must be some mistake. We've not ordered any pizza – and certainly not any Coke.'

'No – the pizzas are yours. There's no mistake, sir,' the man replied. 'They've got your name and address on them. Just take them! We been told to tell you they're from God.'

'It was wonderful how God knew our need and somehow prompted someone – we never found out who – to send us those wonderful pizzas just at that time.'

Time and time again throughout his life, since that early-age commitment to Christ at the Billy Graham crusade, he has experienced God's provision for him.

It was while he was engaged in the prayer time at the pavilion that he prayed conscientiously for his staff. At the same time he asked God to give him His heart and His eyes for the whole world.

God answered these prayers in a remarkable way. In fact, Trevor's prayers, and those of his best mate, had stretched back to the years 1968/9, since when they had prayed for more than fifteen years that God would use them in some major evangelistic opportunity. But, for the last eight years or so, they had stopped praying along those lines because they felt that it was simply not going to happen. Oh ye of little faith!

Eighteen months earlier, Billy Graham had received a call

from two Christian leaders in New Zealand. Off their own bats, and as they prayed together, they had felt compelled to invite Billy Graham to conduct a crusade in Auckland. To their immense surprise and delight, he immediately said 'yes' – which left them in something of a dilemma, because no official invitation had yet been issued. However, they were able to establish a firm base for Billy Graham's ministry in the city and, when church leaders in Australia heard about it, they too were quick to respond with an invitation to come there also. The invitation eventually included the cities of Melbourne, Sydney and Brisbane.

None of these locations was particularly easy, and not least Brisbane, where the mission co-ordinator had been suddenly taken ill. Robert Adsett felt that Trevor was the right man to step into the breach and help them again.

It seemed to Trevor that Robert Adsett had a predilection for making phone calls at unearthly hours! At any rate, it was another midnight phone call which simply said to him, 'Come and get this Crusade off the ground!'

At the time, Trevor was engaged in a sideline venture of building two houses, and he was already on the steering committee for the festival – the name by which the Australian crusades were to be known. Suddenly, he found that he had to drop everything and devote his whole time to preparing for the festival.

A big shock was awaiting both him and the committee just around the corner, in November 1995. A phone call from America disclosed that Billy Graham's doctors had ordered him to cancel his plans to go to Australia on two grounds: first, because in their opinion he would be both too far away and for too long from his medical base; and, secondly, they were concerned for the health of Billy Graham's wife, Ruth, and they felt that he should not be so far away from her.

In the event their wisdom proved well-founded, because shortly afterwards Ruth Graham contracted spinal meningitis and for a short while it was not expected that she would live through it. In this the doctors were to be proved wrong, for she recovered sufficiently to be present at the award of the Congressional Medal in Washington on 2 May 1996 and at the Minneapolis crusade a month later.

For the Australians the news came as a shattering blow. Not only were they well ahead with their planning, but their expectation levels also were high. Melbourne (and, incidentally, Auckland) cancelled. However, Sydney and Brisbane took up the offer of Franklin Graham, Billy Graham's elder son, to come and take the meetings in his father's place.

'It was an incredible disappointment,' says Trevor. 'Everyone had worked so hard for the festival – and as for me, I had expected it to be a particular highlight. For it was Billy Graham who had led me to the Lord at the crusade in 1959.'

The 'Christian life and witness' classes had already attracted 6,500 attenders, and as the groundswell for Franklin Graham got under way that number grew to 9,000. 'Why stop now, we asked ourselves,' says Trevor. 'And in the event we were absolutely amazed and blessed with Franklin's ministry.'

Trevor goes on to say that there were three things which particularly commended Franklin Graham to the Australians. 'We found that he was a man of prayer. It was not unusual for a prayer meeting to last for two hours or more – with everyone on their knees and Franklin asking that everyone in the room should pray.

'Then his concern for the humanitarian needs of the world, through his "Samaritan's purse" ministry, was something that Australians really appreciated. Here was a man who had the additional attribute of practising what he preached in a high-profile way.

'Finally, we had been impressed with his book, *Rebel with a Cause*. Here was a man whose ministry would reflect his understanding of what God had done in his own life. Furthermore, there could be no "skeletons in the cupboard" because Franklin had already opened the cupboard doors!'

In the event, the festival in Brisbane (as in Sydney) was an immense success. It was not a 'Billy Graham crusade'. It was a different animal but equally as effective – and yet geared to today's generation. Franklin Graham preached the Word as his father did. He tended to get straight into his message and spent longer in the instructions to those who responded to his invitation.

A particular joy to Trevor was that his eldest son had become very involved with the festival. 'It was a heart-warming experience,' says Trevor. 'We did the right thing in going ahead.' It was clear to all who heard him that Franklin Graham's ministry was as effective as his father's before him. It seemed that God had laid His hand upon him.

As the news of Franklin's ministry in Australia reached the Minneapolis office of the Billy Graham Evangelistic Association, it caused a total re-think of all future ministry. With that in mind, a group of international leaders was called together in June 1996 for a three-day conference to pray, talk, think and plan, for ways in which the ministry of Franklin Graham might be continued worldwide and into the next decades through the Association. Trevor Adams was included in that group.

It was clear that there are many opportunities and there is much to be done. Although Billy Graham's own strength will not permit him (at seventy-eight years of age) to be as deeply involved in overseas ministries as hitherto, he has given his imprimatur to the continuance of the ministry through his son, Franklin Graham. And Trevor Adams will be there to help him!

14

Escape from the Japs

Richard Galway,* Singapore/UK, 1966
Richard Galway told me: 'I am not proud of my story, but if
it will help someone else to understand how God can redeem
a fallen person like me, then I am happy for it to be told.

'Before the 1939–45 war, I was a deputy manager in one
of the Big Five banks in London. I was also a member of the
Territorial Reserve so, shortly after the outbreak of war, I found
myself "called up" to serve in the Royal Engineers.

'After serving in France and passing through the Dunkirk
experience I found myself, first with Monty's army in North
Africa, then later I was sent out to the Far East, where I served
in Singapore.

'The Japanese army had just landed on the island and were
about to launch an attack with the aim of capturing the island
and taking prisoner all the British servicemen who were there
to protect it. The prospect was not good. The British forces
were smaller than the Japanese. Nor were they as well equipped
with weapons and firepower.'

Six soldiers of the Royal Engineers gathered in a huddle and
reviewed their situation. They were most offended by the fact
that their officers seemed to be more concerned with the
outcome of a polo match than planning for the defence of the
island. It seemed to the six that the true vulnerability of the
island was underestimated and that there was little hope of
survival. For them it seemed there were three alternatives.
They could fight and might be killed; they might be taken

---

* A pseudonym; his name has been changed at his request.

prisoner – or they could flee while the going was good.

They were not enamoured of the idea of being taken prisoner. They had heard that, to the Japanese, to be captured was a disgrace, so the Japanese, by repute, did not treat their prisoners very well. It was not a prospect to which the six were looking forward! Nor did they want to be killed! So, to them, it seemed that the only alternative was to find a means of escape.

As they were on an island, the only realistic escape route was by sea, and the most likely place to find the means of escape was at the harbour. So that was where they started looking. Very soon, under cover of darkness, they had found a small rowing boat – but it had no oars. However, they were still carrying their rifles and they soon found that they could make fairly satisfactory progress by using the butts of their rifles as a kind of paddle.

Paddling out in this way, they could see, silhouetted against the darkened sky, the outline of a Chinese junk. The boat had very high and slippery sides and there was no way they could clamber up from the small rowing boat to the deck of the junk, so they paddled around it, trying to find some way of getting aboard. It was not easy to see in the dark. They did not dare to use a torch for fear of detection; they had to work mainly by touch.

High up on the stern transom, but just within reach, they located a small square hatch. To their delight they found it was open, and they could pull themselves in and get aboard the junk from this unusual access point.

Once aboard, they set to work to try and find out how to make the vessel move. Not one of them had had any previous experience of sailing ships – and certainly none in a junk! After careful investigation they discovered that the vessel did not have an engine, so it would have to be sailed. They struggled to get one of the odd-shaped sails aloft and, as they did so, they let go of the rope which was tying the junk to a buoy in the harbour.

Slowly and ponderously the vessel swung around and started to edge forward. They had no idea where they were going . . . and there came the inevitable shudder and jerk as the vessel ran aground on a sandbank at the mouth of the harbour. Then, to their horror, they heard the deep-throated roar of a motor cruiser coming from behind them and also heading for the mouth of the harbour.

Their immediate reaction was that they had been spotted and now they were being followed, with all the consequences that would result from being captured.

The note of the engine changed and dropped lower as the vessel slowed down. It also became louder as the cruiser came ever closer. Eventually a line flew through the air, and an English voice yelled: 'Grab hold of that rope and pull me in.'

Doing the best they could with the unaccustomed handling of warps from boats, they managed to get hold of the rope and bring the motor cruiser alongside. A tall man wearing the uniform of a captain in the Royal Engineers appeared and leant on the rail at the side of his boat. 'What the hell do you limeys think you are doing?' he shouted. One of the six, a self-appointed spokesman for them all, replied that they had run aground in an attempt to sail out of the harbour.

The captain made it clear that what he meant was to know why they were there at all. The six decided that it was best to 'come clean'. They had been caught red-handed and there was no point in trying to deny the fact. So they told him of their fears of being taken prisoner of war, and of their desire to go somewhere – anywhere – where they could get to safety.

In a different tone of voice the captain said: 'Looks like we're all in this together. For the same reasons I grabbed this motor cruiser, and I want to get to Sumatra. You fellows had better come aboard, and we'll bloody well try and make it together.'

Totally amazed, and realizing that all of them – the captain included – would be candidates for a court martial if they were caught, they were relieved to find a rebel captain who was prepared to aid and abet them in their escape.

He had some of the skills necessary for navigation, and over the next few days he took the cruiser out of the Singapore Straits and into the Malacca Straits, in the general direction of Sumatra. He set a course too far north and they were in danger of running out of fuel before they made a landfall on the north-west coast of Sumatra near the town of Lubukpakam. They found a jetty to tie up to and went ashore to get food and water. Almost immediately they ran into a local inhabitant, who happened to speak English. He told them that the Japanese had just landed on Sumatra, south of the place where they had come ashore. He said that their only chance of escape lay in getting to the port of Banda Atjeh, at the extreme north of the island. This was a major port and he thought that they might succeed in finding a ship bound for Europe. How to get to the port was the big question. It was a long way!

Their local informant advised them that the best route was to follow the nearby railway track. He told them that the line led all the way to the port, but that it was several days' walk away, and there was always the danger that the Japanese might catch up with them. Nevertheless, it was their only hope, and they started out on their long trek.

They had only gone half a day's journey when they heard the noise of a train approaching behind them. Travelling very slowly, the train came to a halt when it reached them, and out of the driver's cab leant a European, speaking a language they could not understand. In seconds he had discovered that they were English, and he changed his language for, like so many of his countrymen, he spoke English almost as well as his own tongue. He told them that he was a Dutchman, working in Sumatra, and that he was one of only a few men on the island who were qualified to drive trains. He had just left the area close to where the Japanese had landed, and he was convinced that he would have no problem with them because of his train-driving skills.

He invited the six men and the captain to jump aboard the train, and they stayed on board until they reached the outskirts of Banda Atjeh. Their Dutch friend was then able to introduce them to another Dutchman, who was prepared to take them in his car to the port and to introduce them to the captain of a Dutch freighter which, he knew, was going to try to join a convoy of ships sailing to Holland.

The journey from Sumatra to Rotterdam was mainly uneventful. The seven of them had to 'work their passage', but this was a small price to pay for their freedom from the Japs.

But they were not so fortunate when they arrived in Rotterdam. There, the German port authorities identified them as British. They were captured and taken to the concentration camp at Dachau as civilian prisoners, and they remained there until the end of the war. Hard though this was, they were quite sure that this was preferable to a Japanese prisoner-of-war camp, so their escape had done them some good.

When the war was over their identities were revealed and the fat was in the fire for all of them. Their names were disclosed during interrogation and it quickly came to light that they were deserters from the Royal Engineers in Singapore. They were all sent back to Britain for court martial and each of them received a severe sentence. But none was as severe as the sentence that Captain Richard Galway received. He was stripped of his rank and dismissed from the service. He also had to serve a long sentence in prison.

From the time of his release until 1966 he lived with a deep conviction of his guilt, and he sank lower and lower into depravity, losing all self-esteem and drive. While he was in prison his wife had divorced him and his family had disowned him. He ended up penniless and started living on the streets of London as a tramp.

Richard Galway takes up the story from this point. 'It was a ghastly life – the more so because I had known better days and had been a respected officer in the Royal Engineers. I could scarcely believe my lot, and I reflected upon my present condition and the dirt and squalor which surrounded me on all sides.

'Even food was hard to come by. Occasionally there were handouts and bits of money that came from begging. But that mostly went on cheap liquor, cigarettes and even methylated spirits. We drank what we could, both to drown our sorrows and to keep warm. Above all, it dulled our senses to our condition and our lot.

'Often we found some of our food in the waste bins attached to the sides of lamp-posts. Scavenging through these, one could often find eatable scraps, which were very acceptable in extreme hunger. Sometimes we found similar scraps in the skips and waste bins outside the restaurants. I had indeed been brought very low, and my lot was unbelievably bad.

'Then, one day, while scavenging through a lamp-post waste bin, I came across a fairly new copy of a glossy magazine called *Decision*. For the want of something better to do, I pulled it out and took it with me to read as I sat on the steps of a building in the Strand. I soon discovered that it was a religious publication – not pornographic as I had hoped. So I threw it away with a curse, and in disgust.

'It fell on the pavement in front of me with an advertisement staring me in the face. The word that caught my attention was FREE! That, at least, was something I was not. Free, yes, from concentration camp and prison, but by no means free in my spirit.

'The advertisement went on to say that there was "Free Admission" to Earls Court Arena where, in that June of 1967, an event was going on with a preacher called Billy Graham. That rang a bell with me, because I had seen advertisements on the hoardings in London saying "Billy's Back", with an odd picture of a man standing up with his back to us! I didn't really know what it was all about, but if I could get into Earls Court free – the event seemed worth the candle.

'When I got to the arena, it seemed to me that everyone had tickets and – for a moment – I was put off. I have to confess that I was not the most elegant-looking of people either. My clothing was somewhat ragged, my hair matted and I suppose

I must have looked like I hadn't washed for weeks – and that was true anyway, because I hadn't!

'As I was looking at the crowds going in, a young man carrying a portable radio came over towards me. I thought, "Here we go, Dick. He's going to tell you to get lost" – but he didn't. With a warm smile, he asked me if I'd like a ticket; so, like all the rest, I now had my ticket also.

'What a shock when I got inside! The place was jam-packed with people from floor to ceiling. The choir was singing as I came in – but that turned out to be a rehearsal, because the affair hadn't started properly yet. My ticket did not seem to be a numbered seat, so I started looking around for somewhere to sit.

'I couldn't believe it when, with a smile, a man wearing a badge which said "steward" approached me and offered to show me to a seat. What was really surprising to me was the way in which he treated me as though I was a normal person, wearing decent clothes and looking clean and smart. But I certainly wasn't! Nevertheless, the people sitting next to the seat I was shown to didn't seem to worry about my appearance, so I settled down to see what would happen.

'It was quite a long meeting. Some of it was singing, some of it speaking. Most of it passed me by, and I didn't really take much notice of it. Then, on to the platform came a stately look-ing elderly man who commenced to sing a solo. His voice captivated me! It was deep, authoritative and clear. I could hear every word: "I'd rather have Jesus than silver or gold. I'd rather have Him than have riches untold. I'd rather have Jesus than houses or land, I'd rather be led by His nail-pierced hand. Than to be the King of a vast domain, and be held in sin's dread sway. I'd rather have Jesus than anything this world affords today."

'That song captivated me. I was in the right frame of mind for what followed: a tall man came to the pulpit and started to preach. He started with a couple of stories and then went on to speak about the blind beggar Bartimaeus and the way in which Jesus came to his life. I learned that the preacher was this "Billy's Back" fellow whose posters I had seen. "It's Billy Graham," said the man I was sitting next to.

'I listened attentively. It seemed that Billy Graham was speaking just to me. And he spoke with such authority. He convinced me that he knew what he was talking about. He told how Jesus could meet the beggar's need. He said that no one was too depraved to be reached by Jesus. "By His death on the Cross, Jesus paid for your sins," he said. "All you have to do is to accept that payment by faith, and to commit your life to Christ." He told the story of a little boy who had made a boat. He had worked long and hard to perfect that boat. Eventually the great day came when it was finished and he took it down to the seashore. Gently he put the boat into the water. As he did so, a puff of wind caught the sails and the boat was carried out to sea and was lost. A few weeks later, to his surprise, looking in a second-hand shop window he saw the very same boat that he had made. Someone had found it at sea and had brought it ashore. With the little money he had, the boy went into the shop and purchased the boat. As he came out, he was heard to mutter: "Now you're twice mine. I made you, and I bought you!" Billy Graham said that we were like that little boat. God had made us, and He had bought us with the blood of Jesus Christ on the Cross. And when he got to the end, Billy Graham said: "Everyone that Jesus called he called publicly. I'm going to ask you to get up out of your seat, and come and stand here at the front. By coming you're saying I want Christ in my life."

'I knew that was what I wanted, so I was one of those who accepted that invitation to go to the front. I was paired up with a marvellous counsellor, who spent a lot of time explaining how Billy Graham's message could apply to me personally. He took some details – not many because I was not able to give him any address. But the most important thing he did was to put me in touch with a local church. As we parted, he promised to pray for me.

'Those prayers have been abundantly answered! The church

I went to set about changing my life and my lifestyle. For the first time since my release from prison I felt wanted – and loved. I felt my sense of confidence returning. I was – and am – still ashamed of the cowardly thing I did when, as a captain in the Royal Engineers, I ran away from my responsibilities, my men and my regiment. I had always felt that I could never regain my self-respect. But God has done it for me.

'That was all in 1967. Now, almost thirty years later, I can say that the change was permanent. God has grown more real to me with every passing day. I have never gone back to the old ways. I have a respectable job, a wonderful wife and a new family (something I never thought I'd have again). And God has used me to tell others of His love and grace – a love which reached all the way into the depths where I was, and a grace to enable me to realise I was forgiven.

'In the meantime I have made such recompense as I could to those I had wronged. I only wish I knew where the six men who ran away with me are. Maybe some of them will read this story and try to get in touch with me. Above all else, I would like them to know what has happened to me. The years from 1945 to 1967 were unbelievably dark. I would never have believed that I could have sunk so low. Yet, at the same time, I would never have believed that I would become a Christian – not, I hasten to add, a religious person! I have a personal experience of the Lord Jesus Christ as my own Saviour, and my only desire now is to share Him with others . . . with you!'

Postscript: The story about *Decision* magazine having been found in a waste bin on one of London's lamp-posts reached the ears of George Wilson. At the time he was head of the Billy Graham Evangelistic Association's offices in Minneapolis, USA, and was managing editor of *Decision* magazine at the time. He jokingly exclaimed: 'Let's put a copy of the magazine in every lamp-post waste bin in London!'

15
Zagreb

Branko Lovrec, Bosnia, 1966

In the war-torn country of Yugoslavia, in the town of Zagreb in the province of Bosnia-Herzegovina, there was a haven of peace and tranquillity. Not that it escaped the bombs and bullets! Indeed, there was more than one occasion when repairs were needed to enable the work to continue.

In their language it is called *Duhovna Stvarnost* – 'Spiritual Unity' – and it is registered as a Christian resource centre which publishes books, distributes tapes and runs a Christian relief ministry.

It is a little surprising to learn that its director is a qualified – and formerly practising – medical doctor. He was deeply involved in his practice and loved his work. But he had reckoned without Billy Graham!

It was during the time that Branko Lovrec was studying medicine in Zagreb that he first encountered the evangelist's name. One day a letter arrived in Zagreb and, as he read it, young Branko learned from a person of Croatian origin (who was now living in California) about the remarkable ministry which was being exercised in America by the young Billy Graham. In those days the country of Yugoslavia was under the rule of President Tito, who had a strict communist philosophy, and individual faith in God was not encouraged.

In spite of that, there was no censorship of letters and the news of the remarkable happenings in America were filtering through. The news was exacerbated by an American preacher who came to Zagreb in the mid-1950s to preach in the Baptist church. In the course of his sermon he mentioned Billy Graham, and this recalled to Branko's mind the letter he had received earlier.

Always of a curious disposition, Branko Lovrec really wanted to know more, but it was not until 1958 that he was able to acquire a small radio receiver. It enabled him to hear the American missionary radio station, Trans World Radio, broadcasting from Monte Carlo in Monaco. For the first time in his life he tuned in to hear the voice of Billy Graham over the airwaves on the radio programme, 'The Hour of Decision' ('HOD').

'The first time I heard his preaching, I liked it very much,' says Branko. 'He had a new style like nothing I had ever heard before, and he appealed to me. I was a young intellectual who was far from satisfied with the dull preaching in the churches I had attended.

'At the time I had already experienced the reality of con-version through one of the ministers of a Baptist church in Zagreb, but I was still very much a "spiritual babe"!'

As such he was sometimes reluctant to accept all that the Bible says. But as he listened to Mr Graham on the radio, and he heard the authority with which he quoted the Bible, Branko came to realise that therein lay the only source of our knowledge of God. That drove him back to read more and more of it – especially as Mr Graham's messages were so relevant to his thinking; and, as time went by, they revolution-ised his life.

Night by night, as he pursued his studies, he found himself praying for this preacher he had never met, yet whose voice he now heard regularly. He says, 'I was so excited by him, and by his message, that I borrowed a small tape-recorder and recorded some of the HOD programmes. Week after week I took them to my room and listened carefully. I translated Billy word for word into my own language. Then I re-recorded the translated messages and played the tapes in my church.

'Billy Graham's preaching so influenced my life that I yearned to convey the same distinctive message to our own people. I hoped that my translation would enable them to understand it, and to benefit from it. God was very faithful to that ministry, and there are those who look back to those days as the time of their spiritual birth.'

Involved in studying as he was, Branko Lovrec nevertheless felt a compulsion to help the young people around him, and he became a leader of the youth group in his church. During those days the youth group flourished.

On the other side of the Atlantic, Billy Graham had returned from crusades held in England, in Scotland, in several cities in Europe, and in New York City. In those crusades he had met people from all over the world and he learned of the dearth of evangelism which seemed to be current everywhere. It was in this context that he had a magnificent dream. He consulted with his colleagues and together they devised a plan to bring as many people together as possible from all over the world to a great congress on evangelism in June of 1966.

Berlin, on the threshold of Eastern Europe, with the Berlin Wall separating the German people of East Berlin from their compatriots in the West, was the city selected for the event. It was held in the great Berlin Congress Centre – known locally as 'The Pregnant Oyster'.

West Berlin itself was in an odd situation. Totally surrounded by the hostile East Germany, a simple corridor (and, of course, the airport) connected it to the rest of the free world. The city itself was divided into three sectors, with the occupation forces of the UK, the USA and France taking responsibility for one of the sectors each. Through 'Checkpoint Charlie' it was possible to cross from West to East Berlin, and to do so was like stepping into a different world.

Its isolation made Berlin an ideal place to hold the congress. Every person attending could not fail to be aware of the tremendous division between those who lived in freedom and those who lived under communism. This created a sense of urgency in all the sessions. It was clear that the Gospel was the only real answer to mankind's problems.

Delegates came from all over the world. Among them were some from South America. They were the very same Auca Indians who, a few years previously, had murdered Jim Elliott and Nate Saint; the two missionaries had landed their small plane to try to preach the Gospel to these unevangelised people.

Now, a few years later, the Indians had found the Lord Jesus Christ as their Saviour. They came to the congress in bare feet, wearing clothes to which they were unaccustomed. They had walked from their village to the nearest airport and, for the first time in their lives, had flown across oceans and continents. It was a traumatic experience for them. At the other end of the scale were the affluent Americans who had put so many resources into the planning, financing and presenting of the congress.

In between came delegates from all over the world. Among these, to his personal delight, was Branko Lovrec. It had not been easy to get an exit permit from Yugoslavia, but God had paved the way, and he was able to come. 'It was my first "live" hearing of Billy Graham,' he says. 'I had been invited because, by then, I was editor of a Baptist Christian magazine.'

Prior to the congress, Billy Graham had held a crusade in Berlin, and Branko had been able to come a few days earlier so as to be present at the crusade. 'I just could not believe it,' he says, 'especially when I saw the multitudes of people responding to the evangelist's invitation.'

Branko had married Mirjana four years earlier, and now he left his wife behind in Zagreb to look after his medical practice while he was away. That work was only one of several activities which kept him busy, and life was rather hectic for him. In addition to the Baptist magazine which he edited, he also translated other English Christian literature into Croatian so that helpful devotional literature would be available to the people of Yugoslavia.

'Medicine, the editorial work, the translation of books and literature and work in my church all came at the same time as, in 1964, my wife and I had our first child, Iva. It put a great strain upon us, and our lives were very full.

'Because I was the editor of the Baptist magazine, I was listed among the journalists who were attending the congress. So I got a lot of extra opportunities and information which would not have been available to me had I been an ordinary delegate.

'One day a journalist from Los Angeles asked me if I would like to meet Billy Graham! It was such a surprise and I was very excited. I found my pastor, Dr Josip Horak (who was also attending the congress), and told him all about it. I asked him to come with me, so that he too could meet Billy Graham. As we talked together, we determined that we would not let the opportunity pass, but that we would invite Billy Graham to come to Zagreb.

'Our meeting with him took place the next day, and we had a wonderful time as he talked and prayed with us. Before we left him, we extended our invitation to him. We were so thrilled when he accepted, and he eventually came to Zagreb in July 1967 – a year later.'

As Branko contemplated that event, he came to the conclusion that it would demand his whole attention. From Berlin he wrote to his wife and told her that he was going to quit his medical practice and devote himself entirely to Christian service.

Soon afterwards dark times came and he and his family did not have enough to live on – let alone do their life's work. Some of his family did not think it right for him to quit his medical work, and he found that they neglected him. Also, his medical colleagues did not understand the reason for what he had done.

'But it worked!' he says. 'Today I look back on those years and see that it was God who gave me the courage then which I might not have today! It was during that period that our two boys were born, and my decision had to be reflected on their lives too. Billy Graham had a lot to answer for! But God was faithful and never let me down.

'Sometimes when the children went to school they were asked by their teachers, and by others in the school, "Where does your father work?" The answer they had to give was not easy since my full-time work was quite unique. I wasn't a pastor, nor a businessman, nor just a writer. I was simply a Christian worker – and how does a youngster explain that to his peers? Many people we met just could not understand that.

'My special loves were literature, evangelism and youth work. I felt that God would provide my needs and that this was a call directly from Him. So, beginning in 1967, I went into full-time Christian ministry. In this I had been greatly influenced by Billy Graham, without whose encouragement, prayers and support I would never have thought it possible.

'To give up my medical work was a crucial decision, which both my wife and I had to make together. But she supported me in it, and we have known ever since that God led us to make the right decision.'

His first task was to translate Billy Graham's book *Peace with God* into Croatian. Branko was aware that this book formed a major plank in the follow-up ministry after a crusade, and he wanted to have it ready in time to use for the meetings in Zagreb. He 'stuck his neck out' and had the book published in his own name. During the communist regime churches were not allowed to publish literature of this type. He was delighted when the book was ready on time.

'It was not altogether a new experience for me to publish a book in my own name. Earlier I had translated two other small books – both by O. Hallesby – *Why I am a Christian* and a book on prayer. I had, therefore, been in touch with a suitable printer – but *Peace with God* was quite the biggest private publishing I had ever been involved in. I ordered 10,000 copies!

'But any doubt I had had in the past was totally eradicated when I saw the response to our work. All 10,000 copies of that book were sold and distributed within three years – and that was a miracle in itself. Yugoslavia had only a very small evangelical constituency, so the disposal of those books was a real success.

'The crusade in Zagreb was a historic occasion for the city. I had the privilege of interpreting for Billy Graham on two of the four occasions when he spoke. I found that to be a terrifying – though a terribly satisfying – experience, and I was afraid that I would miss some of the crucial points. But, happily, that never happened.'

The long-reaching effect of that crusade on the life of Branko Lovrec was beyond his wildest dreams. The crusade affected his whole way of thinking and his whole life. He had at first thought that he might return to medicine once the crusade was over – but that was not to be.

Soon after Billy Graham had gone, Branko established a publishing house with many new books to be translated, printed and published. It was a challenging time for him. He even worked on a Croatian translation of the Living New Testament. That translation was a joint venture in which he was helped by his wife.

'As I had listened to Mr Graham, I realised what a big responsibility had been placed upon our shoulders. We had a ministry both to the people in our own country and to many foreigners who passed through, coming and going on a variety of occupations.'

Just four years later found Branko Lovrec once more involved with Billy Graham's ministry – this time when Billy Graham was in Dortmund, Germany, for the crusade known as Euro-70. On this occasion there were closed-circuit television transmissions from the arena in Dortmund to many other places throughout Europe – and Zagreb was one of the selected venues.

Branko recalls, 'I was responsible for the meetings in Zagreb, and I saw the great potential in using such methods for evangelism. Mr Graham could not be everywhere but, by these electronic means, the next-best possible opportunity was available to us. Indeed, there were those who said that the television relay was better – because you could see so well. Even though Yugoslavia was in the grip of a communist regime, Mr Graham was respected wherever his name was known.

'In addition to the television relays, we were also able to translate and publish his messages, which we took (with permission!) from *Decision* magazine.' From then on it seemed that Branko Lovrec was never far away from the ministry of Billy Graham. The European congress on evangelism came to Amsterdam in 1971. Three years later there was the 1974 Lausanne congress. Once more he had the opportunity to meet Mr Graham.

When the Lausanne congress concluded, the Lausanne Committee for World Evangelisation was formed. To his surprise and unbounded delight, he was asked to be a member of that committee. It brought to his ministry a wider perspective as, through it, he met so many evangelical leaders from around the world. Indeed, in the late 1980s and thereafter his own name was known worldwide, and there was great respect for his ministry and work.

In 1986 Billy Graham held the 'Congress for Itinerant Evangelists', again in Amsterdam, and that event contributed a great deal to the stability of Branko's own ministry. It renewed his faith and commitment to the work that God had given him to do.

'Euro-93', 'Mission World' and the 'Global Mission' opportunities of 1993/4 and 1995 once more made it possible for the crusade ministry of Mr Graham to be effective in Yugoslavia. It was natural that the American team should contact Branko Lovrec for the satellite transmissions to be received in Yugoslavia. Despite the war which was then raging, members of the Global Mission team visited Zagreb with the assurance of their support, encouragement and prayers. Those visits meant a great deal to Branko in his ministry.

Because Billy Graham always spoke in English in those programmes, it became necessary for simultaneous translations to be made, and Branko was invited to fulfil this role in the transmissions.

For Euro-93 from Essen in Germany, no fewer than eight

cities in Yugoslavia were linked up, even though the war was being waged in Croatia. Through the Global Mission, six cities were linked and Branko Lovrec was flown to Puerto Rico to be the official interpreter for the Croatian language. The interpretation for the Global Mission was undertaken at source rather than locally.

This was such a heavy commitment that Branko's son, Matija, was also taken to Puerto Rico to be the 'second voice' and to give his father respite from time to time. 'It was when Mr Graham was in Zagreb in 1967 that my wife had been expecting Matija – now here he was also involved in Billy Graham's ministry!'

Branko concludes, 'Through all that has happened over the years, the most significant event in my life was undoubtedly the 1966 Berlin congress. The last day of the congress was on Reformation Day in Germany and all the participants of the congress marched through the main streets of the city of Berlin. Billy Graham led the long procession, with many other world leaders of evangelism. I was at the end of the procession and was deeply moved. Every one of the messages at the congress spoke to my heart and to my need.

' "Who will go?" they asked. "Who will stand at the gap for my people?" I was approached by an American missionary who asked me, "Can you find someone in your country who could be a full-time evangelist?" I could not answer him at that moment. All around us was the mist and rain, and I prayed and said to the Lord, "Yes, Lord! How can I look for someone else, when you are calling *me*! I will be the one!"

'That evening I wrote a letter to my wife. I said, "I am coming back, not as a medical doctor any more but as an evangelist and missionary to our people who need Christ!"

'That was my decision, and that night I prayed with Josip Horak, my pastor, and asked God's blessing on my decision.

'Now, looking back thirty years later, I know that God never makes a mistake. I see the work developing in publishing and distributing Christian books. We are also able to supply tracts, magazines, cassette tapes and TV messages. On top of that there is the relief work which has run alongside our book ministry and that has grown beyond recognition. I have to say, "God, you are great in Your wisdom and in Your calling of us. Great is Your name and greatly to be praised!" '

16

Rock 'n' Roll Singer

Sir Cliff Richard OBE, UK, 1966
In faraway India on 14 October 1940 a baby boy was born
to Rodger and Dorothy Webb. He was dark-haired and
weighed nine pounds.[1] His father and mother named him
Rodger Harry Webb and he was christened on 2 November
at St Thomas's Church in Dehra Dun.

In the USA, twenty-two years earlier and twenty-four days'
journey away by the ships and trains of those times, a baby
was born to Frank and Morrow Graham. On 7 November
1918 William Franklin Graham Jr made his appearance in the
world.

Half a world separated these two births, yet in a remarkable
way they were to be brought together, the older being an enormous influence on the younger, and the younger bringing his
time and talents to the service of the older.

For Rodger Harry Webb was to be 'discovered' in May
of 1956, when an entrepreneur named Harry Greatorex
took him and others to the Swiss (a pub in Old Compton
Street)[2] because he was turning out to be a fairly acceptable
singer.

Harry Webb had lived most of his early life in India, where
his father was a catering manager. But British rule ended in
1948 and the Webb family sailed on the *Ranchi* for England.[3]
After years of living amidst brown dust, the young Harry was
struck by the green fields and flowers of England.

A year or two later, after completing his schooling in the
suburbs of London, he first heard a recording of Elvis Presley,
played on the radio of a Citroën car parked at the roadside in

Waltham Cross. Harry was transfixed and determined that one day he would sing that type of music.[4] Now he and his cronies were at 'The Swiss' and they were discussing his name.[5] Harry Greatorex believed that the name Harry Webb lacked 'any ring about it'.[6] As a result, the 'great name change' came about. At first they thought of 'Cliff Richards', but then the 's' was dropped, partly as a tribute to the singer, Little Richard, and partly because dropping the 's' would bring added publicity. Every time someone used the plural name, they would have to correct them. That would help to establish the name in everyone's mind.[7]

That name was to become part of the amazing phenomenon of the late twentieth century. Who would have believed that four young men – the Beatles – would achieve international fame? They could have had no idea that, within a decade or two, their kind of music would have been labelled 'great music'! Nor, when they started, could they have imagined that they would become millionaires and that, as a group, they would be awarded the MBE! Nor for that matter would the young Harry Webb – whose name had just changed to Cliff Richard – sitting with Harry Greatorex in 'The Swiss', ever have thought that by the summer of 1995 he would be 'Sir Cliff Richard'!

At some time in 1963 another player was to enter the drama. His name was David Winter, and at the time he was the editor of *Crusade* magazine – a Christian journal which had grown directly out of Billy Graham's crusade at Wembley eleven years earlier. One Sunday he was speaking in the open air in a park near his home when a young man, walking his dog, stopped to listen to him. 'I had Terry Dene, as he was then called, with me,' says David, 'and a couple of days later I had a phone call from the young man. I was very surprised when I discovered that he was none other than the pop star, Cliff Richard. He asked if I would come round and have a chat. I'd never met him before in my life, but I went round and found to my astonishment that he wanted to ask the most incredible –

theological – questions. Nearly all of them related to the divinity of Jesus.[8]

'Now, you know, when you're talking to most people who are searching for Christianity, their questions and objections – or most of them – are often moral and practical. They ask, "Will I have to change my life?" Or they're afraid that they might be thought a nutter. "I don't want to be a religious maniac," they say, or "I can't stand church. Christians are a lot of weirdos." But there was none of that. It was absolutely biblical stuff. He said, "I don't see how you can believe that Jesus is the Son of God, you know. The Bible doesn't teach it." I had to show him that it did.'

Looking back to that time, Cliff himself says, 'I suppose I was upsetting a lot of people, but I'd been doing a lot of reading and had been asking a lot of questions over a period of about three years. Then, having asked all those questions, I came to a point in my life when I thought, "Yes! Yes! I believe in God. That's for definite now. Yes, I do believe that Jesus came and that He died a horrific death so that I needn't be intimidated by death any more. He proved that death, in the end, was not 'king', and that brings us to the third point – He was resurrected." That finally clinched for me, the fact that death was unimportant in terms of eternity and that the resurrection meant that any one of us who died would experience a whole new dimension of living.'

Cliff Richard recalls the day he became a Christian. 'I can only remember that I lay on my bed one night, and I remember saying to God, "God, You know I've spent three years looking for You. I've spent three years arguing and discussing; reading the Bible; reading books about You, and now I believe that You do exist and I believe that Your Son, Jesus, came to this earth to do something very special – not just for everybody, but for *me*." I just remember lying on my bed and saying, "OK, I give in. Jesus, I know You're there. OK, I will say it, 'I want you in my life. Please will you take over my life?' " And I woke up the next day and I didn't even feel religious! But afterwards

– and it took a few months – afterwards I began to recognise that there was a difference in my life.'[9]

'He made his own decision,' says David Winter. 'He does that about everything. And it was his decision, a year or two later in 1966, to accept an invitation from the Billy Graham people, to give his testimony at Earls Court.'

Actually, David Winter had played a part in that invitation, because he had said (on a small postcard he sent to the crusade organisers), 'I think that, if an invitation were to go to Cliff Richard, it might be appropriate, and he would accept.'

The invitation was issued, and accepted, and 16 June 1966 saw the coming together of the two strands of personalities, one born in a remote town in India, the other born on a farm near Charlotte in North Carolina, USA. That meeting was to have an inestimable influence on the life of the young Cliff Richard. It was also the beginning of a ministry together which has taken both Billy and Cliff to many corners of the earth.

Billy Graham says of that occasion: 'I first met him at Earls Court when he came to the meeting one night to sing. I remember greeting him at the door and the great crowd of people that surrounded him. I was absolutely amazed at all these young people. They were screaming and yelling and trying to touch him, and so forth. They don't do that to me!

'I'm sure that quite a bit of cynicism has grown up in Britain about religion in general and evangelism in particular. Because of that, I think Cliff's identification with an American evangelist at that moment in his career might have put some elements of his future in jeopardy. But, in other ways, it might have strengthened it too, because it brought him right out. He had to declare himself from then on. The thing that's thrilled me is that he's stuck with it; not only stuck with it, but grown tremendously.'

In the middle of the meeting on 16 June 1966, Cliff Barrows went to the microphone and said: 'Cliff Richard, we're delighted to have you here. Let's welcome him this evening as he comes.'[10] To tremendous applause, Cliff Richard went to the microphone. He says: 'Even thinking about it now brings me out in a cold sweat! I gripped Billy's lectern and tried to steady myself. I was worried that my legs might not hold me up! Then I tried to move my arms and found I couldn't. I had pins and needles.' When it was all over, he was so nervous that his arms remained in their outstretched position.[11]

He needn't have worried. His testimony was clear and to the point: 'The opportunity doesn't come very often to be able to actually confess Jesus Christ with one's lips to so many people at one time. I have never had such an opportunity before but it is a great privilege to be able to tell you that I am a Christian. I can only say to people who are not Christians that until you have taken the step of asking Christ into your life, your life is not worthwhile. It works. It works for me.[12] I know I have been quoted in the press as saying that I am a Christian. I would be the first person to say, "Don't believe everything that you read in the papers", but this – believe!'[13] Then, with Tedd Smith, Billy Graham's regular pianist, accompanying him, he sang Stuart Hamblen's song, 'It is no secret, what God can do'.[14]

But his ordeal was not over when he had finished on the platform. News was received that several thousands, who had been unable to get in, were outside the arena. So Cliff and Billy Graham climbed out of a window overlooking the panoply in front of Earls Court, and there Cliff sang and spoke to them as well. But this time it was more 'his thing'; he was much more at home with the audience outside.

Cliff recalls the trauma he went through in making the decision to come to Earls Court. 'I had to make a big decision, and that decision was: if I lose fans, then it wasn't going to matter to me. The most important thing at that time was for me to tell the world that "Yes, I was a Christian," and that it had made big differences in my life.'[15]

The weekly Christian newspaper, *The Life of Faith*, reported the event in its issue of 16 June 1966: 'At the Earls Court meeting this evening, Thursday, Cliff Richard, the popular film

actor and pop recording artist, will sing "It is no secret". Cliff
Richard is a keen Christian.'

Several national newspapers had quite a bit to say about
the event:

> Screaming teenagers had to be dragged away from pop
> singer Cliff Richard last night, [but inside the arena] there
> was not a murmur from the mainly teenage audience as
> Cliff, wearing a dark brown corduroy jacket, grey
> flannels and thick horn-rimmed spectacles, stepped to the
> rostrum. Billy Graham said: 'It is wonderful that they
> waited here to hear him talk about Christ. It had a
> tremendous impact on the young people.' Cliff Richard
> said: 'I think to be a Christian today is very relevant and
> necessary to life. Once, when someone else had a hit
> record and I didn't, I said, "Drat it." Now I have learned
> that we can't always have what we want.'
> *Daily Sketch*, 17 June 1966

> Cliff Richard told the many young pop fans: 'I can only
> say to people who are not Christians that, until you have
> taken the step of asking Christ into your life, your life
> is not worth while. It works – it works for me.' Billy
> Graham gave the 25-year-old singer credit for his courage
> in appearing. Later Cliff Richard spoke of rumours that
> he planned to give up show business to teach religion.
> 'I don't want to be in show business all my life,' he said.
> 'But I have commitments for some years yet. When I do
> give up I won't wear a dog collar, but the idea of becom-
> ing a religious instructor appeals to me.'
> *Daily Express*, 17 June 1966

> Cliff, minus the twanging of beat guitars, sang a simple
> gospel song 'It is no secret' for the Billy Graham crusade
> at Earls Court, London. Afterwards he spoke and said:
> 'Anyone who thinks a Christian is soft can think again.

It took me a long, long time to pluck up enough courage to tell the world "I am a Christian." But when I did I knew I had scored. Now I can make something out of my life.'
Daily Mirror, 16 June 1966

Cliff has joined the Billy Graham set. He has said he plans to become a divinity teacher. When he retires, that is. Cliff did go behind a microphone at Earls Court – but not to sing. His message to the other young people there was that Christianity was relevant to their way of life.
Daily Mail, 17 June 1966

. . . the cynics began to call it a publicity gimmick. 'They were bound to,' says Rhona Churchill in the *Daily Mail*, 'but were they right?' [She goes on to tell how she met Cliff at Pinewood Studios, where he was working on his new film with Robert Morley and Peggy Mount.] 'He was a soft-voiced, polite, gentle and modest lad.' He told her that he was thrilled by the size of the audience but 'scared to death'. He added: 'You could see I couldn't rehearse that testimony. If I had it might have sounded like an act. So I went forward knowing what I wanted to say but not how I would say it. I steadied myself by gripping the lectern. Then, when I tried to move my arms I found I couldn't. I had pins and needles!'
Time and Tide, 6 July 1966

Cliff was back again at Earls Court a year later, when Billy Graham returned for a brief follow-up crusade to the 1966 meetings. In the meantime World Wide Pictures, which had made several films for Billy Graham, had decided to make a film centred on the crusade in London. Cliff Richard was invited to take the leading role of Jamie Hopkins. In the film he became the drug-runner and thug whose girlfriend was converted at Earls Court. It was not a film which neatly tied up all the loose ends, with Jamie Hopkins becoming a Christian. The audience was left to provide their own ending to the story. But Jamie, in the film, did attend a meeting at the arena, and succeeded in wangling his way past the platform security, on to the platform itself. There, Jamie Hopkins (alias Cliff Richard) found himself sitting near Billy Graham.

The film, called *Two a Penny*, turned out to be something of a problem for Cliff. 'Here I was,' he says, 'playing this rather snide character in the film. I was supposed to appear cynical and critical of the whole set-up. I must have played the part well, because afterwards I received at least one furious letter from someone who said, "You call yourself a Christian, and yet you behaved in that appalling way during Billy's address!"[16] Actually, Jim Collier, the director of the film, had given me a bunch of cards which I put into my top pocket. Each card had an instruction from him. Whenever I removed a card and read the instructions (for example, "Think that the audience must be a bunch of sheep to take all this in") the cameraman, who was hidden in the foliage on the platform, would know that I was about to switch on the acting!'

The film received its première at the Prince Charles Theatre in London, and it gave Cliff a chance to give his testimony in front of many of his contemporaries. 'You know,' he said, 'those last moments as Jamie Hopkins were very close to my own experience. A few years ago I asked the same sort of questions myself, and the answers I got . . . well, ultimately they changed my life. Maybe you're full of questions, too: about God, about who Jesus Christ really is, and what all that means, if anything, to you. Like Jamie, I hope you are honestly looking for answers, and that you will take your first step towards your own spiritual adventure.'[17]

'Stars of screen, stage and song mingled with eminent Church leaders,' said the *Daily Cinema* in a full centre-page spread of the event. 'Hundreds of Cliff Richard fans watched the VIP arrivals, who included Dora Bryan, Cilla Black, Norrie Parramor, Sandie Shaw, David Jacobs and Pier Angeli – as well as Ann Holloway [cousin of Stanley Holloway] who played the ingénue lead.'

It was a glittering and sparkling occasion, followed by a reception in a church hall next door. *That* was nearly a disaster! It was arranged by the publicity agents for the film 'in the name of the Billy Graham film people'. So far as drinks were concerned, they had laid on all the usual accessories that they would provide for an ordinary film première in London. They also included a young lady entertainer of doubtful presentation!

Fortunately the Billy Graham people recognised the problem before the guests arrived and, by the time the film ended, everything was sorted out. The bottles of hard liquor had disappeared, and now everything was in keeping with a Billy Graham event!

Billy Graham's influence on Cliff Richard was to have dramatic repercussions. Soon after the crusade ended, Cliff took a decision to quit his career and to take up teaching. There were some around him who encouraged him in this move, but there were others who regarded this decision as a disaster. For most of his fans it was staggering news.

David Winter, who still remained close to Cliff, says of that time: 'He wanted to be a teacher. I was always against it, really, I must say. But he did his O-level and passed it, much to his satisfaction. Then he spent two months at Oak Hill Theological College to study the Bible. They also helped him to articulate his faith. He even had the promise of a place at the Trent Park Teachers' Training College.'

One thing that influenced Cliff was the constant question about the compatibility of his Christian faith with the show-business world. It troubled him that he might give the wrong impression to, and lead astray, his teenage fans.[18] He also felt a compunction to 'do something' with his life, and he knew that many Christians regarded the entertainment industry as ungodly.[19] This was in the days when Christians did not go to the theatre or to 'picture palaces' (as the cinema was dubbed); they did not dance, did not smoke or drink, did not swear, wear make-up or do a whole list of other no-no's that they had compiled! All this meant that a life in show-business was virtually unthinkable.

Many before him in the show-business world had given their lives to Christ. Almost all of them had provided Christians with a happy ending to their story, by quitting their profession.[20]

David Winter says: 'Then along came *Two a Penny*. During that time we spent a lot of time talking about it – and with the amazing director, Jim Collier. He also took the line that Cliff would be quite wrong to pull out of something in which he could use the gifts and talents that God had given to him.'

Cliff was encountering a lot of different viewpoints that were influencing him. Billy Graham himself pointed out the value of a witness in an otherwise dark environment. Jim Collier (as a part of the Billy Graham set-up) was urging him to stay where he was and use his position for God in the area where God had placed him. David Winter was pointing out to him the advantages and value of giving a living testimony among those in the show-business world. In the magazine he edited, David had chided those who withdrew from the arts and then expressed their dismay when other viewpoints became predominant. He persuaded Cliff that he had two immeasurably valuable assets: his performing talent and his audience. Put together, those two factors could be a powerful force for good.

In the end it was Jim Collier who tipped the balance:[21] 'Look what you can do,' he said. 'You can't throw all this away.'[22]

As he listened to Jim, Cliff finally made his decision. 'You can only do what you feel is right, and what people say doesn't add up to me. I don't know what God has in mind for me in the future, but at present I am sure I am doing His will where I am. I can only say, "Here is me, this is what I am," but really in the end what matters is how people respond to Jesus.'[23]

Looking back on that decision from the perspective of later years, it is abundantly clear how right he was. It would be hard to know the number of personalities in the show-business world who have become Christians as a result of Cliff's testimony.

He has never failed to be faithful to the message that God has given him.

At the Wembley Stadium in the summer of 1989 he drew more than 72,000 on each of two nights. In the middle of his performance he exclaimed: 'The best I can do is not going to change your lifestyle in any way. It's not going to mean anything in any great eternal terms. And I always feel that, if I have one thing to offer that's of any value at all, it's the message that God exists *and that Jesus is alive and He can be yours if you want Him!*'[24]

He moved into a song which concluded:

> ... And all that I am
> And everything I'll ever be
> Is because of You
> Because You're in my heart!

The partnership between Billy Graham and Cliff Richard has continued over the years. Cliff receives regular invitations from Billy to sing at crusades all over the world, and he has been to Germany, Holland, Tokyo in Japan, and many other places. In Britain, in 'Mission England' of 1984/5, the 'Mission to London' of 1989 and the 'Mission to Scotland' in 1991 Cliff had a major role. An outstanding occasion was the opening night of the Crystal Palace meetings in 1989, when a total strike of tube- and bus-drivers deprived the capital of all its public transport. In spite of that, an over-capacity crowd of some 30,000 were there to hear Cliff sing and give his testimony, as well as to listen and respond to Billy Graham's preaching.

Earlier, in 1973, he had been deeply involved with Billy Graham in Spre-e 73. Conceived as a youth training event, it had been inspired by Explo 72 in Dallas, Texas, a year earlier and was itself to be the source of inspiration for 'Christaval 74' in Essen, Germany, as well as the great 'Eurofest 75' in Brussels. At Spre-e 73, Cliff had both taken part during the week and held a full-scale concert on the Friday night. On

Saturday he sang with Johnny Cash at the closing meeting in Wembley Stadium.

He was a participant in the great congresses in Amsterdam and elsewhere. He has shared his faith on radio and television. He has had his own television show, and he has communicated his faith by every means available to him. He has always been faithful and has used every opportunity to include a comment that 'none of this would have been possible without my faith as a Christian'. Billy Graham has said that Cliff Richard is an evangelist in his own right – a different style from Billy's own, but an evangelist nevertheless.

His influence as an evangelist has not been restricted to large gatherings alone. On one occasion he accepted an invitation to visit the home of a young man who was celebrating his twenty-first birthday. There were some 125 youngsters packed into the three ground-floor communicating rooms of the house. Cliff sang for about forty minutes and then talked for another twenty minutes. He then answered questions that the young people fed to him. In response to two of these he gave wise and significant answers.[25] The very sophisticated son of the local estate agent asked: 'If I wanted to become a Christian, how would I go about it?'[26] Cliff replied that he could think of nothing better than to recommend reading the first chapter of the Epistle to the Romans and the Gospel of John. Three weeks later this young man followed Cliff's advice, gave his life to Christ and became an effective Christian in his school and, later, in his work.

Another young man asked: 'If I became a Christian, would I have to go to church?'

Cliff replied: 'No! You wouldn't have to go to church. Becoming a Christian is not about going to church. It's about finding Christ for yourself, and giving your life to Him.' He continued: 'But I will say this: after you've become a Christian, you might find you want to be around others who are Christians also, and it *might* just be that you would most easily find them in church!'

Cliff has also been the instigator of a series of Gospel Concerts. Assisted by his good friend and colleague, Bill Latham (Cliff had gone to live in the home of Bill and his mother, Mamie, many years before, and they had become 'family' to him[27]), a series of these concerts has been held year by year, with the proceeds going to The Evangelical Alliance Relief (TEAR) Fund. This all came about when Cliff learned a big lesson from the Bible: 'I discovered that the Bible actually says, "To whom much is given, much will be expected in return." So God says, "OK, Cliff Richard, if you have more money than somebody else, I will expect *you* to give more money away. If you've got more time and more talent, I will expect you to give more time and more talent to Me." '[28]

That time and talent seem inexhaustible as he travels around the world communicating his faith by word and song. Billy Graham was once asked by John Capon if he felt Cliff could learn from Billy's own experience of communication. Billy Graham replied: 'Not much! I think Cliff communicates as very few people can communicate. I've seen him communicate at a little private dinner-party. One night we had some very interesting people together, here in London, and we got on the subject of the deity of Jesus Christ. Cliff made one of the clearest presentations from the biblical point of view about the deity of Christ that I've ever heard. The people there had expected *me* to say it!'

Cliff recognises that, by the world's standards, he possesses a lot. But he regards all of it as 'on loan'. He says, 'If we really say that we love God, then somehow or other we have to show that we love other people. Because otherwise how can we prove that we love Him? You can't *see* Him; other people you can see, feel and touch.'

As a result, he has devoted some of his travelling time to visiting needy areas. Once the late and beloved George Hoffman took Cliff with him to Bangladesh. George said: 'After spending days out at, say, a hospital station, I can remember him being at a reception centre for kids. He came back at the end of the day and he spoke to one of the nurses and he said: "You know, what I've seen today makes me feel as though I want to give it all up and come out here and work." The nurse turned to him, and very quietly she said to him, "Can you give an injection and put a person on a drip?" He said, "No – I'd be horrified!" And she replied, "Well, you go back home and raise money for us to do it!" '[29]

Sometimes Cliff has felt an element of guilt in all that has come to him. An interviewer once asked him about that on a TV programme. 'The only reason we're doing this programme, and why I'm on it,' replied Cliff, 'is because I happen to be Cliff Richard, the rock and roll singer who has fame and fortune. It would probably be more valid to find somebody who's out of work and who's a satisfied Christian human being. They would probably have more to say, and probably say it more powerfully – on television – but then, who would watch it? That's the thing, you see. It's no good criticising me for things like that, because if the ideal was to take place, no one would watch!'

Cliff says: 'I have always wanted to do things well. My original hopes and ambitions when I first started were just to survive the next week – the next record! Now I've always tried to make every concert the *best* concert and every record the *best* record. Every time I make one I think, "This is going to be the best!" Then the world goes by and you realise there's still more to do.' Cliff has become a perfectionist in all his presentations.

Just recently, on a 'This is Your Life' programme featuring Helen Shapiro – a contemporary of Cliff's – he appeared with her and recounted how both of them have the same strong faith. He finished movingly: 'We are both in the same business . . . and we both have the same Father.'[30]

In 1996 Cliff Richard hosted a specially produced TV programme featuring Billy Graham. Carried by television stations in countries across the world on 14 April, it was beamed into the British Isles by Sky TV. It was a fast-moving programme in a contemporary style. Using Cliff as host demonstrated, in a dramatic way, the fact that he was as well known as Billy Graham himself. Remarkably, he did not sing. He left that to the group D.C. Talk and to pop and rock star Michael W. Smith. It was an outstanding programme through which many found Christ as their Saviour.

Finally, a personal reminiscence: the location was the Wembley Arena where Cliff Richard was singing as part of his 'Hit List' tour. We were amused, in our dotage, to see great-grandma, grandma, mother, daughter and grand-daughter, all bopping along to the music. Often they were all dressed alike, in Cliff Richard sweatshirts or emblazoned T-shirts. One and all had come to enjoy this remarkable 'young' man who had spanned the generations. Although at that time fifty-four, he was still thought of as 'young' by all and sundry! Somehow he had broken the barrier of communication and was able to straddle the age-range without difficulty. Cliff had just finished taking his last bow. His song had been a testimony:

> Open your eyes on Saviour's day
> Don't look back or turn away
> Life can be yours if you only say
> He is coming, He is coming
> On Saviour's day.

'You don't look the type who normally come to concerts like this,' said a voice behind us. 'Do you often come to pop concerts?'

We had to confess that this was a 'one-off' for us. We explained that we came to this concert because we knew Cliff Richard. 'What, *really* know him?' came the astonished response. We explained that we worked for the American evangelist, Billy Graham, and that Cliff had often taken part in Billy's meetings. Then light dawned and they asked if they could shake our hands! It was almost as if they'd met Cliff – by proxy!

In response to the question: 'What would you regard as the biggest influence that Billy Graham has had upon your life?' Cliff replies:

I would definitely have to say that it has been his integrity that has influenced me most. He has shown me that, as a Christian, it is important to maintain that integrity in all that we do – and it's an example that I've tried to follow. His own integrity is cast-iron: he's always stuck by his guns.

The other thing that has influenced me is the way in which he fully devotes his attention to whoever he's with. You know when you are with him that you're the only one who matters to him at that moment. And that's one of the secrets of his success in all his meetings. He devotes himself so completely to his audience that they respond to him. You know, when those eyes of his lock on to yours, you're bound to give him your full attention. He demands that you should give back to him what he has given to you.

So while the world is collapsing around us, Billy manages to keep his head while everyone around is losing theirs! He has a sort of stability that I covet in what I do.

Once, when I visited Dr Billy for some prayer after a meeting, I found him grasping an old gnarled bit of wood. I couldn't think what it was for, so I asked him. He told me that he was concerned that, when he shook hands with people, he might give them a firm handshake. So he was using this piece of wood to strengthen his grip. 'If people don't like you when they first meet you,' he said, 'you'll never establish communication with them.' So his concern is that people should always have the best impression at the outset. He's taught me how important it is to establish that rapport with your audience when you first meet them, because then they'll have a good impression of you, your message, and of your Lord. I've always tried to emulate that. Thank you, Billy!

17

Seven Thumbnail Sketches

'First-person' Stories from *Decision* Magazine

Ron E. Perez

My heart stopped. The police! Shouting to my buddies, I ran, terrified, through the darkness. Footsteps pounded behind me. I crashed into a chain-link fence, invisible in the night. I was trapped! When I whirled around, it was my friend. 'It's all clear,' he panted. 'They're gone.'

We rejoined our comrades to finish the burglary. Sweat stung my eyes as I maintained my lookout post. 'What am I doing here?' I asked myself.

I had grown up the youngest of eleven children. Michigan's auto industry was struggling, and so were we. I fended for myself by swiping penny candy from liquor stores and stealing school supplies from classmates.

As a teenager, I succumbed to peer pressure and became involved in more serious crimes. My friends and I burgled automobiles, stores and homes. But the thrill and power that I experienced were mixed with dread and fear. I knew that I was headed in the wrong direction.

One night, after the police had questioned me about a car burglary, I knew that I had reached a dead end. I wanted to turn my life around. So I quit stealing; I stopped smoking and drinking. By outward appearances I was a new person.

Inside, however, I felt confused and empty. I searched for a purpose and a meaning to life. Could education be the answer? I decided to find out and enrolled at a local junior college. There I met a professor who took a special interest in me. He gained

163

my trust and admiration. I listened intently when he talked about his personal relationship with Jesus Christ.

After class one day he invited me to a Billy Graham crusade in Pontiac, Michigan. I had heard this preacher on television: such peace and confidence he had! He must know the answers to the questions in my life. I borrowed my sister's car and drove the 70 miles to Pontiac.

When I arrived, the Silverdome Stadium was packed. Billy Graham spoke that evening to thousands of people, but God was speaking directly to me. Before the invitation to receive Christ was given, I was already down the aisle.

I publicly confessed my sins and asked Jesus to come into my heart as my Lord and Saviour. I discovered that Jesus Christ was whom I had been searching for.

Since then God has given my life new direction. After completing my college degree, I joined the Peace Corps on assignment to Belize, Central America. While there I introduced other Peace Corps volunteers to Jesus. Several of them made decisions for Christ.

During my time in Belize, I met Beth Bentrup, a missionary school teacher who was to become my wife. After we married, we worked in southern Mexico with Food for the Hungry, Inc., co-ordinating a sponsorship programme for children in poverty-stricken villages.

After our term was completed, we moved to Florida, where the Lord blessed us with the birth of our son, Jason. In our local church Beth and I are active as teachers and workers, and we are involved in short-term missionary work with Air Mobile Ministries to the Bahamas.

I'm employed as an engineer draftsman and, whether I'm behind a drafting desk or at an open-air meeting in Latin America, I want to tell others what the Lord has done for me. Isaiah 38:17 reads, 'In your love you kept me from the pit of destruction; you have put all my sins behind your back' (NIV). I praise God for delivering me from my sins when he gave me new life through His Son, Jesus Christ.

Seven Thumbnail Sketches

Dr Raymond Damadian

There is a mistaken impression that science and God are not compatible. As a scientist and a Christian, I believe that to be wrong. Science ought to unite men and women with their Creator rather than separate them from Him.

I have always had an interest in maths and science. Even though I studied violin at the Juilliard School of Music for eight years, until I was sixteen, when I entered the University of Wisconsin on a Ford Foundation Scholarship, I chose mathematics as my major. And four years later, when I graduated from college, I continued my scientific pursuits when I entered Albert Einstein College of Medicine in New York City.

It was during my first year of medical school that I discovered it is possible to have a personal relationship with God through Jesus Christ when a friend, Donna Terry, invited me to the Billy Graham crusade at Madison Square Garden.

That was in 1957, thirty-five years ago, and I can't remember what Dr Graham said. But I remember that we were sitting in the highest balcony – we could hardly see Dr Graham from there – and by the time the invitation was given to go forward, I was convinced of the Lordship of Jesus Christ and I went forward to give my life to him.

My faith has been a foundation for my life ever since. I married Donna in 1960 after I graduated from medical school. We have two sons and a daughter, all grown now, and I'm pleased that they too are believers.

When I began my professional career as a professor of biophysics at State University of New York Downstate Medical Center, the recognition that God is the source of creativity and scientific insight was responsible, I believe, for the contributions I made to present-day understanding of cell theory, and ultimately to my invention of what today is known as the MR scanner, or MRI.

This machine scans a person's entire body non-invasively, using radio signals and magnets rather than X-rays. With the aid of computers, a picture is created that gives exquisite detail of the interior of the body. The machine is used to detect all diseases, but its greatest use is in searching for cancer.

From the outset I was told that making a machine like this couldn't be done. Funding agencies considered the project nonsense, and they thought that I was a fool for proposing and promoting the idea. During the early years of my struggle, my critics almost seemed to be right. But I didn't give up trying. In looking back now, I am certain that I can attribute my willingness to go ahead with the MR scanner to my ability to trust the Lord. The Holy Spirit was working in me, enabling me to withstand all that I had to withstand in order to get the job done.

My associates and I achieved the first successful human MR scan in July 1977. Eleven years later I was honoured by President Ronald Reagan for that achievement when he awarded me the National Medal of Technology. In 1989 I listened in disbelief as my achievements were recounted at my induction into the National Inventors Hall of Fame. Humbled by the fact that I was deemed worthy of inclusion in the Hall alongside the legendary heroes of my boyhood – Thomas Edison, Alexander Graham Bell, Samuel Morse and others – I knew that it was God who gave me the insights to invent the MR scanner.

My position as the Chief Executive Officer of FONAR Corporation, the company I founded in 1978 to produce MRI machines, gives me opportunities to present the Gospel message in scientific circles. It's a delicate task, because sometimes my audience is hostile to the subject of God! Yet many people are receptive. Every morning at FONAR we have a voluntary prayer meeting for the employees. We have forty to fifty who attend; most are unbelievers looking for answers. A number of them are close to accepting Jesus Christ as Saviour.

Every person is trying to find a purpose for existence. Personally I find joy in sharing with people my greatest discovery of all – that the highest purpose a person can find for his or her life is to serve the will of God.

Isaac Bonful

To celebrate Christmas with my friends, I bought four bottles of schnapps, six bottles of whisky, four bottles of dry gin and a case of forty-eight bottles of beer. I also bought a goat for feasting.

That Christmas Eve of 1959, my friends came to my house and we started a drinking spree that lasted all that night until daybreak. In the morning I prepared myself for church.

I was a member of a church in Accra, Ghana, and attended church services and Bible classes regularly. But I drank heavily and chased after women.

At the church service that Christmas Day, it was announced that a Billy Graham crusade would be held at the Accra Sports Stadium in January 1960. When I returned home, my friends and I continued drinking and feasting to celebrate the birthday of someone we had never met and did not know personally.

I announced that Billy Graham, the renowned world preacher, was coming to Accra to preach and that they were all invited to attend. My friends laughed at me and cracked all sorts of jokes, which nearly discouraged me from going to the crusade. But thank God I went.

When the day of the crusade came, I went to the stadium at 2 p.m. and found the place already filled. I took a seat on the ground at the front.

When Billy Graham started preaching, I could feel the presence of God. Just before making the invitation for people to come and accept Jesus Christ, he said, 'You are following somebody's wife. Stop it and come to accept Jesus Christ as Saviour and Lord. You will never regret it.'

It was as though Billy Graham knew me personally and was telling me what I had been doing. I had been flirting with a married woman, and I had been thinking of going to her after the crusade meeting. I bowed my head in shame and tears flowed from my eyes.

When Mr Graham made the invitation for us to pray, I was already in prayer, sitting condemned before God. Then when the invitation was made to accept Jesus Christ, I believe I was the first person to go forward to the platform.

I found a great change in my life when Jesus Christ came in. I stopped drinking and following women. It was a dramatic change! Through attending Bible studies and prayer meetings, and by God's grace, I started to grow spiritually.

In 1967 I received a letter from the International Bible Reading Association (IBRA) in England, asking me to become their travelling representative to churches in Ghana. I was to promote daily Bible reading with their notes 'Light for Our Path'. After praying for three months, I accepted the position.

IBRA sent me to Trinity College, where ministers in our established churches are trained. After a year I started travelling extensively to churches of many different denominations all over Ghana.

In 1974, after two years of theological training, I started to pastor a Methodist church. In the fourteen years of my ministry I have been blessed wherever I have been a pastor. I have felt a call to itinerant evangelism and have been invited by churches and groups to preach and conduct revival meetings.

I thank the Lord for making me what I am today.

Rev. Gipp Forster

I drifted on the streets of some of Canada's major cities for many years before I met Christ. I lived with drugs and booze . . . travelled with pimps, rounders, hookers and others.

One day in 1965, when I was twenty-eight, I lay on the beach at English Bay in Vancouver, British Columbia, having already been to places such as Australia, New Zealand and the highlands of New Guinea. I was running and never had any intention of stopping. Vancouver was just a stopover.

Billy Graham was in the city at the time, although I was not aware of it until a 'tinker bell' came to the beach, handing out fliers about the forthcoming Billy Graham meetings. A 'tinker bell' is a clean-cut type with white teeth and honest money to spend and who is all wrapped up in advanced education.

In those days I was into the occult, so I thought I would have some fun with this fellow. I challenged him to read a book on the occult and, if he did, I promised to go to a Billy Graham meeting. He accepted, took the book and left. Later in the week he was back. I fired questions at him about the book and he answered them all. My honour was at stake, so that night, with a .45 pistol stuck in the back of my belt, I went to the Crusade. I thought I would be facing maybe 500 'tinker bells'; instead, there were more than 25,000.

I fought Mr Graham's message. However, the Spirit had other ideas. Before the night was over, I surrendered my life to Christ.

Love for the Lord was immediate; loving Christians took ten years longer. I moved to Victoria, the capital of British Columbia, to get away from the heat of the streets. I met and married Dawna, a cocktail waitress, and both of us tried to live a straight life. She wasn't a Christian then, and I was not living like one. But in 1972 I attended Emmanuel Baptist Church. Norman Archer was the pastor. I challenged Archer to take the church to the people, instead of the people to the church. I urged him to enter the inner city to learn the culture and the language of the streets. Through Norman's encouragement the 'Mustard Seed' ministry began – with a prayer stool in a tiny closet in the poster store I owned at the time. Our purpose was to help the street people of Victoria in any way possible and to share the Gospel with them. People from all walks of life began to use the prayer closet.

Today the 'Mustard Seed' operates out of a storefront on Pandora Avenue in Victoria. In 1980 it was recognised as the first street church of the Baptist Union of Western Canada; I was ordained to the ministry in 1983.

The 'Mustard Seed' feeds more than 10,000 people each month through its food bank. Its outreach draws street people from all over, and our workers are both inside and out on the streets. A weekly Narcotics Anonymous meeting is led by a former drug-user. We have radio spots on a secular station each day. There are support groups and we take street kids into our own homes. The little storefront is usually packed Sunday afternoons and Wednesday evenings. And there is more. The 'Mustard Seed' has reproduced itself in Calgary, where the First Baptist Church is the sponsoring body.

Our children – we have two natural and one adopted – have grown up with the street ministry. They have gone farther in school than Dawna and I did – neither of us graduated from high school. Our adopted daughter, now twenty-five, came to us with a grade five education when she was seventeen. She is now taking fourth-year honours psychology at the University of Victoria.

As I look back – and forward – on what God has given Dawna and me to do, I can't help but think about the people just beyond our doorstep. We tell them about a compassionate Christ they can identify with – a Christ who had bare feet and dusty clothes. He slept on the ground and knew what it was to be hungry and spat on, to be treated like garbage.

We want these people to know that Christ loves them. We don't talk about where they have been, only where and what they can be in Christ Jesus.

Norma Symonds

The counsellor was pretty and neatly dressed, an eighteen-carat church member if ever I saw one. With my own unkempt, haunted appearance, I must have looked an unpromising assignment that night in 1966 at the Billy Graham crusade at Earls Court in London.

'Do you want to accept Jesus Christ as your Saviour?' she asked. I nodded. I was eighteen years old, a prostitute and a drug addict. I bit back tears. When I was seven years old, my mother told me that I was illegitimate and had been adopted. From then on I felt as if I belonged nowhere, to no one.

I ran wild with a gang of boys, vandalising, skipping school, beating other kids and running away from home. At age eleven, with a pretty face and above-average height, I became a prostitute. I did this not only to earn money but for kicks, and now I know that I was also looking for love. Then, while involved in a satanic cult, I got hooked on drugs.

At age fourteen I became pregnant. Even though my parents placed me in a home for unwed mothers, the cult leader smuggled drugs to me. Soon after my fifteenth birthday the baby was born. He was deaf and had curvature of the spine. Yet he was mine to love. I named him Bruce and made plans to raise him, but my parents signed the necessary forms and one morning Bruce was taken from my arms.

After that I moved to London to look for a 'straight' job. Since I'd never worked at anything for more than a week, I finally returned to prostitution. The money I earned kept me in drugs.

This way of life went on for three miserable years. When I walked into Earls Court in 1966 to hear Billy Graham, I was desperate. But I left with the hope that God would provide a way out: 'If we confess our sins, he is faithful and just to forgive us our sins, and to cleanse us from all unrighteousness' (1 John 1:9 KJV). What a sweet taste those words had.

Soon I was linked with a church and staying with a family, but I spoiled it. When the police came looking for me on a soliciting charge, I ran.

Then, one night, at the Embankment Underground Station, a preacher climbed on to an upturned crate and spoke while someone else passed out leaflets. A few days later I wrote to the address on the leaflet, outlining my circumstances and asking for help.

A colleague of the preacher met me, and I told him I was sick of my way of life. He said, 'Only one person can help you. Do you know who he is?'

I nodded and tears started to fall. Then I prayed, asking Christ to take total control of my life. He did. For a long time I seemed to take a step back for every two forward, but I sensed a slow unfolding of God's purpose for me.

Soon I met Paul, from Australia. As our relationship deepened, I felt I should tell him about my past. He listened, and then asked for time to think it over. Two days later he came back, took me in his arms and said, 'Jesus has dealt with your past and I am sure he means for us to be together.' We were married in 1970, with my parents present to hear how God had worked in our lives.

I now have four children. I am an accredited volunteer worker with the probation service and work among young offenders, telling them that new life in Christ is possible.

God has wiped away the hurts and guilt of the past. I have been able to contact my natural mother, as well as the son I was forced to give away.

God's healing can reach to the troubled depths of the human soul and make everything new. He has fulfilled his promise that 'all things work together for good to them that love God, to them who are the called according to his purpose' (Romans 8:28 KJV).

Tom Bradley

It was a routine call: a man with a gun. As officers with the Charlotte, North Carolina, Police Department, my partner and I answered the call. When we arrived and got out of our squad car, the man opened fire on us.

I had been shot at before, but this time, after the gunman was arrested and I was thinking about it, I asked myself, 'Where would I be if I had been killed?' Unable to answer my own question, I asked, 'God, if a person can know whether he is going to heaven or hell, I want to know.' That was the first real prayer that I had ever prayed.

I had gone to church regularly as a young person. I didn't get into trouble and had many good friends. But in spite of regular church attendance and a good moral home life, I had never accepted Christ as my Saviour.

When I took up weight-lifting, some of the men with whom

I worked out were police officers in Charlotte. They encouraged me to apply for a job with the Police Department. After I was hired, my goal in life was to be the toughest and strongest cop in the city.

I soon earned a reputation for being tough on the job. In fact, I was sued several times for my over-zealous actions, and I was even charged with and tried for brutality.

In 1968 I met Beverly Blankenship, who was a Christian. After we married, I attended church with her when I wasn't working Sundays. I knew enough about God and the Bible to convince people that I was OK spiritually.

But in the spring of 1972 I was not a happy man. Even though I had a good and faithful wife and two fine children, I was miserable. That was when the man opened fire on my partner and me and I first considered the possibility of death.

That same afternoon as I left police headquarters, a sergeant asked if I could help him at the Charlotte Coliseum the following week, April 5–9. Billy Graham was going to be conducting a crusade, and several militant groups had threatened to storm the platform. I was stationed at the foot of the steps, where I was to stop anyone who tried to disrupt the meetings.

For four nights I listened to the Gospel. I had asked God for some answers, and He was allowing me to listen to those answers – and get paid to listen. On Thursday night, after listening to Mr Graham's message and a testimony by Norm Evans, who was with the Miami Dolphins football team, I asked Jesus to forgive all my sins and to be my Lord and Saviour. Before leaving the Coliseum, I bought a Bible, which I read through in less than six months.

I remained with the Police Department for the next four years. During that time God led me to a growing church and a pastor who was willing to invest his time discipling me. In June 1976, God showed me that he wanted me to go to Bible School to prepare for the ministry. So at age thirty-five I returned to college to complete my undergraduate degree. I went to Bible College and later to seminary.

In the spring of 1981 I still had no idea where God was leading me. I was active in a local church and preached in some high-rise apartment buildings and in a juvenile detention centre. I was still praying about what God would have me do when I met Billy Simmer, founder and president of Good News Jail and Prison Ministries. He believed that I was the man to start a new jail ministry in Bristol, Virginia.

Beverly and I both knew that this was where God wanted us. I am a prison chaplain and directly minister in two institutions in Bristol. During the past years I have seen more than 700 inmates come to Christ and 1,000 make recommitments. More than 14,000 inmates have attended Sunday worship services and 22,000 have attended Bible studies and Christian videos. Recently I have been named a regional director for Good News Jail and Prison Ministries.

I could not have known, on 6 April 1972, what God planned for me. I am glad that He has shown me one step at a time the path He has picked out for me.

Makoto Yamaya

Right now I am in what I call my 'happy decade'.

One day in the fall of 1980 I sat in the Tokyo Korakuen Stadium in Japan, not to watch a baseball game but to see a miracle. A few days before, my uncle Sokichi Mori had telephoned and said, 'Let's go see a miracle, shall we?'

'Miracle?' I asked.

He said, 'My wife's friend is a clerk at a Christian bookstore, and she invited us to come to see a miracle.'

I knew nothing about this friend, but I suppose she must have been a faithful Christian, practising friendship evangelism. The strange but interesting term 'miracle' was her word to express an evangelistic service to be held in the stadium. Anyway, I decided to go.

I was not a religious person. My family's background is Buddhism and Shintoism. I had attended a religious kindergarten, where I was taught that God exists and that Jesus Christ is His Son. So I knew about Him, but I didn't know I could have a personal relationship with Him.

I felt as if I were walking in a dark valley, like Christian, the traveller in John Bunyan's *Pilgrim's Progress*. I did not know the true meaning or purpose of life. I wondered why I had been born. Why did human beings have to live if there was nothing after death? If God existed, as I had learned in kindergarten, then where was He? I was just like a traveller who had fallen into the slime pit.

It was cold the day I went to the stadium. But inside it was filled with warm sounds of music. I was surprised to hear so many people singing joyfully in one voice.

That day I heard Billy Graham. It seemed that he was preaching the Gospel just for me. Through his strong words I learned that I was a sinner on the way to hell. But at the same time I came to know that the Son of God had shed His holy blood for redemption of my sins.

I confessed my sins before God and accepted Jesus Christ as my personal Saviour. Truly it was a miracle, for I received heavenly life! I thank God for Billy Graham and his service in Tokyo.

Now I have a personal relationship with God. Every day I study God's Word, read devotional books, pray and listen to learn God's will for me. In my devotional time I read stories of other Christians all over the world. These teach me and are helpful to me.

In April 1988 I graduated from Seikei University, then entered the college for Salvation Army officers. In 1990 I will finish my courses and become a full-time worker for the Lord in the Salvation Army.

All of Japan is an open field for evangelism. Less than 1 per cent of my country's 121 million people have any knowledge of the Lord Jesus Christ. If God opens the way, I hope to become involved in active evangelism here. Our country is a fertile field and needs much prayer. Economically it is strong, but spiritually it is weak.

I'm Going To Ask You . . .

Now that I know the true meaning and purpose of life, I want to tell others. The answers are all in the Holy Bible: 'Thou shalt love the Lord thy God with all thine heart, and with all thine soul, and with all thy might' (Deuteronomy 6:5, KJV). This is the purpose of my life. God loves me and I love Him. I know the love of Jesus Christ.

I was saved in 1980, and in 1990 I became a Salvation Army officer. That's why I have called this my 'happy decade'. It was given to me by God.

18

A Dangerous Life

Vikta Giovanni,* UK/Italy, 1973

God's hand reached into the very heart of the Mafia! It
happened at Spre-e 73 – a youth training event held at Earls
Court in August 1973. Standing for 'Spiritual Re-emphasis'
(Spre-e was never written without the hyphen), many thousands
of young people (and some older ones) from all over Europe
were trained to take their faith 'out on to the streets'. There
they would witness to anybody they met.

One young girl, somewhat pimply-faced and not particularly
attractive, went out on her own. She was confident, innovative
and adventurous. Her assigned street was no less than Park
Lane in the West End of London. A more distinguished street
would have been hard to find! Full of top-class hotels like
the Dorchester, the Hilton and the Grosvenor House, many
of those who walked up and down were from other countries
and from a variety of ethnic backgrounds. This young woman
was somewhat intimidated by what she saw and decided to
take refuge by going into one of the hotels. She chose the
Dorchester!

Little is known about her, but it would seem that she was
experienced in hotel life. Somewhere along the line she must
have learnt that hotel lobbies and reception areas are not exclu-
ded to those who have legitimate business. All we know is that
she entered the hotel with a degree of confidence which was
noticed by a man sitting at one of the tables near by. 'She
seemed to come in without any specific reason, for she went

---

* Surname changed to protect his family.

neither to reception nor to the concierge's desk – which she might have been expected to do if she had come to visit one of the guests.' Instead she walked the length of the lounge area as though looking for someone she expected to meet. 'To my surprise, she stopped at my table and said, "Excuse me, but may I sit and talk to you for a few minutes?"'

Vikta Giovanni (not his real name for, like the Ayatollah Khomeini's *fatwa* on Salman Rushdie, the long arm of the Mafia is still looking for retribution and revenge) was taken aback. It was not unknown for young ladies to approach gentlemen sitting on their own, but they usually did so in the street – or learned a room number from the porters and then called on the telephone. To proposition a gentleman in full public view, in the lounge of so illustrious a hotel, was totally unexpected, and Vikta (usually called Vikkie) was intrigued. He indicated that she might join him and asked if she would like a cup of tea.

Seeking to explain herself, the young girl told Vikkie that she was part of a massive event taking place at Earls Court. She told him that she had been assigned the task of inviting people to attend the evening's public event at the arena, when Billy Graham would be speaking. Her description of her assignment was not strictly true, for the purpose of 'going out on to the street' was for the young people to share their faith by means of the booklet *The Four Spiritual Laws*. It has not been explained satisfactorily how she came to be on her own. The plan was that all those going out should go in pairs – partly to encourage each other, and partly to ensure their safety. But this girl (whose name is unknown) was on her own, and she did not attempt to share the booklet with Vikkie. Instead, she simply gave him an invitation to come to Earls Court that evening. 'I was more and more intrigued,' Vikta says in heavily accented English. 'She did not tell me much about the event, but what she did say aroused my curiosity. One thing astounded me – that a young girl like her should have the courage to stop and talk to me the way she did – and I thought the English were reserved and did not speak to strangers until they were introduced!'

Vikta lived in London, but he originated from the extreme south of Italy. There he had become involved (as had his father before him) in the machinations of the Mafia. His contribution to their criminal activities was sufficiently committed to justify his promotion within their ranks. Eventually he was sent to work with Mafia interests in the British Isles, and he was now the treasurer of the Mafia in the UK. Never grudging in their hospitality, the British Mafia had provided accommodation for their treasurer at the Dorchester Hotel during his visit to London. His main business had been concluded earlier that Tuesday morning and now, at teatime, he was relaxing in the hotel. That evening he was looking forward to visiting a theatre, and he had planned to stay a few extra days in London 'to take a bit of a holiday'.

After a while the girl excused herself and, leaving a leaflet and invitation with Vikkie, walked out of the hotel. He never saw her again – and indeed only heaven knows who she was!

'I looked at the leaflet I held in my hand. The invitation was much more personal and as I read it I thought "Why not?" and I decided to go to Earls Court that evening to see what it was all about.'

Vikkie was not prepared for what he found there. He had arrived fairly early at the arena, but he found a long queue already formed. In the course of his whole life he had bluffed his way through many situations, and now he set about finding a way to beat the queue. Eventually he found an open door at the back of the building and he followed others (actually Spre-e workers!) who were using that door. 'I suppose I was fairly intolerant of ordinary people. In my own organisation I was "the boss" and my buddies looked after me; I was treated with kid gloves. So, when I got to Earls Court, I was unconsciously looking for special treatment. If that was not forthcoming, then I was left to my own devices.'

With time to spare, he walked around and found a

comprehensive exhibition area where many Christian organisations were displaying their wares and their ministry. He was surprised to find it so well done. It promoted a state of mind which left him asking questions and inspired a readiness to listen. He had never seen so many young people all in one place. But the overpowering impression was one of astonishing happiness and serenity that he saw on their faces and the way they behaved. They were singing, too! It was a strange environment for him, and he found his curiosity stimulated.

'My invitation did not show a numbered and reserved seat, so I asked a big, red-faced man (who wore a badge which said "Chief Steward") where to go. He directed me to the balcony upstairs. "I think you'll be more comfortable there," he said. "Downstairs here, it's bedlam with all the youngsters around." So I made my way up the escalator, where another steward directed me to a good seat – right in the front row of the balcony.'

Vikkie was not impressed with most of the music which filled the first half of the programme. He *was* impressed, however, with a Swedish choral group called the Choralerna. Their excellence captured his attention and imagination, and he settled back to listen and enjoy the music.

When that part of the programme concluded, a young man came on to the well-lit platform. He was leading an elderly man who was wearing a maroon smoking-jacket and dark-blue slacks and a bow-tie. 'For an old man, I thought he looked very natty,' says Vikkie. It was 'interview time' and Phil Herbert, the MC, had brought the ninety-four-year-old evangelist, Lindsay Glegg, on to the platform. Vikta's attention was grabbed the moment the interview started.

Phil Herbert turned to his guest and said: 'Well, Mr Glegg, you have just received a wonderful welcome here and we are very glad to see you. May I say particularly because of your jacket! Isn't it beautiful?' (Applause)

Mr Glegg replied: 'You're not too bad yourself!'

Phil Herbert continued: 'Mr Glegg, as long as I have known

you, I've always been impressed with your attitude. The way you dress obviously means that you think Christians should not be dowdy and shabby, is that true?'

'Yes, that's quite true. In my early days my father said to me, "Now you're going into business. What's it going to be?" One day I said, "A Managing Director." He replied, "So dress like one." So I, the fair-haired boy, was always well-dressed, and I found it a great advantage.'

Phil Herbert asked: 'What sort of things would you be wearing in those days?'

'Well, when I went out to the slums to preach the Gospel, I *always* wore a frock coat and a top hat and a marvellous white waistcoat. They came from miles around to see it!

'We had some great preachers in those days: mighty preachers. There were great meetings to talk about the Lord's return, and they formed a society for preaching about the second coming of our Lord. What a prospect that is! What a thrill!'

Phil Herbert said: 'One final question, Mr Glegg. You seem to have got so much out of life. What can you say tonight as your last words to us so that we can remember this special occasion?'

'I would like everyone to have a passion for souls. I wrote in my Bible many years ago: "Oh! For a passionate passion for souls." There it is, in my Bible. Oh for the love that Jesus had! Oh for a Pentecost! My cry is: "Others!" Hallelujah!'

Vikta says: 'I've always dressed well and I was intrigued that this obviously religious man should consider it so important. I particularly liked the bit about the frock coat and top hat! How quaint! Then I looked around at the thousands of youngsters in the arena and thought, "You've all got a lot to learn!" Most of them were tattily dressed, and many of them looked like they hadn't washed for weeks. It was the *excellence* of Lindsay Glegg that got through to me. I was glad that to be religious didn't mean that you had to look scruffy.'

There was some shifting of scenery after the interview, and

181

a team of young men carried a wooden reading-desk on to the platform. 'There seemed to be a great deal of precision about where it had to be,' says Vikta. 'But once it was in place, there was a great flurry of activity as, surrounded by a posse of bodyguards, Billy Graham came on to the platform. I was comfortable with the sight of those bodyguards! It was something I was used to. But I was not so comfortable with the arrival of Billy Graham. I thought: "Here we go! Steel yourself, Vikkie. They're about to get to you." '

Vikta doesn't remember a great deal of Billy Graham's message that first night. He was more involved in watching everything that went on. He was impressed by the silence and attentiveness of the young people all round him and on the arena floor below. 'Mine was a watching brief that first night,' he said. 'And, as the evening went on, I knew I was going to come back. There was too much to absorb that first night – both organisationally (because I was impressed with the excellent way that everything was done) and in the competence of the speaker. I had to leave before the end of the meeting, but I firmly decided to return.'

In fact, he could not come back again until Thursday night; he had various commitments in London which occupied his time. He was so impressed with what he heard on that second occasion that he went straight back to his hotel and wrote to Billy Graham:

> If Spre-e hasn't done anything for anybody else in this vast crowd, it has certainly been worth everything for the change it has made to me. Everything that has been said and done in these last few days has been meant for me, with my problems and hangups. I can't explain now everything that has happened, all I can say is that Spre-e was, if only to help me. God's richest blessing upon you. Vikkie.[1]

Then, on the Friday night, he went back again. He learned that the final event would take place at Wembley Stadium on the Saturday with Johnny Cash, but he had a flight out of London on Saturday morning – a flight he was never to take!

Cliff Richard was the featured singer on Friday night, along with the Swedish choir. Vikta was not 'into' much of the pop scene, but he found Cliff Richard an interesting person. 'Here I saw someone at the top of the "pop" world, yet he was religious! All that went before paled into insignificance as I listened to Cliff. His presentation made me ready to listen attentively to Billy Graham.'

As Cliff Richard left the platform, on came Billy Graham: 'He out-performs anyone I ever saw,' Billy said, referring to Cliff, to tumultuous applause! Mr Graham continued:

> Tonight is an important night, a night of decision, a night of commitment. This week could be the beginning of a great movement. I've never been to a place where so many Bibles were being held up!
> But the end is coming. Jesus Christ predicted it 318 times in the New Testament. I don't mean the end of the earth or the human race, but the end of the world system. I believe His coming is near and we are going to enter a kingdom like Utopia. Are you able to stand up like Cliff Richard does and say, 'I'm a Christian?' Tonight, present your bodies as a living sacrifice.[2]

The evangelist did not mince his words about the immorality around in this day and age:

> There are different kinds of love, affection, friendship, and there is sexual love. The Bible says: 'Obey your parents.' If they're Christians, you should do that. If they're not, you should honour them. Man has taken sex and perverted it until today it's on the verge of destroying us. You say, 'It was easy for Paul to control his sexual desires. He didn't have to contend with the

advertisements, the posters, the films, the plays which confront us every day.' No, he didn't. And it is only possible to live a clean life today because of the dynamic power of God's love in your heart. God loves you, and that makes you valuable.

A crucial decision confronts you tonight. Many lives here face decisions of commitment. Many of you stand at the crossroads. You must answer the question, 'What are you going to do with Jesus Christ?' Do you know that you have eternal life? If you were arrested for being a Christian, is there enough evidence to convict you?

Do you want to make sure? Do you want to know? The whole of Spre-e might be just for you. The chance may never come again. I'm going to ask many of you, hundreds of you, to stand and commit yourselves to Christ.

Vikta was deeply moved. 'I hadn't been there at the end of the meeting earlier in the week,' he says, 'so I was totally unprepared for what happened when Billy Graham concluded his talk. Consequently I had to watch in astonishment as hundreds of people from all over Earls Court responded to Billy's invitation to 'stand up, wherever you are, and commit yourself to Christ'. I looked at the faces of those who stood in my area of the seating. It was clear that they were determined and that they meant business. It disturbed me and I was challenged.'

Then before he could do anything else, something was happening on the platform.

'The big, red-faced man, whom I had met the first day, came to the microphone. He told us that he wanted our help.' Vikta tells how Henry Hole, the chief steward in question, told the audience that the arena had to be cleared of the thousands of chairs that evening. The Earls Court authorities had quoted a sum of £3,000 to do the job. Henry Hole said that he had a better idea: 'Will you all stand up. Now turn around and pick up the chair you have been sitting on. When I give you the word, please carry it to the right-hand side of the hall. When you get there, some of the stewards will meet you and will show you where to stack the chair you are carrying.'[3]

Henry Hole then gave the word for the exercise to begin. Vikta says: 'I watched in amazement as this extraordinary plan was put into effect. Within five minutes the entire floor of the arena was cleared of chairs. It was a stroke of genius and I thought to myself, "We could use that red-faced man in the Mafia!"

'But, even as I was reflecting upon what I had just seen, I saw that, in the midst of all this kerfuffle, people were still going forward to the front. The movement of all those chairs had not got in their way at all! What impressed me most was the way these religious people did not compartmentalise their faith and separate it from the reality of everyday life. These people did things well. They were not wimps. Suddenly I realised that this was my last chance to be one of them.'

At that moment, Vikta became one of those who stood. The message had challenged – convicted – him, and he was ready to take the right path from the crossroads.

'Like a rocket, I was out of my seat and heading towards the nearest staircase to get down to the ground floor in time! They had said there were counsellors there, and I wanted to get down to see one. I don't think I was the last to come forward – but I must have been very near to the end.'

It was then that a miracle occurred. Along with all the others who came forward, Vikkie was 'paired up' with a counsellor, but the one assigned to him just happened to be a leading barrister. His counselling went along on the normal lines until the counsellor got to the question on the counselling card: 'What job do you do?'

Vikta decided to take the bull by the horns! 'I work with the Mafia,' he said. His counsellor was startled and, at first, thought he was being 'had'. Understanding the baffled look on his counsellor's face, Vikta re-emphasised, 'I am not joking. I really do.'

185

The normal counselling pattern went 'out of the window'! Vikta's counsellor realised that he had a 'hot potato' on his hands and that something drastic needed to be done. Leading Vikkie away from the counselling area, he took him into one of the many private rooms around the arena. First the counsellor prayed with him. Then he asked him about the consequence of his decision for Christ – for such it turned out to be. 'When I came forward,' says Vikkie, 'I didn't really know what the reason was. But on my way down to the front I said to myself: "Vikta! This is the moment of truth for you." I asked myself why I was going forward in this way, and I understood that it was to respond to Billy Graham's presentation of Christ as my Saviour. I knew it would have incredible implications for the future of my life!'

His counsellor talked with him about his involvement with the Mafia and learned about the senior and responsible post he held. It was clear that, from this moment onwards, the Mafia had lost its representative and that recriminations would follow. What concerned him most was the possibility of actual danger to Vikta's life.

Instead of the flight he had expected to take, Vikta found himself on the way to the south of England. He was taken to the home of Judge Ruttle, a Christian judge who was an enthusiastic supporter of the crusade. Vikta didn't know the significance of his host's occupation at the time, but he stayed there for a short while until suitable arrangements could be made for the next stage in his rehabilitation!

There could not have been a better home in which to stay. Henry Ruttle was not unused to complicated situations. He had been involved in controversy on the bench and was widely known for his extrovert personality, as well as for his strong Christian faith. He had undergone a life-changing Christian conversion at seventeen years of age while he was a student at Wesley College in Dublin. Subsequently he became a schoolmaster and a vigorous rugby player (he once played in a trial match for the Irish national side and was described as 'the best forward who never won a national cap'[4]).

He had served in the RAF during the war and became a deputy judge advocate, handling courts martial. After demobilisation he became active in the Church Assembly, where he took up the cudgels on behalf of anti-Romish idols. He was used to difficult situations, and he relished the opportunity of helping Vikta Giovanni.

Details concerning the next months are still sensitive and cannot be given – even twenty-three years later there is a danger that, even today, the long arm of the Mafia could reach out to harm innocent people. In outline, however, after spending an extended period in Judge Ruttle's home, arrangements were made for Vikta to move on to a Christian training centre in L'Abri in Switzerland. There, the director, Francis Schaeffer, was the only person aware of Vikta's background. In L'Abri they sought to realign his life and helped him to learn how to decide God's will for his future.

Among other things, this involved changing his identity. His name was changed and his circumstances were revamped. In subtle ways his appearance was changed, and eventually he went to live in America where, today, he continues to serve the Lord. Neither his name, his ministry, his location nor any further details of his story can be related.

Today he says: 'That life-changing experience at Earls Court in 1973 probably affected me more than it would another person. So much has changed in my family and in my own life that I am bound to look back and say, "Was it all worth it?" The answer to that question must be an unqualified and resounding "Yes". I have never looked back, even for one minute.

'All the trauma of changing my life so dramatically was nothing to the experience of Christ in my life. He has been totally real to me in a way that nothing else I had experienced before had been real. All the power, wealth and importance of my former life have nothing to compare with the "treasure I have laid up in heaven".

'I thank God for that little pimply-faced girl who came and had tea with me at the Dorchester. I don't know who she was: I don't suppose she would have had any idea of the dramatic change in my life to which she had contributed. All I know is that she was an "angel from God" who brought His message of salvation to me in an unexpected and unbelievable way. And all the others who played their part – Choralerna; Cliff Richard's testimony; the smartly dressed ninety-four-year-old who was still "going strong"; that red-faced steward with his big chair-moving exercise; Billy Graham's message that had reached into my heart; my miracle counsellor who understood my situation; the judge in whose home I stayed; L'Abri and all those who contributed to my new identity. Life was never the same again – and I thank God for His grace and mercy which reached out to a sinner like me. He can do the same for you!'

19

Second Row, Piano Side

Chonda Pierce, USA, 1979
(Note: All quotations are from the cassette tape, 'Live from the Second Row Piano Side', and are used with permission)

The audience rocked with laughter as Chonda Pierce told of her experiences as a child.

She had been brought up in the home of a pastor of the Church of the Nazarene, and there was a certain strictness which was essential to her parents' way of life.

> I grew up in church. Most all my life I grew up sitting on the second row piano side, rain, snow or shine. Even if your body is in a cast, my mother will wheel you in and lean you against the wall. But you are *not* going to miss church! You know what I'm talking about? How many of you had mothers like that? Dress you up? Are you still going to therapy? We had beautiful memories growing up second row piano side.

Chonda, however, always saw the funny side of life, and it was not altogether surprising, therefore, that when she grew up she became a comedienne. She saw humour in so many experiences of life.

> Back in those days, in my denomination, we had district superintendents. They were, like, your dad's boss, or a something: head of a few churches. I never figured out what they did. All I knew was when they came to town

189

my parents were a nervous wreck. They tried to get us to go and stay with somebody else on those Sunday afternoons!

There was this one superintendent I would never forget who came with his sweet wife. They were having Sunday dinner with us and we passed the mashed potatoes, and the green beans, and the corn-on-the-cob, and that sweet lady started cutting all that corn off the cob. I hollered across the table, 'What's the matter with you, lady? Ain't you got no teeth?' My mother started crying.

Then, after lunch we took them to the living-room couch where my little sister would quote a few scriptures and my brother would play a chorus on the trumpet and my big sister would play a song on the piano. Then we would sing a few songs. I had the opening poem that day, which was my mother's first mistake. I was four or five years old at the time. I had memorised the poem she wrote. It went:

We hope you like our singing, we're glad that you are here,
We want to fill your visit with happiness and cheer.

Isn't that sweet? But something came over me. Carnal sin, I think! I looked at the district superintendent and said:

We hope you like our singing, we're glad that you are here,
Now let's go into the kitchen and have a glass of beer!

My mother fainted, bless her heart. I am telling you, visitation was a big deal! Such precious memories in the second row piano side!

Chonda, her brother and sisters would go into their father's church. There they would line up all the hymn-books and preach to them as though they were the congregation. That was all right, until their father became the pastor of a church that had a baptistry. Then the inevitable followed; they had to have a baptismal service, and Chonda says: 'That day we baptised twenty-seven hymn-books. After that, my father always locked the church door!'

> I remember the first church my daddy ever pastored was in South Carolina. In those days the church and the parsonage were just side by side. You know what I'm talking about? My brother and my sisters went next door to check out the new church. We found all these little tiny glasses over there, so we went out there on the front porch, and we took two brick-o-blocks and a big wooden plank, and we played the American TV show 'Gun Smoke Saloon' all day with those little communion glasses . . . till the ladies' fellowship came over!

Chonda, a lively thirty-five-year-old, was born in Covington, Kentucky, USA. The peripatetic nature of her father's calling meant that the family moved to wherever his church was located. So, for almost fifteen years, the family lived first in South Carolina, then in Tennessee. It was in Nashville that she met David Pierce, who was to become her husband. They now have two lovely children, Chera Kay and Zachary.

> I remember, you know, back then we had a television but I just didn't know 'cause we kept a blanket over it. We all remember those days, don't you? I thought it was some kind of strange coffee-table, but sure enough, every now and then on Friday night we could take the blanket off and watch TV. We were wild! We could watch kind of three wholesome things in our lives all the time. There was some television evangelist who was popular at the time, or Andy Griffiths, or some news documentary about whatever was going on in the world. But TV like it is now, we would just be allowed to watch Andy Griffiths!

It is often the case that, for those who are able to raise a smile from the experiences of life, there is an element of sadness and tragedy through which they have passed – and in this Chonda is no exception.

The news reached the family one day that her eldest sister, Charlotta, had been killed in a road traffic accident. Death had been instantaneous and, although for the victim that is a blessing, it always leaves a deep trauma for those who are left behind. When the telephone rings and the policeman says, 'I think you should be sitting down before I proceed further,' the heart immediately constricts and life seems – instantaneously – to stand still. So it was for Chonda and her family when the news reached them. There is an immediate tendency to ask: 'Why, God? Why us?' and there is a temptation to blame Him for what has happened.

They had only just come to terms with Charlotta's accident when her youngest sister, Cheralyn, came home from school listless and pale. She was obviously unwell, and it was thought that she might have some type of 'flu. However, a visit to the doctor disclosed that tests were necessary to determine exactly what was wrong.

Just a few days later came the shattering news that Cheralyn had a form of leukaemia which gave her only weeks to live. Just twenty-one short days after the diagnosis, the cancer had galloped ahead and she was taken from them.

I will never forget a little eight-year-old girl who brought her baby dolly in for the healing service. She walked in with this baby doll. You know, its leg was missing, and the little eyes were rusted and some of the hair was missing. This little girl laid her doll on the altar and knelt down beside it. As the pastor and some of the folks came to pray for others they came to this little eight-year-old with her favourite baby doll.

Now I will never forget the pastor being so concerned at not wanting to hurt her feelings or discourage her in the slightest, but he looked at her and said, 'Honey, I need to explain to you. I'm not quite sure that Jesus will heal your baby doll.' She said, 'Oh, I know that, pastor, but He can heal my broken heart.' Isn't that the truth? I'm so thankful that I learned that, as a child growing up, because when the tough times came He really did heal my broken heart.

This second tragedy, so shortly after the first, left a terrible void in the family life. The news was so shattering to her father that he could no longer face life within the family and he packed his bags and moved out.

My daddy had been a good pastor, but somewhere in all of that hurt and anger and disillusionment, he packed a suitcase one Saturday and walked out – of the church and of his marriage, and there sat me and mum, second row piano side.

Round about the same time, her brother married and moved away, so Chonda and her mother were left very much alone. Life was not easy, and they had to sell their home in order to find a way of surviving, both financially and emotionally. At the beginning of 1979 they moved into a one-bedroom apartment. Chonda says: 'I felt alone and abandoned.'

I also remember my mother's prayers. You know the prayers I'm talking about. Now there were those when I came in late at night. I would walk down the hall an hour late. I should have been in an hour before and that last board in the hallway creaks, and your mum knows you were late, and she begins to pray out loud. 'Now, Lord, you know I don't want to have to kill Chonda, but if I have to, Lord, give me the strength to do it.' You know what I'm talking about? And there were those other prayers that I remember hearing my mom pray. 'Lord, have patience with Chonda, she's hurting, she's discouraged, she's angry. Have patience with her, Lord.' And He did as my mom prayed. And I've never in my life forgot those prayers as I sat in the second row piano side!

Then, at about the same time, came the news that there was to be a great crusade in the Vanderbilt Stadium in Nashville, and that the evangelist would be none other than Billy Graham. 'Because my father had been a pastor, the name of Dr Graham was certainly heard of around our dinner table.' Occasionally there had been a television programme which Chonda had watched, and she had seen his name on many books in her father's personal library.

'My mother suggested that we should go along to the crusade one evening. Although we were both so lonely, she never failed to live a godly life before me,' says Chonda. 'But I was very reluctant. I was still very bitter from all that had happened to us. I thought that "hanging around" in church all of my life had brought me nothing but pain and this gnawing loneliness. But, to keep peace with my mother so that she wouldn't nag me every night, I went with her.'

When they arrived at the stadium there were more than 50,000 people there, and Chonda was awe-struck. First it was empowering to see so many people singing. 'They sang "How great thou art" and "Just as I am" like I'd never heard them sung before! As I watched, hundreds of people went forward, and some of them seemed to be shedding tears. It made me see a much bigger and bolder picture of God Almighty.

'It was all so moving that I don't even remember breathing. Whenever the name of Billy Graham had been mentioned in our home, it was almost as though he was considered a prophet. My mother had said, almost all of my life, that Billy Graham is the nearest thing we will have on this side of heaven like the Apostle Paul! He was an incredible preacher and really illuminates true integrity.'

Chonda recalls that the effect of that crusade meeting in

1979 was to change the whole character of her life. It was the first time she had heard Billy Graham in person. 'I went forward *four* times,' she says. 'Four nights in a row! At first it was just so that I could get a better look at him! I was desperately in need of a hero, and in Billy Graham I had found one. Dr Graham preached a message one of those nights in which he repeated, several times, "You are not alone." He planted a seed in my heart that renewed my faith in life and, most importantly, in God. I knew that I would survive if I could rely on His strength and ask Him to forgive my sins and to be the Lord of my life.'

It would have been difficult for her to have grown up in a pastor's home, where she had heard the Gospel from the time she was a baby, if she had not already known Christ as her Saviour. What happened at Nashville, during the crusade, was in some ways more of a rededication of her life than an initial commitment to Christ. *Now* she was prepared to do something about it.

I admire my mother. She's one of the heroines in my life. She's just a neat lady and she taught me such beautiful biblical truths growing up. Things that have stayed with me for years and years. I find myself passing them on to my same little young 'uns. I felt some of them might help some of you who have little ones. You may want to write these down. They're so good. Eat all your carrots. They're good for your eyes. It works for me! Don't make faces like that or it will get stuck that way. Which is true: I used not to look like this!

Then there's that wonderful little question that my mother asked me two or three times a day, just about on a regular basis. 'Do you want your face slapped?' And if one time you said, 'Sure,' then you *would* get your face slapped! And this same little Nazarene mother had a saying that I heard most all of my life. 'If the Lord had meant for you to have holes in your ears, He would have

195

put them there!' And that all-time favourite saying is the best one I think I had learned to pass on to my children: 'Always wear clean underwear in case your car is in a wreck!' So important!

'It didn't all happen at once. Over the next sixteen years there were building blocks laid one upon another on the foundation that had been laid in 1979. My immediate response was to be less bitter, less sarcastic. God faithfully met me at my needs. I had some wonderful church leaders and counsellors to help me – because I still faced depression, resentments and pain from my past.

'I had lost so much so quickly – but the guidance of those who helped me enabled me to see that I was not alone in my struggles. I learned from those who have suffered much worse than me, and I have been inspired by their strength and inner peace. That can only have come from my loving Heavenly Father.'

The loneliness that Chonda had experienced did not vanish immediately. Nevertheless she had now learnt the source from which strength could come. She learned that she needed to saturate herself in God's Word and surround herself with resources that would guide her closer to Him. 'It is amazing to take a step back and to look at the handiwork of God in my life,' she says. 'I have never regretted the decision I took then.'

The year is now 1995. In the intervening years Chonda had learnt that God continued His faithfulness to her, and year by year she grew in the grace and knowledge of the Lord Jesus Christ. She thanks God that He brought her husband, David, into her life. Today he is the spiritual leader in her home and she constantly thanks God for him.

As a Christian comedienne she has the opportunity to speak in a wide variety of places. She performs equally effectively in a church sanctuary and in a county fair. Several times she has been a performer at the world-famous Grand Ole Opry.

'This was a tremendous honour to me,' she says, 'because I have been a fan of Cousin Minnie Pearl for most of my life.'

> I thought one of the most hilarious things was when I called my sweet mother and told her to watch TV. I was to be on with country and western singer Garth Brooks, and they told me that there could be as many as 40 million people watching. Mom was so excited! Thrilled! Just as she finished congratulating me and telling me about the family members she needed to phone right away, she said suddenly, 'Honey, that's wonderful, but who is Garth Brooks?' I suppose the show went well, because I was invited back a few more times. I even had my picture taken with Garth Brooks – just for Mom.

One day, out of the blue, Chonda had a telephone call from her manager to say that an invitation had arrived for her to visit Fort Lauderdale in Florida, where members of the Billy Graham team were gathered for a Team and Staff Conference (TASC). It was one of a regular series of TASCs which took place every three to five years. Many of those who attended it believed it to be the 'powerhouse of the team'. God always met with them in a very real way. Devotional times, prayer times, biblical expositions and reports were balanced by times of supreme fellowship. And one evening was always devoted to relaxation and a time of fun. Sometimes this was indigenous fun, with various team members sharing stories about one another. Sometimes it was concentrated in a film presentation, specially made by their colleagues at World Wide Pictures, with help from Roger Flessing and others.

On this occasion there were to be two visitors. One brought a couple of ventriloquist's dolls and kept the team entertained with their antics. And the other was Chonda!

When she got the invitation to appear as a comedienne at the team's fun evening, Chonda says: 'I was ecstatic. That night, at supper, I told my daughter, "Mommy is getting ready

to meet someone that I have wanted to meet for sixteen years."
My daughter quickly said, "Oh, wow! You're gonna meet
Carman!" [Carman is a popular contemporary Christian music
artist.] I said, "No, Chera, I'm going to meet *Dr* Billy Graham."
She was very concerned and said, "Mom, have you been
sick?" '

Going to Florida was an excitement all by itself. But, to add
to that, the possibility of meeting Billy Graham really 'blew'
Chonda's mind. 'I was so excited, thinking about the possibility
just of shaking his hand. I didn't want to get my hopes up that
I would actually have a chance to interact with him, or that
he would even be there at all to hear my performance.' The
evening turned out to be an evening of the most sanctified of
fun.

'As a comedienne I work hard to communicate effectively
so that what I have to say will be heard with clarity and ultimately it will evoke a hearty laugh. Many of those who work
in comedy feel that timing is everything! I tend to agree. Timing
is indeed everything. Our God has an impeccable sense of
timing. He sends just the right people at just the right time.
When we are seeking Him – He is always on time. Recognising
His work, relaxing in His care, and accepting His will. We can
truly see God being God . . . at the *right* place and at the *right*
time.'

Skilfully Chonda carried her audience through all of her
experiences. There were so many stories that had the Billy
Graham team members laughing until their ribs ached. Then,
with scarcely a change of pace, she had driven home a serious
point that was a lesson to everyone: laughing one minute, but
real tears from emotion the next. She led the group through
those funny and embarrassing experiences which have made
her such an outstanding comedienne, then a moment later she
was telling them about the tragic loss of Charlotta and
Cheralyn.

Then she moved on to how her whole life had been changed
through the ministry of Billy Graham at Nashville's Vanderbilt

Stadium in 1979. And she described the reality of her experience with Christ today. It was powerful, enthralling and fascinating as she carried everyone with her through her story.

Then, at the end of the presentation, 'There was Billy Graham,' she says. 'He stretched out his arms to hug me – it was like a daddy telling his little girl at the end of a long day at school that everything was going to be all right. His favourable response to my presentation and his kindness towards me was a true affirmation for me, personally, that God had His hand on my life since 1979 – and even before. I was humbled to know that me, this funny girl from a little church in Tennessee, would one day have the chance to make Billy Graham laugh, and I was amazed and touched to see him cry with me as well.'

> Months and months later – my mother doesn't have a clue where that photograph with Garth Brooks is – but she does have a picture in her living room. It is an eight-by-ten photo of her little girl, arm in arm with Dr Billy Graham!

It seemed to Chonda that having that opportunity to share in this ministry with the group at TASC had reminded her that nothing is too big for God! She adds, 'And no one is too small for God to use and care about. After that meeting in Fort Lauderdale I returned home with renewed strength and commitment to "be about my Father's business".' And those who listened to her may have thought that it was only the fun they were going to have – but they went away inspired, enriched and blessed by this little comedienne from Tennessee.

She has the last word – as she so often does! Asked if she has *ever* regretted her decision to accept Christ and to follow His leading in her life, she replies with one word – which is emphasised heavily in her writing – 'NEVER!'

20

Diminutive Medium

Eva Close, England, 1982

> I'm only four feet eleven,
> But I'm going to heaven
> And it makes me feel ten feet tall!
> They say I'm not too strong,
> But I've known all along
> I've got the Greatest Power of all!

So sings Evie Tournquist in one of her Gospel Song albums. Little Eva Close would echo those sentiments with great fervour! She *never* found it easy to see over the heads of people in front of her!

She lived in Blackpool at the time of Billy Graham's mini-crusade in the town in 1982. The local churches there heard that he had accepted an invitation to be the honoured 'banquet' speaker at the annual Christian booksellers' convention which, at that time, was held in Blackpool each year. A group of leaders was called together and they decided to extend an invitation to Billy Graham to conduct a one-night-only meeting in Blackpool's Winter Gardens.

Once the announcement was made, it soon became clear that one night would be insufficient to accommodate all those who wanted to come, and a plea was sent to Mr Graham that he would extend the meetings by an extra day and that it could be treated as a crusade – with prayer groups, counsellors being trained, Operation Andrew and a proper choir. To their delight, he agreed.

Blackpool was regarded by some as the 'sin city' of the

north! First and foremost it was a holiday town, and along the Golden Mile were endless attractions, culminating in the Pleasure Beach with its great variety of rides. On the seafront itself were many booths – some of which housed the famed gypsy palm-readers, fortune-tellers and mediums of all sorts. Eva Close was not one of these – but she might well have been, for she too was a medium.

'There *is* a power: there *is* an anointing in spiritualism,' she says. 'Make no mistake about it. It's counterfeit: but it's there. The devil is a real person and he gives a power that makes strange things happen. But it's counterfeit power. I've been there and I've seen it. And I know it's evil.'

There came a time in her life when she proved for herself the truth of 1 John 2:27: 'As for you, the anointing you received from Him remains in you and you do not need anyone to teach you. But as His anointing teaches you about all things *and as that anointing is real*, not counterfeit . . . remain in Him.'

In March 1982 she went to the Winter Gardens in Blackpool to hear Billy Graham. It was then that she came to see that the spiritualism which had engaged her attention over a number of years had been of the counterfeit variety.

Born at around the time when the Second World War had broken out, in the village of Witton Park, near Bishop Auckland, almost all of her life has been spent in the north-east of England.

Witton Park – 'Jam-Jar City', as it was called – was where she and the six others in her family grew up. When the children went to the pictures at the local cinema, they took with them four washed and dried jam-jars as the price of their admission; hence the strange nickname of the village.

Her mother had brought her up from childhood to believe in spiritualism; it was something in which her mother was very interested. Eva herself started going to a spiritualist church when she was twenty-eight years old. She soon became aware that there was a power which enabled her to receive and give messages. That could have led her to a professional career as a medium. Mercifully, however, she was spared that – chiefly because, as a housewife and mother of three daughters, she found spare time at a premium.

She continued going to the church for about five years. Then she stopped attending any meetings, but she still conversed with 'spirit guides', who became like real people in her life. 'I became terribly depressed,' she says, 'and from time to time even contemplated suicide.' Then she and George moved back to Blackpool, and once again Eva started to attend various spiritualist churches. 'One night, after giving a man and his wife a message, they approached me and asked if I would be willing to start a development group in my home. "We like your style," they said.'

A few days later, while ironing, she had the television on and was watching an interview with a man called Billy Graham. The interviewer said that he was an evangelist. 'I didn't really know what an evangelist was,' she says, 'but it sounded like an uninteresting programme to me, and so I switched off the television set.'

A short while later, her daughter (who was twelve at the time) came home and said: 'Mum! Billy Graham is coming to Blackpool and I can get some free tickets.'

'Get me five,' Eva replied.

She goes on: 'I don't know why I asked her to do that. I suppose it was because I was clutching at straws to get myself out of this terrible depression.'

It was 3 March 1982. On that day Eva had twisted her ankle and it was very painful. Nevertheless she was so eager to go to the Winter Gardens that she crammed her shoe on over a swollen and bruised foot and hobbled into the car and down to the town with the rest of her family.

Looking back on it today, Eva says, 'I believe that twisted ankle came from the devil. He wanted to stop me from going to hear the Gospel!'

But worse was to come. George, her husband, went off to park the car while her three daughters went into the Winter

Gardens to get the seats. Somehow or other she and George got separated; they missed each other, and no one knew why. When he returned, he made his way into the auditorium to join the three girls. Meanwhile Eva was left outside. It was 6.40 p.m.

'I waited and waited for George, but he never came,' she says. 'I began to wonder if I should tell a policeman – or just go to a café and wait for the meeting to finish. My mind raced in every direction. Eventually, at 7.30 p.m. I was so upset that I broke into tears. I just wanted to get into the hall.'

She became very distressed and was full of fear that something dreadful had happened to him: maybe he had been mugged or had had an accident of some sort. She imagined him in the emergency ward of the Victoria Hospital! Then someone came out and said that the Winter Gardens was already full and that everyone outside would have to go to the video overflow next door.

'I didn't care,' says Eva. 'I just knew that I had to get into that meeting. It seemed that a voice was saying to me, "Go in . . . go in . . . go in . . ." repeatedly.' In the end, she went in and took the first available seat she could find in the overflow – and it was right in the centre of the front row.

As she sat down, a strange peace came over her and all her fears disappeared. She stopped worrying about George; she felt sure that he was all right.

Billy Graham was already speaking by that time. 'As I listened to him, I found that I had never experienced anyone who could talk like that before. It seemed as if he was speaking to me alone. I hung on to every word and soaked it all up like a sponge.

'Then Billy Graham said, "Do you need Christ in your heart?" As I listened to him, it seemed that the devil had me riveted to my seat. Here was Billy Graham telling me how much Jesus loved me – and *I* didn't think I was very lovable. Then again he said, "Do you need Christ in your heart?" "Sit tight, Eva," said the devil! "It's emotion; don't yield to it, Eva."

'Then, a third time Billy Graham said, "Do you need Christ in your life?" Immediately the devil said again, "Sit tight, Eva," but this time I managed to beat that voice and I flew to the front.

'Soon after I had finished being counselled, I breezed out of that building on cloud nine! It was, to me, an elation, like being in a hovercraft. I felt twenty feet tall and above it all. Amidst the vast crowd leaving the five auditoriums – the meeting had been relayed to four other large halls in the complex – I managed to find the rest of my family, and I hugged them all. All I knew was that, as the hymn says, I was "lost in wonder, love and praise". It was a total mystery to my family. I kept on talking about it, and they thought I had gone insane! After that night, my feet hardly touched the floor again for the next six years!'

Eva found that she had innumerable battles with the devil, for he was a hard master to dispose of. He was loath to let her go. 'My husband and my daughters thought I had gone insane because of the change in me. I was always reading the Bible and singing about Jesus!' But she declares that, from the moment of her conversion on, she had never been more sane and was in full possession of all her senses.

She soon became involved in numerous Christian activities: she was invited to join the Board of Women Aglow, and she also did a lot of street preaching with Teen Challenge. 'This latter included witnessing to those I suspected were druggies and alcoholics – also glue-sniffers.' They all called her 'Mrs Eva'. On one occasion she got too close to a glue-sniffer. When she got to her car, she was overcome with the fumes and felt quite silly. When she got home, still feeling its after-effects, she said to George, 'I'm high tonight!'

Once she talked to a young man on the street, and afterwards someone came up to her and said, 'Did you know that he had an open knife in his pocket?' It was sometimes dangerous work.

At the end of the six years of euphoria and ministry she had an attack of shingles. At the same time, some problems developed in her family which she needed to deal with. 'Having found that all his other ploys didn't work, the devil now tried to attack me through my health and my family,' she says.

'George advised me to give up my work with Women Aglow in order to allow me space to recover.

'But even with these setbacks, I found that Christ was sufficient and that He could help me. My response to these setbacks was so different from the response I used to make. Then I would swear and blaspheme. Now God had so cleansed my mind that the very idea of using such language was foreign to me.

'At first it seemed that my love for Christ had grown cold. But I discovered that, although I was not side by side with Him, as I had been since I found Him, I was hanging on to the edge of His robe. I knew, and was totally assured, that He'd be able to pull me back.

'The devil had a field day during those times. I'd always been used to hearing "voices", and there were times when some dreadful swearwords and blasphemies came into my mind – always the worst ones! I didn't feel very holy as I went to Bible study that week. The devil said to me, "The pastor knows what you're thinking. He knows all those dreadful words." And I began to believe that I would be kicked out of the church. That went on for about seven or eight weeks.

'I remembered that, earlier on, my family had told me they thought I was insane. Now I was beginning to believe that they might be right after all. I thought that perhaps I needed a psychiatrist. Then one day I'd had enough. I went upstairs and fell on my knees. I prayed that God would cleanse me.

'I heard a tremendous voice which said: "It's not *your* battle – it's *My* enemy." A picture came into my mind. It was of a black circle, surrounded by a great circle of light. It seemed that Christ was saying to me, "Fight to get out."

'So, using Scripture, I began to fight, and then it came to me that Christ had already won the battle. It was a wonderful victory! I didn't need a psychiatrist! It was a lie which the devil had tried to sell me. I'd already got all the equipment I needed to win the fight. And from that moment on, I have left it all to Him, and He's always been faithful to me.'

Eva has grabbed every opportunity to tell others about her lively faith. One day she was in her local Fine Fare supermarket, wearing (as always) her badge which declared 'Jesus: my hope', when she passed an attractive girl demonstrating a microwave oven. She stopped and told the girl that she had bought one the previous week, and that she was very happy with it.

'That was nice of you to come and say you liked it,' said the young girl. 'Most people only stop when they want to complain.'

As she left the girl, Eva found herself looking back at her. 'She's a very tall and lovely girl to look at,' she thought to herself. 'I must talk to her about Jesus.' So she went back and discovered that the girl's name was Janice.

Eva told her all that Christ had done in her own life. As she did so, Janice's eyes filled with tears. 'I used to go to a Methodist church,' she said, 'but I looked around and it seemed to me that everyone there lived a worse life than I was living. So I gave it all up. What do I need to do to put it right?'

Eva told her that she needed to ask God to come into her life. 'I'm simply a knocker on doors,' said Eva. 'The rest is up to you,' and she gave Janice a tract that would help her to find Christ for herself.

Another day she was going to the butcher's. As she went in, she was singing some choruses quietly to herself and the lady in front of her said, 'You sound happy and you look happy. Are you singing hymns?'

Eva explained that she was singing choruses, not hymns. The lady said, 'I do not know how to get through today. Can you help me?' Eva told her that the only solution to her problems was to ask Jesus into her life.

One day there was a lacecraft party at her pastor's house. About twenty-two people were there and the room was full.

On the other side of the room, Eva saw a lady, and the Spirit of the Lord seemed to say to her, 'Eva! Talk to that lady,' but it was easier said than done. Eva was sitting at the back of the room, and the other lady was sitting at the front. In between were lots of chairs and people.

Then, without warning, the meeting ended and everyone stood up. Most of them moved their chairs in such a way that there was now a clear passage across the room. Eva was unimpeded on her way to talk to the other woman, who told Eva that her name was Mildred. She told Eva that, whenever anyone tried to talk to her about Jesus, she always wanted to shout, 'Get away from me!'

'Then she told me that she hadn't felt like that when she saw me coming over.' Eva was able to talk to her about Christ – but without any certain conclusion.

The following Sunday morning, Mildred's daughter ran up to Eva in church and asked, 'Whatever did you say to Mother the other night? She kept us up until three in the morning asking questions about the things you had said to her.'

Eva told her, 'We must pray for her because your mother is going to get saved.' And, a little while afterwards, she was. Now she goes regularly to Eva's church.

In her own way Eva has become an evangelist too. Like Billy Graham, she is called to tell others about Christ, and she does so whenever she gets the opportunity. She has spoken to several ladies' groups and at meetings in lots of churches. Her testimony has inspired many people.

One day, in a supermarket she dropped some heavy tins on her toe. She danced around in pain for a little while, and a man near by, who had been watching, remarked: 'Go on, I'm waiting for you to swear.'

She replied: 'I used to do that all the time. But now I'm a Christian and the Lord has cleaned me up. Hallelujah!' The man looked at her quizzically, shook his head and walked away. But she had faithfully witnessed to him.

At home, her daughter thought Eva had lost her sense of

humour. 'Once upon a time you liked a really good laugh at a filthy or dirty story,' she said one day.

'I assured her that I still had a sense of humour – but a clean one now. Tell me a simple and clean joke and I will laugh!' replied Eva. 'I still love a good story – but it had better be clean,' she says!

Once she was at a relative's wedding celebration. A man was there, telling dirty jokes. 'So I walked out,' says Eva. 'My brother asked me why I had done so and I replied, "I cannot praise God with my mouth and listen to that stuff with my ears!" '

With a long, drawn-out gasp of 'Ohhhh!' she declared, 'I've never, never, never, *never* regretted the decision I took at that Billy Graham meeting in Blackpool. I praise God for him, for it was he who introduced me to my Saviour.

'After I became a Christian it was like seeing a three-dimensional film when I read John 14:6 the next time. Jesus said, "I am the way, the truth and the life. No one comes to the Father except by me." It jumped out of the page and hit me between the eyes. A real 3-D experience. In the past when I was a medium I listened to spirits: now I listen to *the Spirit*, and I'm training to become a Christian counsellor! I know without any doubt that I am heaven-bound and will see Jesus. Praise the Lord!'

21
Dream Machine

Jean Lupton, England, 1985

Exuberant! That is the only word to describe a meeting with Jean Lupton. She exudes that exuberance from every part of her being. And talk! You can't stop her – and it's mostly about what God has done for her in her life.

Jean always enjoyed riding motorcycles. Her greatest delight is to work in the firm she founded. Motorcycle enhancement was the nature of the business: 'Dream Machine', a motorcycle paint-spraying company. All work was welcome, but the firm's expertise lay in the finishing and customising of trimmings. They did this both for the motorcycle trade and for the various works' race teams.

That's not exactly the image one would have of this petite lady, nicely dressed, well-groomed and well-spoken – in a Derbyshire manner! But she has her head screwed on the right way. She is a good businesswoman with a shrewd understanding of what makes it all tick.

She enjoyed her work, but she always knew that there was more to life than she had experienced thus far. It was, therefore, with a jolt that her whole world was to be shattered when she was involved in a ghastly accident. She was with a young man called Andrew, who was driving one of the firm's delivery vans at the time. Jean never really knew what happened because it was so sudden. The saddest part of that accident was that Andrew lost his life. Jean survived, although she suffered serious injuries. These included at least thirty fractures of her right leg from the foot, through the knee, to the thigh. It seemed impossible that she could ever be put together again. For Jean,

209

however, that scarcely mattered compared to what had happened to Andrew. That tragedy was to live with Jean for all of her life.

She was not a 'religious person', but in the extremity of her need, she prayed 'to her "distant uncle", God,' for help, because that was how she thought of God. To the astonishment of the doctors, five days later the bones in her leg had gone back into proper alignment and the healing process could begin.

It was a long time before she was back to normal – but the world of motorcycles called and, as soon as she could, she was back in her business. In her absence her partner, Steve, had kept the business going smoothly. Steve was a different person from Jean. He was happiest getting his hands covered in prime dust or wearing a paint-spraying mask. He knew his job well and he was skilful in directing the work for all their employees.

Steve could probably have done Jean's job, although it is unlikely that she could have done his! She kept a close tab on all aspects of the business and made sure that it was efficiently and well run.

Shortly after the accident, the firm passed through great financial problems. Apart from Steve, Jean had a colleague, who was the managing director of the company. During her absence in hospital, he ran up enormous debts and the firm was on the brink of receivership and liquidation. Jean will never know how it was pulled around, but later she was to see it as the hand of God in her life. At the time, the situation was saved by careful management, and the business continues today.

Jean Lupton was born in Nottingham some forty-six years ago. Her father and mother were not particularly religious people, although her mother did teach Sunday school. 'So I had to go, didn't I?' says Jean. 'Jesus was a story-book character, and there were lots of other lovely stories we were told – but I was convinced that all the God-stuff belonged to the past. It was not relevant for us today.'

Then, one day, some Anglican nuns came to the church and talked about Jesus as though they really knew Him. That surprised Jean, because she didn't know how you could know Jesus today. 'In any case,' she says, 'when they left, it was as though they had taken Jesus with them. It was all back to normal at the Sunday school! By the time I was eleven, anything to do with church was thoroughly boring. There they used a different language and the men all wore such strange clothes!'

Her teenage years were a bad experience for her. She became pregnant when she was eighteen and, because she wanted to do 'the right thing', she married her boyfriend (the father of her baby). That marriage turned out to be a disaster. He was cruel and violent and often got in trouble with the police. 'I thought that marrying him would put it all right, but at twenty-four I left him for the sake of my life. Everything went wrong. God remained like a distant uncle to me – except when I was in trouble. Then I knew what to do. But now, I thought, I've totally failed.'

Then, when Richard, her son, started school, Jean went to work at a local hotel, where she was responsible for the conferences and promotions. She did so well that she was promoted to sales executive. It was a wonderful promotion for her, but the manager resented her success.

Through those conference bookings, however, she met a man called Mike, and she started living with him. He was into motorcycles and, although Jean had never ridden one before, she was soon hooked and was invited by BMW to a motorcycle launch at Donnington Park. 'A big event came about during that launch; it was to change the whole direction of my life,' says Jean. 'For the first time I was invited to ride – as a passenger – on a motorcycle. I had never been on such a machine before.' There were to be demonstration tests for journalists. Then afterwards she was to organise the dinner at the hotel. To her distress, the manager of her hotel would not allow her to attend the meal. But Mike had other plans.

He had the dream of running a motorcycle showroom in Long Eaton, near Derby, and he persuaded young Jean to help him. The exercise turned out to be very successful. Enthusiasts

211

could not believe that a woman could run a motorcycle dealership, but Jean was successful and so Mike decided to expand and start other showrooms. By then Jean's love for motorcycles was established; she took lessons from the RAC and learned how to ride.

Mike's vision exceeded his resources and, before long, he was heavily in debt, so that Jean lost her job as the business went into receivership. Steve (who was destined to have a long association with Jean) had been the service manager at the business and he wanted to stay on with Mike and Jean. So they started working on ideas for another business. Using his business expertise, Mike persuaded the Allied Irish Bank to advance a loan of £2,000, and 'Dream Machine' was founded.

Steve was so dedicated to the work that sometimes he didn't go home at night – even if he had a home to go to! He would curl up in a sleeping-bag on the floor of the factory. He, Mike and Jean pulled together to make a success of the venture. By then Jean had money, good holidays, nice clothes and a good car. Through it all, though, she felt that something was missing.

Then into that syndrome came astounding news from her young, seventeen-year-old brother. He had decided upon a complete turn-around in his life and announced that he had become a Christian! A month later, that news was compounded by her mother, who announced that she too had become a Christian. Jean was flabbergasted! 'Here was I, thinking that my old mum was a wonderful Christian because she had been a Sunday school teacher. Now she was telling us that all that counted for nothing. What really mattered was a personal relationship with Jesus Christ. It was all double-dutch to me, and I didn't understand it at all!

'Both of them had "got religion" and I couldn't believe it. Whenever I met them, I felt awkward and guilty in their presence. I found the whole thing hard to understand.

'Until that dreadful day in 1983. One of my salesmen, Andrew, was driving our Volkswagen delivery van. He was twenty-six years of age. In another Volkswagen van, coming towards us, was a twenty-two-year-old man. He was late meeting his girlfriend and he overtook four cars over a double white line. The last car he overtook was on a blind bend. As he came around the corner, he was right in our path and heading straight towards us. I thought, "I'm going to die".'

It was a head-on collision and Jean's legs were trapped in the wreckage. Beside her, Andrew was still and silent. Jean soon realised that he was dying. Then suddenly she remembered that they had just filled up with fuel and she was sitting over the tank. It would take a single spark and the whole lot could go up in flames. She was terrified and cried out, 'GET ME OUT!' It was at that moment that a surprising thing happened to her. She describes the sensation: 'I felt as though someone came and put arms around me and whispered in my ear "It's all right: I'm here with you." I couldn't see anything, but it felt like a warm bucket of love being poured over me and, as it happened, I passed out.'

It took the fire brigade more than an hour to cut Jean free of the wreckage. But they managed at last and she was rushed to hospital. When they examined her, the doctors shook their heads at the badly fractured leg. At one point they even considered the amputation of her leg. 'That Wednesday night,' says Jean, 'I was kept in intensive care and I stayed there all through the next day. Then on Friday morning they X-rayed me again and found that my leg was broken in at least thirty places. They said it would need a *long* operation and that it could not be done until Monday. Then, they said, they would cut the leg open, plate it, bolt it, screw it, wire it and put all the jigsaw back together again. It was then that I was informed that Andrew had been pronounced dead on arrival at the hospital.'

Monday came and Jean describes how she lay on the ITC bed, being looked over by the consultant and his team of students. 'They were like a lot of little chickens flapping around their mother hen! They talk over you as if you aren't there!' It was with a real sense of satisfaction, that Monday morning, that they found an operation was unnecessary. Jean was all

ready for the operating theatre – 'gown, socks, nil-by-mouth'
as she says – when the surgeons asked for a final X-ray.

As the consultant looked at the X-ray pictures, he exclaimed:
'I just don't understand what's happened to this lady's leg. I
can only describe it like this. Imagine a boiled sweet, in a wrapped paper, being hit by a toffee hammer and shattered. Now
it looks as though someone has picked up the two ends of the
twisted paper and pulled so hard that everything has gone back
into its rightful place. It's *amazing* – and we don't need to
operate!'

Jean takes up the story. 'As the consultant, and his inevitable
students, examined me and saw that none of their plans to
operate would be necessary, I shouted for the nurse and asked
her if what I had heard was true. She confirmed that it was
true. I felt like I'd been robbed! "What about my operation?"
I shouted!

'I rang my mum and told her what had happened. She didn't
seem at all surprised. "There were seven churches praying for
you over the weekend," she said.' So was it a coincidence that
it all happened at that particular time? 'No! I've come to believe
that it was "God-incidence"!

'While I was in hospital, Mike, with whom I had been living,
had gone wild. He virtually tried to do me out of my business,
my house, and everything I owned, except my horse – Guinness
– who became the most stable "man" in my life! I went up to
the stables early one morning after not being able to sleep for
worry. As I watched the dawn break and saw all the beautiful
colours, I cried out again, as I had in the van, "What am I going
to do?" Then that same feeling of security and peace came over
me, as though Someone cared.'

Within ten days, everything had turned around. From that
dawn experience she derived a new strength, and she determined to make a comeback. It was amazing, to her, the way
that everything fell into place: the people in Dream Machine
backed her; the bank backed her; Steve backed her. People they
owed money to said that they would back her and were

prepared to wait for their money. There were thirty-five people working in the company by then (there are sixty now). The bank manager was amazed at the accuracy of the cash-flow forecasts. Once again Jean felt as though Someone was helping her.

'When Christmas came, I had thought more about all that had happened to me, and I said to my mum: "I know that God is in all this." My life had been saved (the police said that they were amazed that I had got out of the accident alive); my leg was saved; without doubt my livelihood was saved; and I began to think what God could do if I gave it all to Him. So I started to search for God.'

First Jean tried to find the answer by going to church in Long Eaton. But church after church that she tried, left her feeling grim. She couldn't find an answer in any of the churches. 'Are you supposed to *suffer* it – or can you enjoy what God has to offer?' she thought.

Then, one day, her mum invited her to go to Sheffield to attend a meeting at which Billy Graham would be speaking. 'Here we go,' Jean thought, and the only attraction to her was that the meeting was to be held at a football stadium; that rather intrigued her. Her mum invited her to travel with her party in a church-booked bus from Long Eaton. 'On a *Saturday* night, when you're supposed to be going out and enjoying yourself?' Jean exclaimed. 'I could really think of something better to do. Anyway, I'm used to fast motorcycles, and fast cars.' So she asked, 'Why should I come?'

'To hear Billy Graham,' her mum answered.

'Well! I think my mum must have prayed,' says Jean. 'For some reason that I could not determine at the time, I accepted her invitation and found myself on the bus.' But when she saw the vehicle in which she was to travel she could hardly imagine a more decrepit bus. By today's standards it would not have been allowed on the road. 'But I was committed – so I had to go. I left behind all the things I would like to have done that Saturday night and found myself in this rickety old bus that is chugging up the motorway at forty m.p.h.! It was a case of shaking, rattling and rolling all the way – with a load of religious weirdos! I felt aggravated and wondered what insanity had prompted me to come!'

When they arrived and passed through the turnstiles, she was not prepared for what she found at the stadium. There in front of her was a crowd of around 45,000 in the packed stadium. Every seat seemed to be filled. In addition there were many thousands of chairs on the football field itself. 'There must be something about it, to have all this lot here,' she thought.

She tried to steer clear of the other members of her bus party but found herself directed, with them, to those very chairs on the pitch. She could not believe that the football stadium authorities could have been so foolish as to allow chairs on the sacred turf like that! She remembered thinking, 'What, in heaven's name, prompted this madness? Why had the Sheffield football club allowed this desecration?'

She looked around her: here she was, the managing director of a company dealing with motorcycles, sitting in this religious meeting where everyone seemed to be enjoying themselves. Nevertheless the singing was most impressive, and Jean settled down to listen.

'Billy Graham said his bit,' she recalls, 'and I can't really remember very much except when he got to the bit where he said, "If you want to commit yourself to Christ; if you want to join yourself to Jesus; if you want to be reconciled to God – then come forward and stand at the front of the platform."

'I said to my mum, "If I go forward, will you come with me?" And there I was, the managing director of this macho company, walking to the front with my mum. I felt like a little child.

'All of a sudden I was confronted by a teenager – with a clipboard – who asked me to tell her what I knew about Jesus. So I told her what I knew. She said, "You know more about Him than I do!" I replied that I knew all *about* Him but I hadn't *got* Him.

216

' "Let's say this prayer," she said, and repeated a prayer that sounded a lot to me like a wedding vow – "I'll be yours and you'll be mine . . ."

'Anyway, I said the prayer and nothing happened; nothing was changed: there were no angels flying; no bells ringing; my face was the same, and no hairs were growing on the backs of my hands! "That's it then," I thought. "It hasn't taken!"

'I walked out of the stadium and back into that old rickety bus – but suddenly it had turned into Starship Enterprise! Smooth and fast down the motorway it ran as we drove home. The people all around me were still the same people – but now they all seemed nicer and lovely!'

That all happened on 22 June 1985.

After she got back to Long Eaton, Jean resumed her search for a church. 'Someone told me about Christ Church in nearby Chilwell. So I went there, and I had the same feeling as I had had when I walked into the new Sainsbury's superstore in Beeston. "This is *good*; I like this," I thought, and I found myself enrolled in a Christian basics course. When I attended for the first time, they told me that I needed to buy a Good News Bible in order to follow the course. I tried at the local large bookshop in Long Eaton but I couldn't find any Bible – let alone a Good News Bible. All I could find anywhere was a white Bible, the sort of thing you give for a christening present – and that didn't seem very appropriate! So I borrowed my mum's Bible and took my friend Janet with me to the course. As we stood outside, plucking up courage to go in, she said, "If anyone bangs a tambourine or shouts 'Hallelujah!', we're off!"

'As we went into the room, a young man was sitting there, wearing a tracksuit, and there was an Old English Sheepdog sitting on his lap. We could hardly see him peeking out from behind the dog – but, from what we could see, he didn't look in the least bit like a vicar! At the very start he gave us a page number to find, and it was Romans 1. I remember thinking how helpful it was for him to give the page number. Then, as he read the passage, I said to myself, "This is all about today."

Previously I didn't think anything came from God unless it was in old, Shakespearean English! This Good News Bible said the same things, but in today's language. I found I couldn't wait for next week's Christian basics course *and* I was looking forward to going to church on Sunday. What a different person I was!'

As Jean listened, she began to wonder whether she had done everything backwards. First she had committed her life to Christ. Then she went to church. Then she read the Bible, and finally she prayed. It seemed to her that it should all have been the other way around.

After attending several of the Christian basics classes, she said to herself: 'OK, God, now we're getting someplace. Now it's up to You to use me!' She began to realise that, after a prayer like that, anything might happen. 'You should never pray a prayer like that unless you are ready for the unexpected to happen,' she says.

Twelve months later, almost to the day, 1 October 1986, in the middle of the night she had the inspiration to open a Christian bookshop in Long Eaton. She had remembered how impossible it was to buy a Bible in the town, let alone any other Christian books. When she awoke the next morning, the feeling was still with her, and on the way to work she called in at the newsagent's to ask about a problem with her newspaper bill.

Next door but one to the newsagent's was an empty shop with a 'For Sale' sign outside. Jean says, 'A very strong thought came into my head which said, "That's the shop." Oh dear me! I rang Mum (after all, she's got a direct line to God, hasn't she?). I asked her, "What do you do if you think God's talking to you? How do you know it's God?" After all, it could be the other one, couldn't it? It seems that God always gets a bad press. It's always the Devil that's on TV. It was Martyn Lewis who complained on TV that we never got to hear the good news. Well, I can tell you the good news – God is alive today and He wants very much to control our lives if we will let Him.

'Anyway, Mum said, "Let's pray about it. Then, when

you've prayed, you'll get confirmation from an unexpected source." That encouraged me to ask the estate agent to send me details of the shop, and they arrived in the post on Monday morning.

'I had just decided to go down to the town and look inside the shop when Steve came into my office. I told him that I was going out to look at this shop and that I was thinking of buying it with the compensation money I had received from the accident. Earlier that year, when Steve had heard that I had become a Christian, he had exclaimed: "I can't believe you're so naïve as to believe in God!"

' "What are you going to sell in that shop?" he asked me. I told him that, if I told him, it would bring him out in a rash! "Go on: try me!" he urged.

' "It's going to be a Christian bookshop," I said.

'He reacted instantly and said, "I'll go in with you on that!"

'I just couldn't believe my ears. "But Steve," I said, "it's a 'so naïve to believe in God' type of shop."

' "I know," he replied. "Come on, let's go and have a look at it."

'As we drove down the road, I thought of my mum's words – "*Unexpected source*"! What source could have been more unexpected than that?'

Steve actually borrowed £10,000 from his bank to invest in the shop. He paid the interest on that loan as well! Jean realised that Steve really had no hope of ever getting a penny back! But she felt that this was ample and adequate confirmation of her vision, and she was now *sure* that this was God's will.

The next Sunday Jean went to her church and spoke to a local disc-jockey named Simon Mayo; he attended her church regularly and was a Christian. Jean invited him to come and open the shop. He asked what date that would be and, off the top of her head, Jean said, 'The fifteenth of November.' But when she said that, it was only a date that came into her mind. Simon Mayo said he could manage that. Jean wanted to get the shop open in good time for Christmas, so she went ahead and booked advertising without so much as a thought about getting books! 'I knew all about motorcycles,' says Jean, 'but nothing at all about books.'

Then her mum introduced her to a man called Patrick. Now Patrick knew all about books. So she and Steve went around to see him at his home. As they talked, it came into Jean's mind to ask him if he would help to open the shop and be its manager.

Before he replied, he went out of the room and, when he came back a few minutes later, he was smiling all over his face.

'Where did you go?' Jean asked him.

'I went to phone the people who had been praying that you would offer me that job, and I told them they could stop praying now,' he replied.

'That group had been praying for six months for a Christian bookshop to open in Long Eaton, and I only knew about it last Thursday,' says Jean.

The solicitors told her that it would take at least six weeks for the conveyancing. She told them that she had planned for the opening to take place in less than four weeks! Then the surveyors said that the walls needed to be damp-proofed and that the windows and doors would have to be replaced before the shop would be usable.

Then the book suppliers told her that it would take at least six weeks before her account could be authorised and opened. 'In any case,' they said, 'the books you want should have been ordered last March.' Everyone kept telling them that to open on time would be an impossibility.

'But they counted without God!' says Jean. 'On the Wednesday before the Saturday opening, there was just a cement-mixer sitting in the middle of the floor. Then, as the builder pushed it out he told me that, with new plaster and cement, we could not decorate for three months.

' "But we are opening on Saturday," I said. He tut-tutted, shook his head, and walked out. On Wednesday, in the shell of the shop, there was no decorating, no carpet, no books, no lighting and no counter. I thought that I was going to look foolish on Saturday when Simon Mayo arrived. So I rang mum. "Pray!" I said!

'At lunchtime that day a man, whom I had never met in my whole life before, walked into the shop carrying overalls over his arm. He told me that he had been praying when he suddenly had this urge to come down to see if any help was needed at this new shop. "When the Lord calls you, you just have to get up and do something about it and get on with it, don't you?" he said; and he put on his overalls, got hold of some paint and . . . started painting! Many other people arrived to help, and by Wednesday night we had finished the decorating. On Thursday morning the carpets arrived. Thursday afternoon, the shelving was put in and the lighting was completed. During this period, a lot of book orders started to arrive, all the packages being delivered to the Dream Machine factory. On Friday morning we started bringing them down from the workshop and putting them on the shelves.

'That Friday night we had a small dedication service in the room above the shop. I had remembered that the compensation money had come from the accident in which Andrew had died. It seemed right, therefore, to dedicate the shop to the memory of Andrew. He had not been a Christian, nor did he have a Christian funeral. He was cremated and his parents, who were not believers, wanted no hymns and no prayers. It broke my mother's heart to feel that God meant so little to them. So I felt that, even if the shop saved just one person from dying without Jesus, then Andrew had not died in vain.

'At 10 p.m. the door opened and in walked the joiners with the newly built counter. It only just went through the door by a whisker – and there they were, muttering all the time that it was a good job it was going to be a Christian bookshop. Nothing short of a miracle would make it ready on time! It was midnight when we put the sign up over the shop, and we called it "Insight". It felt like putting the candles on the cake!

'The next morning, at ten past ten, Simon cut the tape. It

should have been at 10 a.m., but there was a ten-minute delay because the stereo speakers were still being screwed into place.

'On Saturday afternoon the joiners came in and, when they saw the lovely counter, the carpeted floor, the well-lit bookshelves and the beautiful floral decorations and they heard the stereo music, their mouths dropped – the miracle had happened!'

'Insight' was to have many unexpected ministries. For example, one day the lady at the fish-and-chip shop across the road came in to see Jean's mother (who was working as a volunteer in the bookshop). She was terribly distressed by the violence, the drug-taking and the awful language used by the teenagers from the school across the road and she said she could not take it any more. Jean heard about this and went straight away with Joan (from the fish shop) across the road to the headmaster's study. There, Joan told the headmaster about their concerns over the young people, and Jean offered the room over the shop for the use of the school Christian Union. It so happened that the window of the headmaster's study faced directly through the school gates to the Insight bookshop! As Jean spoke to him, all she could think about was that the shop had been put in exactly that place for this special purpose!

The following week, a group of girls from the Christian Union at the school were having their first meeting in the room upstairs when some boys rampaged through the shop and even went upstairs and created havoc there. They pulled down the curtains and threw sugar all over the floor. They said they would be back to do more damage the next day.

When they returned the next day, they were confronted by Jean. She was there to 'sort them out' and when the first boy came in, Jean was surprised to find that all her aggressive spirit had disappeared and she heard herself telling them that she was going to start a club for them. Only twelve would be allowed to join at a time, and she explained that there would be a membership card for each one of them. She later discovered that the boys had a respect for her because they had often seen her as she parked her 750-c.c. BMW motorcycle outside the shop. It seemed that this had impressed them greatly!

The next day, twelve of them turned up. Jean opened the room above the shop as the club room and told the boys that they had to make their own rules. She herself would only insist on one rule: 'No Smoking' – because of insurance problems with a bookshop. They themselves made up nine other rules, which included 'No swearing'! Jean felt that it was very biblical, because there were twelve people and ten rules!

She provided them with a simple lunch – and a Coke – and each day gave a little talk about God. She used the 'What's the point' booklet and, following that, she explained His plan for their lives. For fifteen months they continued to come – all boys – and she witnessed to them by every means possible. Once they came to her home and she showed them the film *The Cross and the Switchblade*, the story of Nicky Cruz, the New York gangleader. That was exactly up their street; they could identify with that, and they could appreciate the story that Nicky Cruz had to tell. Afterwards she gave each one of them a ride around the estate on her bike – and that was a real winner!

Later, Nicky Cruz came in person to Derby and Jean hired a minibus to take them all along. At the end, they all went forward to meet him. Later she also took them to a Billy Graham live-link satellite mission in Nottingham.

Over the fifteen months around twenty boys came up to the club – but never more than 12 at a time. One or two of them became Christians as a result, and none of them thereafter was any trouble to the lady across the street. As they grew up and left school, one or two of them were given jobs at Dream Machine. Some who worked there moved on to other good jobs. But it was a special ministry that started and grew up within the bookshop.

Then, as the twenty boys all left school, at the end of fifteen months, it all stopped. At any rate, the lunch club came to an end, having fulfilled an unusual ministry. As for the lady across the road, she was never troubled again by the youngsters, and she herself came to realise that there was something special in the message of 'the shop across the road'.

The first twelve months at the bookshop were very difficult and were not without their problems, but Jean felt that God would help them to overcome. Then one day, walking up an aisle in the bookshop, Jean's mother looked down at the floor and saw the pattern of the dove of peace glowing on the carpet. She looked around to see where the sunlight might be coming in to make this image – but the day outside was cloudy and dull; there was no sunlight. Nor was there any reflection from any of the inside lights. To Jean's mother it seemed like a message from God. The bookshop was there to bring peace into the lives of those who used it. At any rate, from that day onwards, everything seemed to go well and the bookshop held its own.

All the time, as Jean looked back to that one meeting at which she had heard Billy Graham in person, she grew increasingly hungry for more of God, and she wanted to learn more about Him. She found a Christian training centre in Farnham and went there for a weekend every other month for a whole year. Each weekend had a different theme, and one weekend dealt with the needs of living as a single Christian. She found that that weekend helped her beyond her wildest dreams.

She had been married and divorced at a very early age, and when she became a Christian she had asked God to give her a new partner to share her life with her. She felt that God's reply to her was that *He* would be her partner for the time being. She felt that it was His promise that a husband would eventually come along but that for the meantime she needed to trust and be patient.

Then in May 1991 it all came together. Through a remarkable series of events she met and, in May 1992, married Jonathan Lupton, a man she had met through a committee meeting on 'Church Planting' at her church.

Jean tells how, at the wedding reception, someone rushed

in to tell them to go outside – and there, across the sky, was the most vivid rainbow Jean had ever seen. 'I was reminded once again that God says, "I always keep my promises." That gorgeous rainbow stayed there for half an hour and we had our wedding photographs taken beneath it.'

Jean has said that if her life was like a television programme, then *before* she went to hear Billy Graham, it would be like a programme in black and white. *After* she found Christ at the mission, the programme had changed to glorious technicolor!

In 1995 her tenth 're-birthday' as a Christian was celebrated at a meeting in Sheffield to commemorate the tenth anniversary of the Billy Graham mission there. At the meeting she gave her testimony of what God had done in her life and they gave her a special birthday cake. She told the many hundreds of those attending how real that decision was in 1985 and the continuing thrill she had of being a Christian today.

No one can know, except God, what chain of events will be linked together once a life is committed to Him. Jean's story is but one from among the 6,172 people who responded to Billy Graham's invitation at Sheffield. Altogether 80,519 people came to Christ at Sheffield and at the 150 centres linked by the television Livelink Satellite Mission throughout the UK. Jean's prayer is that her story from that mission will lead others to a similar discovery of what Christ can do in their lives.

22

Rock Band Evangelist

Alex Bowler, England, 1989

'McKenna's Gold', one of the finest bands of the 1980s, was belting out its version of Rock 'n' Roll from the stage. With his fingers flying over the guitar strings, young Alex Bowler was well on the way to becoming Britain's fastest bass-guitar player. He loved his music. He revelled in the noise, the rock beat and the deep 'thump' of the bass.

Seven years later, from a platform in a large tent specially erected for the purpose, in the town of Taunton, a young evangelist was preaching the Gospel. He did so with all the fervency of an old-time sawdust-trail evangelist – a modern-day Billy Sunday, some were saying. His name was Alex Bowler!

The catalyst between these two diametrically different scenarios was another evangelist named Billy Graham.

Born in Matlock in the 1960s, young Alex grew up in the culture and music of a pop and permissive generation. In spite of that, he was encouraged by his parents to sing in the local church choir, and from that inauspicious beginning his love of music grew.

He was eleven years old when he attended a children's mission in his Taunton Church. The mission was led by an evangelist from the Scripture Union whose name was John Inchley. One evening, when the opportunity was given, young Alex was among those who prayed the prayer to become a Christian.

'I did not really understand what it was all about,' says Alex. 'I thought it simply meant that I should love my enemies and that, as a Christian, this should show in my life. I thought it also meant that I accepted the fact that Christ was alive and that I should now follow His example.'

Without any *power* in his life to do that, these standards were hard for Alex to keep and live by. He was trying to be a Christian in his own strength, and he soon found out that this did not work, and he failed miserably.

The love of music that had first been instilled through his choir activities began to develop and grow. It was inevitable that his taste should move into the area of modern rock – for that was the sound which excited him and captured his attention. During his fourteenth year he started to play the guitar. He especially loved the bass guitar with its throaty and sensual sound. Later the same year he was good enough to start playing with groups.

When he reached the age of sixteen, Alex left Wellington School, where he had been a pupil, and went to the Somerset College of Arts and Technology to do A-levels in English and History. At Wellington School he was notorious for the part he had once played in a school play: he had been cast as an angel and was supposed to throw an imitation trident at the devil. Prophetic? The climax was supposed to come as the devil disappeared down through the stage trapdoor. Unfortunately, the trapdoor closed more quickly than Alex had expected and the trident glanced off the stage and was deflected into someone sitting in the front row of the audience!

When it came to careers counselling at school, he lasted only a few minutes with his counsellor, who gave up in desperation. He could find no way of advising this addict of rock music who declared his purpose was to become a star in the Rock 'n' Roll firmament!

Alex gave all his spare time to the rock world, from his teens into his twenties. During that time he played in many different rock groups and he became more competent with every day that passed. His object and target was to become the best bass-guitar player in the world!

One day Alex contacted Ted McKenna. Ted was considered to be one of the best rock drummers in the world, and Alex hoped to learn something from him. To his delight, Ted invited Alex, with a guitar-playing friend named Julian, to form a band with him. That band was to become known as McKenna's Gold.

Alex was on cloud nine! He really thought he had made it in the rock world. It was more than he could ever have hoped for, and the pinnacle of all that he had done in rock so far.

While returning to Penzance from a rehearsal at Ted's house in Suffolk, Alex met a girl on the train who was also deeply into rock. It was 'love at first sight' and, before long, an intense, romantic relationship developed between them.

Twelve months later that relationship broke up, but Alex became very lonely and wanted to see her again. He travelled across London to a rock disco he knew of, in order to find her. And there she was! Looking across the smoky room, Alex saw her in a passionate embrace with another man and he realised his whole life was in a mess and that he needed to make a change.

Three days later, Alex passed a Christian bookshop and decided to take a look inside. On the tape display rack he saw a tape by Cliff Richard entitled 'Walking in the Light'. He persuaded the bookshop owner to put the tape on so that he could hear it. Halfway through the second side was a song all about relationships, 'You and Me and Jesus'. Alex started to read the inner sleeve of the cassette as tears welled up in his eyes. The sleeve contained a very moving story about a girl who lived in a caravan and who became a Christian.

'My ex-girlfriend lived in a caravan, too!' says Alex. 'I knew that God had led me into that shop and guided me to that tape. So I bought the tape and went back to my flat. I found I could not listen to the songs without weeping as I became over-whelmed with a sense of God's love for me.'

Alex was so moved with love and compassion for his ex-girlfriend that he drove across London to tell her that God loved her too.

Several days later, on a hoarding, he saw a big poster with the word 'L.I.F.E.' on it. In fact it was the last of a series of posters which had been part of a 'teaser' campaign. The earlier posters had mixed up the letters – each poster leading the reader closer to an understanding of their message. The posters were telling about a series of meetings to be conducted in various venues around London by Billy Graham.

At around the same time, Alex saw Billy Graham being interviewed on television by Terry Wogan. Billy Graham spoke with confidence and assurance when he said he *knew* he was going to go to heaven because he knew the Lord Jesus Christ as his Saviour. That interview made a deep impression on Alex.

He made some enquiries and discovered that Billy Graham would be at Upton Park in West Ham, east of London. He decided to go to one of the meetings. On that first occasion he was struck especially by the *joy* on the faces of all the people around him. He was particularly moved by the worship segment of the songs before Mr Graham stood up to speak. The music was his tempo and appealed to him.

He was riveted by the preaching of Billy Graham, but he did not respond to the invitation to go to the front. He just felt he wasn't ready to take such a step.

Alex decided that he must go and hear Billy Graham preach again, and the next venue was to be the Crystal Palace in south London. On the night he chose, there was a major bus, tube and train strike in London, so it was a struggle to get there. Rather like the story in the Gospels of the sick man whose friends stopped at nothing to bring him to Jesus, Alex was determined to get to Crystal Palace and to let no obstacle come between him and his objective – little knowing that the outcome would be a total change of direction for his life.

So, difficult as it was, he nevertheless made it – along with more than 30,000 others who had also beaten the strike to assemble the largest crowd that the Crystal Palace had ever seen.

As Billy Graham stood up to preach, Alex found himself compelled to listen. 'As I listened to him,' says Alex, 'it all became clear. That night I too *knew* that Christ had died for me. I believed in my heart that God had raised Him from the dead, and the message became real to me. I knew I needed Jesus as my Lord and Saviour.

'When Billy Graham gave his invitation to come to the front, I immediately walked down the steps, and there I stood, near the front of the great crowd. As I stood there, I knew that I was a lost sinner who needed to repent. Strange thinking for a rock musician! I remember hanging my head down as I realised the purity of Jesus and the depth of darkness in my own life. I just wanted to give my whole life to Jesus Christ.

'Other people were still streaming forward and Billy Graham was scanning the crowd. At one point, it seemed, he was staring directly at me. As he did so, God spoke in my heart. I looked into Mr Graham's face and I saw that he had tears in his eyes. I found that I had tears in my eyes too.

'Then, like a lightning-bolt, I received a command from God: "*You are to preach the Gospel.*" It seemed unbelievable, but it was very real to me.'

As people stopped coming forward, Billy Graham spoke to those who were already there. Then he asked them all to bow their heads in prayer and commitment and to confess Jesus as Lord. 'I felt completely free and I *knew* I had been forgiven,' says Alex. 'I was filled with a feeling of joy and peace. Billy Graham said that I had been given eternal life, and I believed that. In short I was Born Again!

'As everyone else left the stadium at the end of the meeting, I stood rooted to the spot. I stared at the podium and said (in prayer), "Lord, please use *me* in that way." It was the first prayer I ever made after I had prayed the sinners' prayer.'

Alex never knew how that prayer would be answered. But it was answered – and almost immediately! Alex came home with a new love in his heart. The love for Rock'n'Roll had not gone – but it was replaced with a new and stronger love. He still loved his music, but he loved the Lord Jesus Christ more, and wanted to tell everyone about Him.

Then the opportunities to evangelise started to arrive. Very soon Alex found himself reaching all sorts of people in a variety of situations. In 1994 he was the evangelist at a tent mission in his home town of Taunton. The highlight of those meetings was the night that his sister and his mother came to the front to accept Christ after Alex had preached. For him it was the seal upon his ministry and upon the call that God had made to him.

Now he has been invited to join the Evangelization Society, to be their evangelist in the south-west of England. He has much to learn and is open to the leading of the Spirit of God in his life and in the opportunities that have been given to him.

Is he an evangelist? Is his call real? In the course of the implementation of his call, he sought counsel and advice from another Christian who had been 'on the road' for many years.

On the day they met the older man gave two hours of his time to Alex before he had to leave for another appointment. That appointment was with a specialist in Harley Street.

When the two hours were up, Alex was given a choice. 'We can either say farewell here and now, or you can, if you wish, ride with me in the car to my next appointment.' Alex chose to ride along.

On arrival at Harley Street a parking meter was soon found. Then another choice confronted him. 'You can either sit here in the car or you can, if you wish, come and sit in the waiting room at the specialist's.' Alex chose the second option, and together they walked up the street to the consulting rooms.

As it happened, the specialist was ready immediately, and the older man disappeared upstairs for his consultation. Returning to the waiting room half an hour later, it was a surprise to discover that Alex was talking to all the people in the waiting room about Christ and was handing out tracts all around.

That urgency of purpose is the mark of a true evangelist. It is the sort of commitment that Billy Graham has always had – persuaded in his life that he had a call from God to proclaim the Gospel, whenever possible and wherever he found himself. That was the true purpose of his life. The true evangelist cannot allow an opportunity to slip by. Every minute must be capitalised for the Lord.

Looking back to those days when he played an angel in the school play, Alex today uses a weapon of a different kind, but this one is totally undeflected, effective, accurate, and sharper than any two-edged sword – the Word of God.

In 1993 he took a decision to trust the Lord for his living and become a full-time evangelist. He founded and formed – with others – 'Salvation UK', a charitable trust which would direct his work under God. The Trust had three objectives: to preach the Gospel to this nation; to work alongside other Christian organisations to pray for the salvation of the lost; and to take the Gospel to the world as the Lord directs.

The last purpose has already been implemented, as Alex has taken the Gospel to Romania and to the streets of New York, and openings continue to come.

Jill Warford – a girl of about the same age as Alex – had gone with him to the meeting when he felt led to start his ministry in Salvation UK. She offered to pray for him and to help him in that work. By profession she was a chartered accountant and her skills were invaluable to him. She was a great support to him too in his ministry, and in 1995 they were married at Taunton. The scripture in Deuteronomy 32:30 had a very real meaning to them: 'If one can chase a thousand, then two can put ten thousand to flight!' Other support in his ministry comes from his friends, Sean and Regia Jenvey. They have already spent some time ministering in Brazil.

Alex and Jill now live in a lovely home with beautiful views across the Quantock Hills, close to Taunton. It provides for them a sanctuary from the rough and tumble of an evangelist's life.

Billy Graham cannot have known what a chain of events he was starting as, unconsciously, he allowed his glance to fall on Alex Bowler from the platform at the Crystal Palace.

23
Not Easy to Respond

Dr Ian Oliver, Scotland, 1991
It was an electronics exam which made all the difference! The young Ian Oliver had not been very successful at school – indeed he had failed his eleven-plus examination – and this did not portend much hope for the future.

It was true that he had gained the prize for 'the best tryer' but never for 'the best achiever'! In fact he imagined that the prize was simply intended as an encouragement to him – a sort of 'wooden spoon' consolation-prize for the person who came in last. Therefore he did not expect anything great to happen to him when the time came for him to leave school.

So he joined the Royal Air Force and trained to become part of an aircrew. But even that did not bring him any achievement or any sense of credit. In his own words he says: 'They felt that I would be better playing the piano than flying aeroplanes!' Perhaps they had some regard for the people above whom he might be flying!

But he had a father who *had* achieved – and Ian was very proud of him. His father was in the police force and, during the Barnes train disaster, had been awarded the George Medal. Young Ian was bursting his buttons over that achievement. His father actually had to go to Buckingham Palace to receive that award, and that day was a highlight for the family.

For Ian, however, failure was a big thing in his life. In order to continue his flying training, he had to pass an exam in electronics. Now Ian knew next to nothing about electronics. The subject had been a closed book to him, although the RAF had done its level best to try to teach him. Now he was faced with this exam and with the assurance that, to continue his aircrew training (and later to do well outside the RAF), he needed some sort of certificate or qualification. The RAF assured him that this was the best way.

From Friday night to Sunday afternoon Ian struggled with textbooks, trying to learn all that he had missed in the subject of electronics. He had the proverbial 'cold towel round his head' and tried to grapple with this totally unintelligible subject. He read and read; he looked at diagram after diagram and followed example after example – until suddenly, at 3 p.m., it all became clear! All the hours of devotion to the study had finally produced a result. Unbelievably, the subject became easy, and he sailed through the exam with flying colours.

From that experience he learned that, if you can really apply yourself to a problem, the chances are that you will be able to solve it – and this became his philosophy throughout his life.

He had been born in Isleworth on the outskirts of London, so he was essentially 'a Londoner'. He was not a religious man, although, from time to time (almost on a regular basis), he did attend church. He also had a friend who was more deeply into Christian matters and encouraged Ian to go with him to his youth club.

'They were teaching us archery there,' Ian said. 'We learned how to pick up the bow and nock the arrow. We learned how to stand sideways on to the target, and to aim at the gold bull's-eye. They showed me how you aim at a point, slightly above the point of the arrow, in order to hit the gold. This allowed for the trajectory of the arrow. But what really threw me was the way in which they were likely to throw a text from the Bible at you – just as you were trying to nock the arrow!'

To Ian it seemed strange that there should – or could – be any connection between archery and being told – at the moment the arrow went 'ping' on its way to the target – 'Behold I stand at the door and knock. If any man hears my voice and opens the door, I will come in and sup with him and he with me.' It left him rather confused, and he found these people to be a little strange!

That did not stop him, however, from accepting an invitation from his friend to go with him to Wembley Stadium one evening, where a fiery young preacher called Billy Graham was holding a series of meetings. Ian's recollection of that night was that it was pouring with rain. But that did not stop him listening to – and remembering – what the preacher had to say. Thirty-six years later he was to meet the preacher in person and he reminded him that, at Wembley in 1955, he had preached from 2 Corinthians 5:20: 'We implore you on Christ's behalf: be reconciled to God.' That message stuck with him over the years, although, at the time, it did not have any immediate effect. He watched as thousands of people responded to an invitation from the evangelist to 'get up out of your seat and come and stand here at the front' as an indication of their desire to follow Christ. This they did – despite the rain – and there they were met by a team of counsellors.

Countless thousands of those counsellors have cause to remember that week-long crusade when, most evenings, the heavens opened and the rain came down! They have treasured Bibles, still damp-marked from the rain. Some of them covered their Bibles with plastic – or held plastic over themselves and their enquirer – in order to protect themselves, their Bibles and their literature from the worst of the elements. But Ian stayed firmly in his seat, high up in the stadium.

After leaving the RAF he joined the police force. He did well and soon progressed in the work he was given. First he served in London, where he has one of his most graphic memories of what the life of a policeman can be all about. He had become an inspector in the force by that time when, one day, he had a call at 2 a.m. to a block of flats in Limehouse. 'I was told that the ambulance service would be there waiting for me – but I was not given any other information. When I arrived at the location, the front door stood open but there was no sign of the ambulance.

236

'So I went in through the open door and was met by an old man and an old woman. Cocking her thumb over her shoulder, the woman said simply: "She's in tha'." I followed the direction she indicated and entered the room, to find a young lady lying on the bed, totally naked except for a light-blue bra (I can't think why that light-blue bra stuck in my mind)! But as I looked at her, I could see the head of a baby emerging and on the point of birth. Obviously there was no time to do anything else, and for the first time in my life I found myself delivering a baby boy!

'At that moment the ambulance service arrived and it was all over! By then it was really me who needed their attentions rather than the girl! Just as I was leaving, having handed the care of the young lady to the ambulance service, she grabbed my arm and asked (in broad cockney), "Wot's yer name?" I told her it was Ian. "Naw. Don' like that. I'll call 'im Jason!" That was in 1972. I've often wondered what happened to Jason after that!'

From London Ian Oliver moved on to Northumberland and then to central Scotland; in 1990 came a move further north to Aberdeen where, despite that eleven-plus failure of earlier years, he became Chief Constable of the prestigious Grampian Police Force!

When you are Chief Constable it is hard to live a private life. Indeed, whatever you do is high-profile and tends to become public knowledge – especially when you do something as public as going forward at a Billy Graham mission!

Thirty-six years after attending the crusade meeting in Wembley Stadium, Ian Oliver (now Dr Ian Oliver) was again in the orbit of Billy Graham when the evangelist arrived in 1991 to conduct a mission in Aberdeen. This time there was no escaping! This was partly because his police force had duties in the stadium, but it was also because, as a VIP in the city, he had received an invitation to a reception which included a ticket to attend the meeting.

Billy Graham gave a powerful message. At the conclusion

he gave his usual invitation to his listeners to leave their seats and come out to stand in front of the platform. In Aberdeen it was both cold and wet but, once again, this did not deter those who wanted to go forward.

Ian Oliver sensed a movement at his side as his wife rose to her feet and started towards the front. Without so much as a moment's thought, he also rose and walked by her side to the front. It was a public witness that could not, and did not, pass without local comment. For him, the move was rather more to support his wife than a personal response to the evangelist's message but, when he got to the front, he too received the literature given to those who had responded.

Ian Oliver told me: 'I was aware that you could not be a part-time Christian. You either *do* or *don't* believe. I found that I had many questions in my mind – many of which have still not been resolved. But I know that, as I made that commitment at the mission in Aberdeen, it was a real commitment from which there could be no turning back. In my heart of hearts I knew I now *did* believe and that this fact would make a difference in my life.'

For him it was the culmination of years of peripheral involvement in Christian affairs. He and his wife had been regular attenders at church. Denomination was not as important to him as a church that had a lively spirit and a commitment to the truth. As a result, this led to a diluted acceptance of things Christian, but until he attended the Aberdeen mission he was without any real commitment himself. However, the meeting in Aberdeen made a sufficient impression upon him to make him think about the Bible and to consider its message.

During the years between the time he went to Wembley and the mission in Aberdeen, he had often turned back to the Bible for guidance. He adopted one or another of the many 'Bible reading plans' to help him read through the sixty-six books and, in so doing, read through the Bible about ten times. He says: 'At first I used to read the Authorised (King James) version. The language was beautiful – quite Shakespearean –

but it seemed so remote from today's life. More recently I have started using the New International Version, and that has made the Bible come alive.'

As he read through the Bible like this, questions started to arise in his mind. Many of them he could not resolve. There were places where the Bible seemed to be full of contradictions: there were some claims that he found hard to justify in the light of his experience. Nevertheless he felt that to read the Bible was like providing himself with 'an insurance policy'. 'It was almost,' he says, 'as if I was using it as a spectator rather than a participant. I have recently learnt that participation is so much more satisfying than being a spectator!'

Then came that visit to the mission in 1991. No longer was it possible to escape from the reality of a Christian experience. What happened was not a life-shattering change nor an occasion when he heard 'voices from God'. Nor was it a dramatic conversion in which he had turned from a life without God to a complete understanding of all that God had done for him.

As Chief Constable he could not have been a more prominent enquirer. His faith was sternly tested after his response because there were those who wanted him to 'declare himself'. He was not – and is not – ready to take such a step. There is much that he still needs to fit into place, but he himself knows why he went forward and the change that it has already made to his life.

One of the things that worried Ian Oliver soon after his attendance at the Aberdeen meetings was the immediate flurry of invitations to speak that came to him from churches and groups all over Aberdeen. He found it difficult to respond because, in his own mind, he knew that in many ways he was still searching. He needed to let the message evolve in his life. He needed to ensure that he had not taken the step simply to provide that 'insurance policy' for the future. In any case, there were still major questions in his mind that he had not resolved satisfactorily. There were questions about the Bible; questions about sin; questions about the future life; questions about heaven and hell; and, above all, a need to understand exactly what God meant in his life.

Since his commitment at Aberdeen he had regularly read Billy Graham's monthly magazine, *Decision*. 'My problem is,' he says, 'that most of the stories stop short of recording the real facts of life. There are many testimonies which are printed in the magazine, but so many of them simply tell how God met a particular need without continuing to show that, for the Christian, "everything in the garden is *not* always lovely". The stories leave us on a high point, without going on to say that a Christian too may face tragedies, doubts, anxieties, even sin. I needed to know how to cope with those also.'

He continues: 'I see the most important part of my commitment as translating into my policing the philosophy of my Christian life. Having made a commitment myself, my life has become so much more difficult. Once you have accepted Christ and His sacrifice for you, you can't fool yourself any more. I am aware of how vulnerable I am and open to that extra criticism which follows a person from whom much is expected.'

In some ways, his position as Chief Constable has been his 'thorn in the flesh'. Indeed, soon after his commitment to Christ he was invited to take part in a BBC Radio 4 programme entitled *Thorn in My Flesh*. The implication of the programme was that even important people had a problem with which they had to cope. Ian Oliver described how, for him, the public perception of himself as Chief Constable made it an added burden to life when the public also knew that he had gone forward at Billy Graham's mission.

'My very vulnerability,' he says, 'has become that thorn in the flesh. Nevertheless I seek to let my Christian faith direct me in my policing. For example there are those in the police force who regard God as the "great policeman in the sky". That is, of course, far from the truth. I see Him as a Father leading me away from sin to a life of greater fulfilment. My policing philosophy which I have adopted over the years, is to believe that, whenever it is possible and appropriate, it is better to educate than to enforce. There are times when education is better than prosecution. My faith has some bearing on that, for God is not the God of the periphery. If He is to be involved at the centre of my life, then He will help me to a more effective life in which I can try to measure up to what He wants.

'I'm not sure,' he continues, 'from my inadequate reading of the Bible, whether I understand all that God is trying to say to me. Nor do I understand all the other things that the Bible has to say – for example, about heaven and hell. Is there one or the other? Are we consigned to a future life of glory – or annihilation? I'm not sure if I want to sit on a cloud all day and play a harp! I don't understand about all these things. There is so much more to learn.

'Just recently, in our area, they held a course called "the Alpha course", and I went along to see if it would help me to resolve some of these problems. As I listened to all that was being said, I felt led to act as the "devil's advocate"! I found that, in such a situation, as in others that I have faced since 1991, there was no real answer to the question "*From all that I have been told, what is there to persuade me to come again?*" They really didn't give an answer to that – but if we, as Christians, are to make an impact on the world, we *must* have an answer to that question.

'One other thing about Christians has worried me – especially those who are recently converted. Some of them demonstrate an almost extreme arrogance after their conversion. I am sure that they do not know the harm they do to others. All of us are vulnerable and most of us continue seeking, even after our commitment. That is certainly my experience, and I find it difficult to cope with those who display that arrogance.'

There are some for whom it seems that God has a computer card which He puts into their lives. From the moment of their conversion the change is dramatic, complete and final. For some, it is as though they had already been committed Christians all their lives. To some, even the Scriptures may seem like an open book, while for others there are parts which seem incomprehensible. Some of the most effective Bible teachers today are those who were recently converted and who seem to know what the Bible says and how to get the message across. Harvey Thomas has written a book entitled *If They Haven't Heard It . . . You Haven't Said It*. If we are to communicate the message of the Bible, we must be sure that those who listen to us understand what we are trying to say. If they don't, then all our efforts to communicate are worthless.

Ian Oliver is a great communicator. He has to be as Chief Constable! No room for errors there! There's a saying in the Royal Navy: 'Ninety-eight per cent of the world's problems arise through a lack of proper communication.' But, like a computer, it is what is fed in that comes out: 'garbage in . . . garbage out'. Unlike those new Christians who seem to have that 'computer card' inserted by God, it was not like that for him. No 'computer card' for him! Rather it was, and still is, an uphill struggle to work out the programme of life and to bring all the bytes together! God is speaking to him and the programme *is* working, even though it still has many 'bugs' in it which need to be debugged! Living the Christian life as a Chief Constable is not easy. He is always open to the jibe: 'And I thought you were a Christian!'

If he is asked the question: 'Was it all worth it?', he replies: 'I am now able to say that I *am* a Christian. However weak I may be, nevertheless I know that my commitment was real. Now I am prepared to admit to that publicly, and that alone has made a difference to my life. Perhaps one of my greatest benefits is the many opportunities which come to me in normal life to express my faith. I find that I can often refer to it quite naturally in any talk I am giving. And people are prepared to accept it from me. I get lots of openings to speak on radio and television programmes and, while I cannot give an overt testimony in all of these, I can – and do – make it clear from time to time that my daily philosophy is based entirely upon a committed Christian experience.'

He has discovered that such a philosophy adds a dimension to life that he wishes others could experience. As Chief Constable he cannot be an overt evangelist! But he can, through his life, reflect the faith that he holds. It is implicit in all he does – not that he always does it right. But he strives after that degree of excellence which commends him to others, both in his position as Chief Constable and as a committed Christian.

24

A U-turn

Helen Douglas, Scotland, 1995

Twenty-nine stories thus far, spanning a period of almost fifty years, from 1949 to 1996. Through all of them the constant 'line' has been the ministry of Billy Graham, which has so influenced the lives of every one of them. But what about now . . . and the future? Has it an effect on today's generation?

Young Helen Douglas is a horse-riding addict. Basically nothing was wrong with her world. She loved her horses and tried to get a ride whenever she could. One day, on the beach, her horse was enjoying the freedom of the wide open spaces when, suddenly, it threw back its head and galloped off. 'It was an ecstatic experience,' said Helen, who hung on for dear life. She was not all that experienced, but she knew enough to let the horse have its head and to try, by all means, to stay in the saddle.

Of course it was dangerous. If she had been thrown, she might have been maimed for life – or even killed. It was one of the events in her life that made her aware of the tenuous thread by which life exists. Lately she had been thinking about more lasting matters relating to life. In some way her experience on the beach complemented her search for its true meaning.

In 1995 Billy Graham conducted a crusade in Puerto Rico which was carried by satellite to over 180 countries around the world, and in more than fifty different languages. The set-up was a marvel of modern-day technology, originally conceived, a few years earlier, in the fertile brain of electronics engineer David C. Rennie. He had masterminded the very first satellite transmissions from Sheffield in Yorkshire in 1985. It was used again from Earls Court during the Greater London Mission of 1989.

Since then the use of satellites for Billy Graham's ministry has expanded across the whole world; regionally into the Far East, South America and Europe, this modern technology had been pressed into service to carry the Gospel. It was a natural extension of those projects that, from a single location, *the whole world* should be covered in one series of transmissions.

One of the locations (out of some 150 which were used in the UK), was the little village of Crossford, a short distance from the Royal Borough of Lanark – the biggest market town in that part of Scotland.

Helen Douglas and her family lived in Lanark, and Crossford was not far away and was accessible to them. Mr Douglas senior, who was a builder in everyday life, was not a regular churchgoer, but Mrs Douglas was an elder in the Church of Scotland. So Helen and her older sister, Jill, were taken along to the church by Mum whenever she felt they should be there.

Mrs Douglas taught French and German at the local school, so she was aware of language differences. What she didn't understand was that the different language of the church was virtually incomprehensible to her – almost – twenty-first-century daughters.

'Boring it was,' says Helen. There was not much to inspire her. 'The Church of Scotland was not the liveliest place we ever went to. Even the hymns were boring,' she says, 'they were so monotonous, and the music was very staid and dull.'

Sister Jill, however (currently at university, training to become a dentist), had found something rather different in 1989. In that year she had been taken to a satellite relay of the Billy Graham mission from Earls Court. As she sat and watched that programme, she found herself responding to what the evangelist said. When it came to the end, Billy Graham invited those who wanted to accept Christ as Saviour to come to the front. 'Stand in front of the television screen wherever you are watching this programme,' he said, and Jill was one of those who responded. It was a very real thing to her, and from then on she wanted to live a more effective life for Christ.

In 1991 she had her first (and only) opportunity to see Billy Graham in person. During the Scottish mission of that year, Billy Graham came to Celtic Park, in Glasgow, and Jill made sure she was one of those who attended.

Like so many before her, once Jill had become a Christian, the services in the church became much more easy to understand. She found them geared, generally, to the older population, but there was a lively youth group attached to the church and she became involved in that.

Four years later she heard about the global mission with Billy Graham being beamed by satellite from Puerto Rico. She discovered that a party from the youth group in Lanark were planning to go to the satellite relay at nearby Crossford.

She knew that her younger sister Helen, still at school, had not experienced what she had experienced. When Jill had found Christ, it had made such a difference to her life. So she invited Helen to go with her to hear Billy Graham by satellite. Helen says: 'I'd heard about Billy Graham from Jill, and had seen something about him on the news. I thought I'd like to go and see what it was all about.

'Although I was, sort of, eager to go, I just hoped that I would not fall asleep. I had expected to find it rather boring.'

The thing that impressed Helen about the programme was the music. 'It put me in a good mood to listen,' she says. 'It was so different from what we had in church.'

Helen was captivated as Billy Graham spoke. She listened to him carefully. Above all she was impressed with the forceful way in which he spoke and the obvious air of authority in his presentation. Billy Graham's sermon was on the subject of the Cross.

'Let's think about the cross. Crucifixion was one of the

most terrible of all deaths. It was used by the Romans to execute criminals. Jesus was held in a guardhouse. Then they brought Jesus out of the guardhouse with two other condemned men. A crown of thorns was put upon His head. A few of His friends were there. And the crowd was yelling, "He saved others, Himself He cannot save." The real suffering of Jesus was far more than that. He was suffering, because He was carrying your sins and my sins.

'If you were the only person in the whole world, He would have died because He knows you and He's watched you from the moment you were born. And He says, "I love you." When you're young, you have a tender conscience. The older you get and the further away from God you get, the more dead your conscience becomes. And, after a while, you may have a dead conscience.

'God is saying tonight, from the cross, "I love you. I want you to come to me. I will put my arms of love around you. I will help you solve your problems. I will forgive your sins. I will give you peace and joy and happiness that you've never known if you surrender to my Son, Jesus, on the cross." '[1]

Helen was thinking deeply as she listened, and she felt that, in many ways, Billy Graham was speaking directly to her. Then the evangelist came to the end of his address:

'You have another chance to make a choice. Make it tonight. Jesus said, "Not everyone that sayeth unto me, 'Lord, Lord,' shall enter the kingdom of heaven. But he that doeth the will of my Father, which is in heaven." You can say, "Lord, I try to live by the Sermon on the Mount. I'm not a real bad person." But God says we've all sinned. We all need to come to the cross and repent of our sins. Now what about you? I'm going to ask you to do something that we've seen hundreds of people do.

I'm going to ask you to get up and come. Quickly, right now. You may never have another moment like this when you are so close to the Kingdom of God. You come.'

In some ways, Jill was a little disappointed with the end of the meeting, because when it came to that invitation from Billy Graham, no one moved. And because no one moved, neither did Helen. Jill was praying hard but she was not, apparently, to see the response from Helen she had hoped and prayed for.

With a slightly heavy heart, she and Helen returned to Jill's car and started the drive home to Lanark. They had not gone far – in a silence that seemed to overwhelm them – when Helen turned to Jill and said, 'I thought I should have gone forward tonight!'

Glancing in the rear-view mirror, Jill saw that the road behind was clear. She spun the wheel hard over and did a U-turn to take Helen straight back to the church.

When they got back, most of the people were still in the hall behind the church, having a cup of coffee. It took but a minute or two for Jill to locate a friend and to hand Helen over to a trained counsellor. There and then, on that memorable evening, Helen committed her life to Christ and became a Christian.

It was almost as if God had taken out that computer card in her life and replaced it with another. Her whole life was changed from then on, and she had different desires, a different outlook, different friends and a different ambition.

Indeed, on the way home afterwards, she and Jill were driving behind a car which had an Ichthus Fish sign on the back of it. Helen remarked: 'It's nice to see that Christian sign on a car, and to remember that it dates right back to the ancient days in old Rome.'

Soon afterwards she was able to go with other young people to Carberry Towers. It was a Church of Scotland retreat and conference centre. There she learned many things about her newfound faith, and she began to grow as a Christian. 'Since I became a Christian,' says Helen, 'life has been so much more fulfilling – and I've been happy so much of the time. It's really wonderful.'

It was there, also, that she met Iain, a young man, himself a Christian, with whom she became very friendly, and whom today she counts as her boyfriend. 'It was nice to have someone to share with,' she says. 'I believe God sent him along just at the right time.'

In some ways she gets so excited about the new fellowship she has with other young Christians that she gets herself into trouble. Some of them came to stay at her home for a cousin's wedding. There were too many to accommodate in the house, so three of them – including Helen – slept in a tent in the garden.

In a fit of exuberance she went to dash out of the house on her way to the tent, not remembering that there was a glass door between her and the garden. She bumped into it at speed, and found herself stunned and lying, flat out, in the room. She had only just recovered from that when, walking along the street outside her home, she walked slap-bang into a lamp-post, not once but *twice*! She came to the conclusion that she must not be so heavenly-minded if she was to avoid damaging herself by earthly hazards!

She and Iain have tried to do things together that help them grow in their faith. So they went off to Meltdown: a music festival a bit like Greenbelt, but held indoors.

The future depends upon her grades at school. If she can, Helen would like to become a speech therapist but, if that door is closed to her, she is greatly interested in drama. So she will try to get into a drama school. If all else fails, her interest would lie in hairdressing.

Whatever course her life takes, she is sure of one thing: it will be hand in hand with Jesus Christ as her Guide and Stay – thanks to that satellite ministry by Billy Graham, which led to a U-turn, so changing her life. She is one of the next generation who will carry on among her peers to witness to the power of Christ.

Almost fifty years? Yes! The message that Billy Graham has preached consistently throughout all that period has affected many lives. Those whose stories have been told in this book are but a selection of many tens of thousands whose stories could be told. 'And they all lived happily ever after?' No, not always! Becoming a Christian is no guarantee that you will be insulated against the problems and difficulties – and, indeed, tragedies – that affect all the human race. In those times, you have a power, a strength, a *Person* – the Lord Jesus Christ who, through the power of His Holy Spirit will meet you in your extremity and help you through.

That would be the testimony of those who have already passed on – like Stuart Hamblen. Those who are still active in the ministry – like Peter Pearmain – would testify that Christ is real in the lives of those committed to Him. There are those who have inspired countless thousands of others both to commit their lives to Christ and to serve Him in their daily lives – like George Verwer. There are those who are nearing the end of their lives – like the evangelist himself. But, thank God, there are countless thousands who have a lifetime before them. God alone knows what plans He has for them – like Helen Douglas. And, among them, may even be a 'Billy Graham' upon whom God will lay His hand for the next generation. His ways are past finding out!

Now you have read these stories, it is appropriate to apply them to your own life. It may be that one or another of the stories has reflected your own need and the emptiness in your own life. Billy Graham says that to come to Christ needs only three simple steps:

A – Admit that you are a sinner in the sight of God.
B – Believe that Jesus Christ came to suffer and die, to pay the penalty of *your* sins – both past, present and future – and realise that through His death He has made

it possible for God to forgive you your sins.
C – Commit yourself to God, through Jesus Christ, and
to give your life to Him.

A simple prayer (like this) can help you to take that step:

Oh, God! I am a sinner.
I repent of my sins, and I am sorry for my sins.
I will turn from my sins
And I turn to you.
Cleanse me from my sins, Lord,
And put your Power within, Lord,
For the sake of Jesus Christ Your Son,
Amen.

If you want further help as a Christian, you can write to:

Billy Graham, Minneapolis, Minnesota, USA

25

The Greatest News Ever Heard

A Message from Billy Graham
Christ has risen from the dead. And because He lives, we who
know Him shall live also. In the resurrection Jesus Christ
conquered sin and death, and is alive for ever more. All over
the world, churches are filled with worshippers because there
is an empty tomb in Jerusalem.

We worship a risen, living Saviour, who has promised to
give immortality to all who believe on His name. No longer
do men and women need to stumble in the fog and the darkness
of hopelessness. A Light shines brighter than the noonday sun,
offering hope to everyone who has been born again. Jesus
promised, 'I am the resurrection, and the life: he that believeth
in me, though he were dead, yet shall he live: And whosoever
liveth and believeth in me shall never die.'[1]

Long ago Job asked, 'If a man die, shall he live again?'[2] We
expect death, but we always have a glimmer of hope that
medical science will discover something that will keep us alive
a little longer.

Death carries with it a certain dread. From the day that Abel
was killed, people have dreaded death. It has been the enemy,
the great, mysterious monster, that makes people quake with
fear.

In a discussion of death the Bible always links sin and death.
That is why the Bible says that 'the sting of death is sin'.[3] The
Bible also says that 'sin came into the world through one man
and death through sin, and so death spread to all men because
all have sinned'.[4]

Death stalks the rich and the poor, the educated and the

uneducated. Death is no respecter of race, colour or creed. Its shadow haunts us day and night. We never know when the moment of death will come for us.

Is there any hope? Is there a possibility of immortality?

I take you to an empty tomb in the garden of Joseph of Arimathea. Mary, Mary Magdalene and Salome had gone to anoint the body of the crucified Christ. They had been startled to find the tomb empty. An angel sat on the stone by the door of the tomb and said, 'I know that ye seek Jesus.'[5] Then the angel said, 'He is not here: for He is risen.'[6]

The greatest news that mortal ear has ever heard is the news that Jesus Christ has risen from the dead as He had promised. The resurrection of Jesus Christ is the chief proof of the Christian faith. It is the truth that lies at the very foundation of the Gospel. Other doctrines of the Christian faith may be important, but the resurrection is essential. Without a belief in the resurrection there can be no personal salvation. The Bible says, 'If we confess with our mouths the Lord Jesus and believe in our hearts that God raised him from the dead, we shall be saved.'[7]

In the resurrection of Jesus Christ we have the answer to the great question of the ages: 'If a man die, shall he live again?' The Bible teaches that because Christ lives, we also shall live.[8] The greatest truth that you can ever hear is that Jesus Christ died but rose again, and that you too will die but can rise again into newness of life.

The Bible teaches the bodily resurrection of Jesus Christ. It is not a spiritual resurrection, as some would have us believe. Jesus's very body was raised by God from the dead, and someday we will see Him.

The resurrected Christ lives today but in another very real sense: in the heart of every true believer. Though He is in His glorified body in heaven, yet through the Holy Spirit He dwells in the heart of every Christian. The Scripture says, 'Christ in you, the hope of glory.'[9] The Christ of God, in whom 'dwelleth all the fulness of the Godhead bodily',[10] condescends to live within the hearts of people. This is a mystery that is beyond comprehension and yet gloriously true.

When we come to Jesus Christ, we bring everything that we have. Our bodies with all their members, our faculties, our talents, our time, our money, our possessions, our hearts, our will, are all His.

Our faces become the faces in which the resurrected Christ shows forth His beauty and His glory. Our eyes become the eyes of the resurrected Christ, to exhibit His sympathy and His tenderness. He wants to look on the world's needs through your eyes. Your eyes should never be lent to the devil; they belong to God. Be careful how you use your eyes!

Our lips become the lips of the resurrected Christ, to speak His messages. The harsh, unkind words remain unspoken. Other people marvel at the gracious words which come out of our mouths. When He was on earth, the people said, 'Never man spake like this man.'[11] And this is the One who lives within us. Your lips become an instrument for the expression of His message. His words are spirit and life.[12] The word going forth out of His mouth cannot return unto Him void.[13] Remember, your lips are His; they should never be lent to the devil.

Our ears become the ears of the resurrected Christ. They will be sensitive to every cry of spiritual need. Jesus living in us today listens through our ears and hears the plaintive cry of the world's needs. Take heed to what you hear. Refuse to hear the voice of the tempter or give your sanction to the spread of false reports and idle rumours concerning others. Your ears are Jesus's ears; never lend them to the devil.

Our minds become the mind of the resurrected Christ. The Scripture says, 'Let this mind be in you, which was also in Christ Jesus.'[14] Cultivate spiritual thinking. Your intellect becomes His that He may plan through you that you may be an instrument for the realisation of His purpose. Yield your mind to Him that you may know His secrets and be kept in His will. Never lend your mind to the devil; the mind is the devil's favourite avenue of attack.

Our hands become the hands of the resurrected Christ, to act on his impulse. He will work through us. The living Christ dwells in our hearts and gives us power to live the victorious life. The Apostle Paul said that the same power that raised Christ from the dead is ours to enable us to live for Him.[15]

The feet of the Christian need to tread the narrow path that the Saviour trod, keeping in step with Him throughout the earthly pilgrimage. He lives in you. Let your feet direct you only to those places where Christ wants you to go.

We are to allow the resurrected Christ to allocate our time as His own; to control our money as His own; to energise our talents, our zeal and our ability with His resurrected life; to have complete right-of-way throughout our beings. He does not want an apartment in our house. He claims our entire home from attic to cellar.

Not only does the resurrection give us hope of immortality but it also provides Life with a capital 'L' here and now. Before the resurrection of Christ, the Holy Spirit came upon individuals only on certain occasions for special tasks. But now, after the resurrection, Christ through the Holy Spirit dwells in the heart of every believer to give us supernatural power in living our daily lives. The Scripture says that the same power that raised Jesus from the dead on the first Easter will raise us from the dead if the Spirit lives in us.[16] Call upon His resources. His grace is more than sufficient; He will cause you always to triumph over the world, the flesh and the devil.

Some of you do not know the power of the resurrected Christ. You have never knelt at the foot of the cross and had your sins forgiven. On that first Good Friday Jesus Christ died on the cross in your place. He took your judgment, your sin, your death. Scripture teaches, 'Believe on the Lord Jesus Christ, and thou shalt be saved.'[17] The Bible says, 'The blood of Jesus Christ his son cleanseth us from all sin.'[18]

On the third day Jesus was raised from the dead. That fact is a guarantee that the atoning work of Christ on the cross was acceptable to God in your place.

Now you need to receive Him and to believe on Him. God says that He will clothe you in His righteousness. Everyone can know the power of the resurrected Christ. Through disappointments, tragedies and trials, through all the circumstances of life, the resurrected Christ will go with you, if you will put your trust in Him by faith.

Now is the time to give your life to Christ, to bend your will to His; to let the resurrected Christ come to dwell in your heart and give you supernatural power to meet the problems of the day. So many people are confused, lonely, discouraged. Give your life to Christ. Let Him transform your life so that you will have a glow on your face, a spring in your step and joy in your soul.

First, you need to renounce your sins. Second, by faith receive Him as your Saviour. Will you do that today? If you will, the resurrected Christ will come to live inyour heart.

Postscript

Tens of thousands of people have made decisions for Christ in more than forty-five years of Billy Graham's evangelistic ministry. Today they serve Christ in the Church in nearly every vocation.

The stories in this book are but a cross-cultural selection of many more which might have been told with equal impact.

Month by month, *Decision* Magazine, published by the Billy Graham Evangelistic Association, carries similar stories of the remarkable change which has come to so many lives as a person has confronted Jesus Christ. As you have read this book, it may be that one or another of the stories has made an impact upon your life. If so, the Editor of *Decision* would like to hear from you.

The Editor
Decision
PO Box 779
Minneapolis
Minnesota 55440-0779 USA

A monthly subscription may be arranged from the same address – or in the UK from:

Decision Magazine
PO BOX 2032
Woodford Green
IG9 5AP

Appendix

Crusades and Missions conducted by Billy Graham in the United Kingdom

Greater London Crusade, Harringay Arena, London, 1 March–22 May 1954 (12 weeks), ending at White City Stadium (afternoon) & Wembley Stadium (evening)

All Scotland Crusade, Kelvin Hall, Glasgow, February/March/April 1955 (6 weeks), incorporating more than 2,000 landline relays to centres throughout the UK

Wembley Crusade, Wembley Stadium, London, May 1955 (1 week)

Manchester Crusade, Maine Road Stadium, Manchester, May/June 1961 (3 weeks)

Greater London Crusade, Earls Court, London, 1 June–2 July 1966

Greater London Crusade, Earls Court, London, 23 June–1 July 1967

Spre-e 73, Earls Court, London, 27 August–1 September 1973

Oxford University Mission, Town Hall, Oxford, 30 January–3 February 1980

Cambridge University Mission, Great St Mary's, Cambridge, 9–16 February 1980

Blackpool Crusade, Winter Gardens, Blackpool, 2–3 March 1982

Mission England, Ashton Gate, Bristol, 12–19 May 1984

Mission England, Roker Park, Sunderland, 26 May–2 June 1984

Mission England, Carrow Road, Norwich, 9–12 June 1984

Appendix

Mission England, Villa Park, Birmingham, 30 June–7 July 1984

Mission England, Anfield Road, Liverpool, 14–21 July 1984

Mission England, Portman Road, Ipswich, 24–28 July 1984

Mission England, Bramhall Lane, Sheffield, 22–29 June 1985

Mission to London, West Ham, London, 14–16 June 1989

Mission to London, Crystal Palace, London, 21–23 June 1989

Mission to London, Earls Court, London, 26 June–1 July 1989/
   Wembley Stadium, 8 July 1989 (& 125 Livelink Satellite
   TV centres throughout the UK)

Mission Scotland, Murrayfield Stadium, Edinburgh, 25–26
   May 1991

Mission Scotland, Pittodrie Stadium, Aberdeen, 30 May–1 June
   1991

Mission Scotland, Celtic Park, Glasgow, 4–8 June 1991

Notes

Preface

1. Letter from President Carter's Office dated 7 August 1995
2. From President Carter's statement in the Global Mission Television project

Introduction

1. *Chambers Biographical Dictionary* (5th – reprinted – edition, 1993; first published 1897) published by Chambers. General editor, Magnus Magnusson. p. 615: 'GRAHAM'
2. © The Telegraph Plc, London 1994
3. From *Religious Broadcasting*, p. 8, dated April 1996
4. The magazine *Ministries Today*, published in 1994
5. Julian Huxley, source unknown

1. If Only One Person . . .

Most of the material in the George Verwer story comes from his own pen or from interviews he gave to Noel Stanton, George Rodgers, Mike McManus (sources unidentified), and from the book *The Logos Story* by Elaine Rhoton (used by permission of George Verwer)

1. Information about the BGEA calendar and ensuing results taken from *London Hears Billy Graham* by Dr Charles T. Cook, pp. 35, 36 (published by Marshall, Morgan &

Scott); and also from *The Harringay Story* by Frank Colquhoun, pp. 73 & 74 (published by Hodder & Stoughton)

2. *Introducing Billy*

1. From *A Prophet with Honor* (*PWH*) by William Martin, published by William Morrow & Co., 1991, p. 97, para. 3
2. *et passim* Letters from Mary Currie (née Amies)
3. Letter to John Pollock from Mr J. Rees, para. 2, dated 26 November 1981
4. 'Letters to the Editor', *Christianity Today*, dated 8 January 1996, p. 8. Letter from Donald R. Brown DDS, Bonita Springs, Florida
5. *PWH*, p. 112, para. 2
6. ibid.
7. Quotation: From *Proclaim*, the journal of the Luis Palau Evangelistic Association, February 1996 issue
8. Letter to John Pollock from Mr J. Rees dated 26 November 1981, para. 3
9. ibid., para. 2
10. ibid.
11. ibid.
12. ibid.
13. From *The Christian and Christianity Today* (published by the Billy Graham Evangelistic Association UK) dated 10 June 1966, p. 12

3. *Called to Preach*

This chapter is based upon a written interview with Dr Warren Wiersbe and from the author's own notes. All quotations are taken from the book *Be Myself* by Warren W. Wiersbe (pp. 52–62) published by Victor Books

4. Newscaster

1. *PWH*, p. 102
2. *My Brother Stuart Hamblen* (*BSH*) by Oberia Hamblen, published by Cowman Publications Inc. Source: archives of the Billy Graham Center, Wheaton, Illinois, used with permission
3. ibid., pp. 9 & 10
4. ibid., p. 10
5. ibid., p. 45
6. ibid., p. 42
7. ibid.
8. ibid., p. 83
9. ibid., p. 84
10. ibid., p. 85
11. ibid., p. 86
12. ibid.
13. ibid., p. 87
14. ibid., pp. 104 & 105
15. ibid., pp. 106 & 107
16. ibid., pp. 127–30

5. Wire-tapper

Some of this story is taken from the film *Wiretapper*: World Wide Pictures, California
1. *They Called My Husband a Gangster* (*TCHG*) p. 55
2. ibid., p. 57
3. ibid., p. 58
4. ibid., p. 61
5. ibid., pp. 62–3
6. ibid., pp. 64–5
7. ibid., p. 73
8. ibid., pp. 91–2
9. Letter to the author from Jim Vaus dated 12 March 1996
10. Information from Youth Development Inc. leaflet, published by Worldwide Pictures Inc.

Notes

6. *The Queen's Warrant*

The information in this chapter is compiled from the author's notes of an interview with Dudley Brient in November 1995

7. *Childhood Response*

The information in this chapter is compiled from the author's notes of an interview with Derek Hills on 5 January 1996

8. *Sacrificing Cricket*

The information in this chapter is compiled from the author's notes of an interview with Peter Pearmain on 10 January 1996
1. From *Those Who Came Forward* (*TWCF*) by Curtis Mitchell, published by Worlds Work, p. 226
2. *et passim* Billy Graham's sermon taken from *TWCF*, pp. 25, 27, 29, 30 & 31
3. *TWCF*, p. 226

9. *A Doctor's Story*

The story was composed from letters to the author by Dr David Rowlands in the autumn of 1995
1. *The Harringay Story* by Frank Colquhoun, Hodder & Stoughton, 1955, p. 211

10. *Fish and Meat Pastes*

The information in this chapter is compiled from a transcript of an address given by Ernest Shippam (time and place unknown). Amendments and additions to the story are from correspondence with Mr John Shippam (son)
1. From *Billy Graham* by John Pollock, Hodder & Stoughton (1966 edition), p. 167
2. *et passim* Shippam letter to the author (6 April 1972) from

the Archives of the Billy Graham Center, Wheaton, Illinois, Collection 9, Box 3, Folder 32
3. Letter to Dr Sherwood Eliot Wirt dated 11 September 1961, from the Archives of the Billy Graham Center, Wheaton, Illinois, Collection 506, Box 23, Folder 8

11. No Longer Alone

Note: all the quotations in this chapter are taken from the book *No Longer Alone* (NLA) by Joan Winmill Brown (published by Fleming H. Revell Co.)
 1. *NLA*, p. 9
 2. ibid.
 3. ibid., p. 10
 4. ibid.
 5. ibid.
 6. ibid., pp. 11–12
 7. ibid., p. 12
 8. ibid.
 9. ibid., p 14
10. ibid., p. 15
11. ibid., p. 16
12. ibid., p. 18
13. ibid., p. 19
14. ibid., p. 20
15. ibid.
16. ibid., p. 21
17. ibid.
18. ibid., p. 24
19. ibid., p. 26
20. ibid.
21. ibid., pp. 26–27
22. ibid., p. 28
23. ibid., p. 38
24. ibid., p. 40
25. ibid., p. 43

26. ibid., p. 46
27. ibid., p. 47
28. ibid., p. 50
29. ibid., p. 67
30. ibid.
31. ibid., p. 68
32. ibid.
33. ibid.
34. ibid.
35. ibid.
36. ibid., p. 69
37. ibid.
38. ibid.
39. ibid.
40. ibid.
41. ibid., p. 70
42. ibid.
43. ibid.
44. ibid.
45. ibid., p. 72
46. ibid., p. 73
47. ibid., p. 72
48. ibid., p. 74
49. ibid., p. 75
50. ibid.
51. ibid., p. 81
52. Letter to the author from a Dartmoor prisoner dated 8 March 1957
53. *NLA*, p. 92
54. ibid., p. 98
55. ibid., p. 148
56. ibid., p. 136
57. ibid., p. 137
58. ibid., p. 141
59. ibid., p. 149
60. ibid., p. 151

61. Quoted from a letter to the author
62. Transcript of a tape-recording of the speeches at the celebration dinner, Wembley Centre, UK
63. ibid.
64. *NLA*, p. 152
65. ibid., p. 156
66. Quoted from a letter to the author
67. *NLA*, p. 157

12. *Monk to Minister*

The information in this chapter is compiled from the author's notes of an interview with Alan Wright in October 1995

13. *No! The Pizzas are Yours*

The information in this chapter is compiled from the author's notes of an interview with Trevor Adams in July 1996

14. *Escape from the Japs*

The information in this chapter is compiled from the author's notes of an interview with Richard Galway (a pseudonym) at Earls Court in June 1967

15. *Zagreb*

The information in this chapter is compiled from the author's notes of an interview (by correspondence) with Branko Lovrec in November 1995

16. *Rock 'n' Roll Singer*

The information and quotations in this chapter come from the following sources: *Cliff* by Patrick Doncaster & Tony Jasper (C) published by Sidgwick & Jackson; *Cliff Richard* by Steve

Turner (*CR*) published by Lion; *Which One's Cliff?* by Cliff
Richard (*WOC*) published by Hodder & Stoughton. Other
material is taken from tape-recorded interviews with Cliff
Richard and from his testimony given on the Global Mission
programme (made by the Billy Graham Evangelistic Association). Other information is taken from two documentary
television programmes on Cliff Richard. Cliff Richard's own
comments are taken mainly from an interview with the author
in January 1996

1. *CR*, p. 36
2. ibid., p. 92
3. ibid., pp. 41, 42 & 43
4. ibid., p. 59
5. ibid., pp. 92–3
6. *WOC*, p. 38
7. ibid., p. 41
8. Taken from an interview with Cliff Richard on BBC TV
9. ibid.
10. Extract from the tape of Spre-e 73 on Friday 31 August
    1973
11. *CR*, p. 227
12. ibid., p. 226
13. Testimony taken from the Global Mission programme
14. C, p. 156
15. *WOC*, p. 77
16. ibid., p. 78
17. Taken from the publicity leaflet for the film *Two a Penny*
18. *CR*, p. 228
19. ibid.
20. ibid., p. 229
21. ibid., p. 231
22. ibid.
23. C, p. 160
24. Quotation taken from an interview with Cliff Richard on
    BBC TV
25. C, p. 162

26. Taken from the author's tape-recording of the event
27. WOC, p. 75
28. Taken from an interview with Cliff Richard on BBC TV
29. ibid.
30. BBC Television programme 'This Is Your Life'

17. *Seven Thumbnail Sketches*

Ron E. Perez story taken from *Decision* Magazine (D/BGEA) dated September 1991. Used with permission

Dr Raymond Damadian story taken from D/BGEA dated September 1992. Used with permission

Isaac Bonful story taken from D/BGEA dated June 1988. Used with permission

Rev. Gipp Forster story taken from D/BGEA dated May 1986. Used with permission

Norma Symonds story taken from D/BGEA dated June 1989. Used with permission

Tom Bradley story taken from D/BGEA dated April 1990. Used with permission

Makoto Yamaya story taken from D/BGEA dated December 1989. Used with permission

18. *A Dangerous Life*

The information in this chapter is compiled from the author's notes of an interview with Vikta Giovanni (surname changed to protect his family) in August 1973. Quotations from *Decision* Magazine (published by the Billy Graham Evangelistic Association in January 1974) from the Archives of the Billy Graham Center, Wheaton, Illinois: from the files of Spre-e 73. Used with the permission of the BGEA

1. Letter from Vikta Giovanni from the Archives of the Billy Graham Center, Wheaton, Illinois: from the Spre-e 73 files. Used with permission of the BGEA
2. *et passim* Quotations taken from the tape-recording of the Friday night meeting at Spre-e 73

Notes

3. Quotation taken from the tape-recording of the Friday night meeting at Spre'e '73
4. Comments on Judge Henry Ruttle taken from the obituary notice in *The Times* of London dated 22 September 1995

19. *Second Row, Piano Side*

Apart from the quotations from the cassette tape, 'Live from the Second Row Piano Side', all other information is from notes of an interview (in writing) with Chonda Pierce in February 1996

20. *Diminutive Medium*

The information in this chapter is compiled from the author's notes of an interview with Eva Close on 16 March 1996

21. *Dream Machine*

The information in this chapter is compiled from the author's notes of an interview with Jean Lupton in November 1995

22. *Rock Band Evangelist*

The information in this chapter is compiled from the author's notes of an interview with Alex Bowler in London in February 1996

23. *Not Easy to Respond*

The information in this chapter is compiled from the author's notes of an interview with Dr Ian Oliver in October 1995

24. A U-*turn*

The information in this chapter is compiled from the author's notes of an interview with Helen Douglas in January 1996
  1. Quotations from Billy Graham's sermon taken from a transcript of the Global Mission telecast

25. *The Greatest News Ever Heard*

The sermon by Billy Graham is reprinted from the April 1995 edition of *Decision* Magazine, © 1966 Billy Graham Evangelistic Association, Minneapolis, Minnesota. Used with permission
  1. John 11:25–26, King James Version (KJV)
  2. Job 14:14, KJV
  3. 1 Corinthians 15:56, KJV
  4. cf. Romans 5:12
  5. Matthew 28:5, KJV
  6. Matthew 28:6, KJV
  7. cf. Romans 10:9
  8. John 14:19
  9. Colossians 1:27, KJV
  10. Colossians 2:9, KJV
  11. John 7:46, KJV
  12. John 6:63
  13. Isaiah 55:11
  14. Philippians 2:5, KJV
  15. Ephesians 1:19–20
  16. Romans 8:11
  17. Acts 16:31, KJV
  18. 1 John 1:7, KJV